AF538565

INDIA'S INTERNAL SECURITY

Role of State Governments

INDIA'S INTERNAL SECURITY

ROLE OF STATE GOVERNMENTS

Pushpita Das

First published in 2024 by
PENTAGON PRESS LLP
206, Peacock Lane, Shahpur Jat
New Delhi-110049, India
Contact: 011-26490600

Typeset in AGaramond, 11.5 Point
Printed by Aegean Offset Printers, Greater Noida, U.P.

ISBN 978-81-968722-0-5 (HB)

www.pentagonpress.in

CONTENTS

ACKNOWLEDGEMENTS

The resilience of India in the face of myriad threats and challenges to its internal security has been a fascinating subject. While it is a common knowledge that the Union government has been primarily responsible for maintaining the security of the country, the state governments have also played an important role in ensuring public order and security of the citizens. It is said that every conflict starts at the micro level, but if not addressed effectively at that level, it has the potential to blow up and manifest itself as a severe security threat for the entire country. In this respect, various affected state governments have attempted at resolving conflicts and building peace at the ground level. While some of these attempts have been successful others have not accomplished the desired results. The contributions of the state governments, however, have remained sparsely discussed in the academic narratives. That is why there is a need to address this lacuna and this book endeavours to do so. It brings to the fore the efforts of the state governments in safeguarding internal security in India.

This book would not have been completed without the encouragement and support from my colleagues and administrative staff at the MP-IDSA, and I offer my heartfelt thanks to all of them. A few of them deserve special mention. First of all, I would like to express my wholehearted thanks to Brigadier Pradeep Chhonkar who graciously discussed the topic with me and offered his valuable inputs. In fact, his inputs helped me in firming up my initial arguments. I also offer my deep gratitude to late Dr. S. Kalyanaraman for being a patient sounding board. His insights and analysis helped me in getting a better understanding and a unique perspective on the subject. I express my sincere thanks to Amb. Sujan R Chinoy, Director General and his administration for providing me with an enabling environment to conduct the study. I am also thankful to my colleagues, especially my centre members for their intellectual inputs. I convey my thanks to library staff, Mukesh, Hitakshi and Vikrant, for their assistance. Finally, my sincere thanks is extended to the three anonymous referees who perused the manuscript and provided constructive comments and suggestions which vastly improved the content of the book.

I hope the readers will find this book informative and a useful addition to the existing literature. I take responsibility for any error or deficiency that remain in the book.

New Delhi **Pushpita Das**

3 November 2023.

ABBREVIATIONS

ADCs	Autonomous District Councils
AFSPA	Armed Forces Special Powers Act
AICCCR	All India Coordination Committee of Communist Revolutionaries
AICCR	All-India Co-ordination Committee of Revolutionaries
AISSF	All India Sikh Students Federation
ANSAM	All Naga Students' Association Manipur
AOB	Andhra-Orissa Border
APCCCR	Andhra Pradesh Coordination Committee of Communist Revolutionaries
APSALTR	Andhra Pradesh Scheduled Areas Land Transfer Regulation
AR	Assam Rifles
ARC	Aviation Research Centre
ASUK	Alliance for Socialist Unity Kangleipak
ATSUM	All Tribal Students Union, Manipur
ATTF	All Twipra Tiger Force
BFSR	Battle Field Surveillance Radars
BJP	Bharatiya Janata Party
BRGF	Backward Regions Grant Fund
BSF	Border Security Force
BTFK	Bhindranwale Tiger Force of Khalistan
BUPC	Bhoomi Uchched Protirodh Committee
CAPFs	Central Armed Police Forces
CATs	Concealed Apprehension Techniques
CBI	Central Bureau of Investigation
CCP	Code of Criminal Procedure

CCS	Cabinet Committee on Security
CIAT	Counter-Insurgency and Anti-Terrorism
CID	Criminal Investigation Department
CIJWS	Counter-Insurgency and Jungle Warfare School
CoBRA	Commando Battalions for Resolute Actions
COBs	Company Operated Bases
Cor-Com	Coordination Committee
CPA	Calcutta Police Association
CPI (M)	Communist Party of India- Marxist
CPI (M-L)	Communist Party of India- Marxist Leninist
CPI	Communist Party of India
CPOs	Central Police Organisations
CRPF	Central Reserve Police Force
DAKMS	Dandakaranya Adivasi Kisan Mazdoor Sanghathans
DOC	District Organising Committee
DRG	District Reserve Guards
DRI	Directorate of Revenue Intelligence
DRP	District Reserve Police
EFR	Eastern Frontier Rifles
FGN	Federal Government of Nagaland
GDP	Gross Domestic Product
GER	Gross Enrolment Ratio
GGI	Good Governance Index
GMP	Gana Mukti Parishad
GSDP	Gross State Domestic Product
HAC	Hill Areas Committee
HDI	Human Development Index
HHMD	Hand Held Deep Search Metal Detector
HHTI	Hand Held Thermal Imagery
HPA	Hill People's Alliance
HPC	Hmar People's Convention
HRF	Hmar Revolutionary Front
IAY	Indira Awas Yojna
IB	Intelligence Bureau

ICDS	Integrated Child Development Scheme
IEDs	Improvised Explosive Devices
IEP	Institute of Economics and Peace
IM	Indian Mujahideen
INF	Islamic National Front
INPT	Indigenous Nationalist Party of Tripura
IPC	Indian Penal Code
IPFT	Indigenous People's Front of Tripura
IRBs	India Reserve Battalions
IRF	Islamic Revolutionary Front
ISI	Inter-Services Intelligence
ITBP	Indo-Tibetan Border Police
JWCI	Jungle Warfare and Counter Insurgency
KCF	Khalistan Commando Force
KCP	Kangleipak Communist Party
KDF	Kuki Defence Force
KIA	Kachin Independence Army
KIA	Kuki Independent Army
KIF	Kuki International Force
KLF	Khalistan Liberation Force
KLF	Kuki Liberation Front
KLO	Khalistan Liberation Organisation
KMAS	Krantikari Mahila Adivasi Sangathana
KNA	Kuki National Army
KNO	Kuki National Organisation
KNV	Kuki National Volunteers
KRF	Kuki Revolutionary Front
KSF	Kuki Security Force
KYKL	Kanglei Yawol Kanna Lup
LMGs	Light Machine Guns
LORROS	Long Range Reconnaissance Observation System
LWE	Left Wing Extremism
MAC	Multi Agency Centre
MCCI	Maoist Communist Centre-India

MGNREGS	Mahatma Gandhi Rural Employment Guarantee Scheme
MHA	Ministry of Home Affairs
MI	Military Intelligence
MLR&LR	Manipur Land Revenue and Land Reforms
MMS	Midday Meal Scheme
MNF	Mizo National Front
MPF	Modernisation of Police Force
MPI	Multidimensional Poverty Index
MPLF	Manipur People's Liberation Front
NCRB	National Crime Record Bureau
NEMF	North East Minority Front
NER	Net Enrolment Ratio
NFG	Naga Federal Government
NIA	National Investigation Agency
NLFT	National Liberation Front of Twipra
NNC	Naga National Council
NNPG	Naga National Political Group
NREGS	National Rural Employment Guarantee Scheme
NRHM	National Rural Health Care Mission
NSCN-IM	National Social Council of Nagalim – Issac-Muivah
NSG	National Security Guard
NTRO	National Technical Research Organisation
PAC	Public Affairs Centre
PAP	Punjab Armed Police
PCPA	People's Committee against Police Atrocities
PESA	Panchayats (Extension to the Scheduled Areas) Act
PGA	People's Guerrilla Army
PLA	People's Liberation Army
PLGA	People's Liberation Guerrilla Army
PMEGP	Pradhan Mantri Employment Generation Programme
PNG	Passive Night Vision Goggles
PREPAK	People's Revolutionary Party of Kangleipak
PRIs	Panchayati Raj Institutions
PW	People's War

PWG	People's War Group
QRT	Quick Reaction Team
R&AW	Research & Analysis Wing
RCS	Ryuthu-Coolie Sangathans
RGM	Revolutionary Government of Manipur
RIAD	Remote and Interior Areas Development Programme
RJC	Revolutionary Joint Committee
RMSA	Rashtriya Madhaymik Shiksha Abhiyaan
RPCs	Revolutionary People's Committees
RPF	Revolutionary People's Front
RSU	Radical Student Union
RYL	Radical Youth League
SAD	Shiromani Akali Dal
SAP	State Armed Police
SAPA	Special Armed Police
SC	Scheduled Caste
SCERT	State Council of Education Research and Training
SDG	Sustainable Development Goal
SEZ	Special Economic Zone
SFJ	Sikh for Justice
SGPC	Shiromani Gurudwara Prabandhak Committee
SIB	State Intelligence Bureau
SIMI	Students Islamic Movement of India
SLCC	State Level Coordination Committee
SLOG	State Level Operations and Intelligence Group
SLRs	Self-Loading Rifles
S-MAC	State-MAC
SOG	Special Operations Groups
SoO	Suspension of Operations
SPO	Special Police Officers
SRC	Screening and Rehabilitation Committee
SRE	Security Related Expenditure
SSA	Sarva Shiksha Abhiyaan
SSB	Sashastra Seema Bal

SSDCM	Sixth Schedule Demand Committee, Manipur
ST	Scheduled Tribe
STF	Special Task Force
TAC	Tribal Advisory Council
TADA	Terrorist and Disruptive Activities (Prevention) Act
TCOC	Tactical Counter-Offensive Campaign
TLR &LR	Tripura Land Revenue and Land Reforms
TMC	Trinamool Congress
TNV	Tripura/ Tribal National Volunteers
TRA	Tripura Resurrection Army
TRMP	Tripura Rajya Mukti Parishad
TRPC	Tripura Rehabilitation Plantation Corporation
TSR	Tripura State Rifles
TTAADC	Tripura Tribal Areas Autonomous District Council
TUJS	Tripura Upajati Juba Samiti
UAPA	Unlawful Activities (Prevention) Act
UILA	United Islamic Liberation Army
UNC	United Naga Council
UNLF	United Liberation Front
UPF	United People's Front
URF	United Revolutionary Front
VDS	Village Defence Scheme
VVF	Village Voluntary Force
WPR	Work Participation Rate
WSO	World Sikh Organisation
ZRA	Zomi Revolutionary Army

1

INTRODUCTION

India, since its inception, has faced a number of violent conflicts in the name religion, ethnicity, caste, language, class, etc. These conflicts are the outcome of the fact that India is a multi racial/ethnic, multi lingual, and multi religion/sectarian nation with widespread social and economic disparities. These disparities gave rise to a sense of deprivation amongst the affected masses, which manifested itself as extreme intolerance against different religions, ethnicities, languages, castes, etc. Such extreme sentiments coupled with poor governance and absence of speedy resolution resulted in the eruption of violent conflicts demanding autonomy or secession in different parts of the country.

Significantly, India had to confront three major internal security challenges in Jammu and Kashmir (J&K), Telangana and the Northeast almost immediately after independence. Beginning with J&K, the indecision of Maharaja Hari Singh to accede to either India or Pakistan gave an opportunity to Pakistan to attempt a forcible accession of the princely state to its territory. This failed attempt forced India to militarily confront Pakistan resulting in the war of 1947-1948. Since then Pakistan has been trying unsuccessfully to change the status quo either militarily or through cross-border terrorism by sending in its own terrorists into J&K.

Meanwhile, the Communists, who had been spreading their influence in the country by taking up issues affecting the peasants, started instigating them to rise in revolt against the Indian state. Consequently, in 1948, India had to face its first post-independence communist led peasant revolt in Telangana (erstwhile Hyderabad State). For the next three years, the Communists continued with their agenda of people's revolution and tried to destabilise the nation through violent means. This phase of Communist-inspired violence ended after they decided to abandon their revolutionary methods and participate in the general elections of 1952. Even as the embers of communist revolution were dying down, the Naga rebels formed the underground Naga Federal Government (NFG) in March 1956 and started the longest running secessionist movement in the country.

These three sets of violent conflicts, in fact, became the template for future insurgencies and terrorism in the country. In the Northeast, inspired by the Naga rebels, the Meiteis and Mizos too asserted their 'distinct ethnic identity' and raised the banner of revolt against the Indian state in the 1960s. In subsequent years, large scale illegal migration from Bangladesh triggered 'sons of the soil' agitations, which soon morphed into raging insurgencies in Assam and in Tripura. Naxalism (later on Maoism/Left Wing Extremism) raised its head once again in the form of violent peasant insurrection in rural West Bengal in the late 1960s. Although the communist-led insurrection was tackled in the state by the mid-1970s, it soon spread to Andhra Pradesh, Chhattisgarh, Jharkhand, Odisha and Maharashtra in 1980s and 1990s, becoming one of the most potent internal security threats to the country.

The 1980s also saw the emergence of religion based militancy in Punjab. Sikh militants demanding separate Khalistan unleashed a reign of terror in the state and neighbouring areas before the separatist movement was decidedly contained in the early 1990s. As the Khalistan movement was raging, J&K witnessed a separatist movement in 1989. While the movement was indigenous in the beginning, it soon transformed into cross-border terrorism as Pakistan started sending in its own *jihadis* to shore up the fledgling separatist movement in Kashmir. The Pakistani terrorists, however, did not limit their terror activities to Kashmir but carried out attacks in the rest of India. The attack on Indian Parliament in December 2001 and the bomb blasts in Mumbai in November 2008 are cases in point. Terror attacks gradually increased in the Indian mainland by mid-2000s as home grown terror organizations such as the Students Islamic Movement of India (SIMI) and the Indian Mujahideen (IM) cropped up. These organisations, especially the IM carried out a series of attacks including bombings in public places ostensibly to avenge the demolition of a disputed structure (the Babri Masjid) in Ayodhya in 1992 and killings of Muslims during the Gujarat riots in 2002.

These internal security threats have had an immense adverse impact on the socio-economic and political life of India. Insurgencies and terrorism undermine the political stability of the country by disrupting governance and challenging political authority. Loss of lives not only creates fear and a sense of insecurity among people, but it also questions the ability of the government to protect the life and properties of its innocent citizens. Prolonged conflicts result in widening of disparities among regions and communities, which leads to increased polarisation and communalisation of the society and breeds distrust and intolerance among the populace. Thus, social harmony and cohesion is severely affected, which ultimately hinders nation building efforts.

Violent conflicts also disrupt economic activities, discourage investments and hinder development. Targeting and destructing critical infrastructure and assets such as transportation and communication networks, power plants and public facilities disrupt supply chains, which have a long term negative impact on the economic growth of the country. Combating these internal security threats also drains the country of its resources. In fact, the economic cost of violence for the country is huge. According to the Institute of Economics and Peace (IEP) Report, India's economic cost of violence was 6 per cent of its Gross Domestic Product (GDP) in 2022, which is phenomenal.[1]

It is therefore crucial that India proactively tackles these threats to safeguard the well-being, stability, and progress of the country. Addressing internal security threats requires a comprehensive approach involving intelligence gathering, law enforcement, community engagement, socioeconomic development, and political initiatives. However, before discussing the institutional and structural arrangements to tackle internal security threats, it is important to discuss the difference between public order and internal security.

Public Order and Internal Security

India is a democratic country where public dissent is welcomed and even encouraged because it not only provides a vent for airing legitimate public grievances and frustrations but also keeps the government in check, thereby maintaining harmony in the society. However, when this avenue for dissent is exploited by partisan politics resulting in extreme polarisation, they more often than not degenerate into violent conflicts and public disorder. Inability of the administration to implement the rule of law and to promptly resolve the conflict results in insurgency or terrorism.

These insurgencies, militancy and acts of terrorism cost the country dearly, impacting its politics, economics, security and psyche. These violent conflicts keep the political leadership preoccupied and distract them from nation building efforts. Economic growth and development become a casualty thereby plunging the affected areas into a cycle of poverty, frustration and violence. These conflicts also ensure that the armed forces remained engaged in internal security duties rather than being stationed at the borders defending the country against external aggression. The unending saga of violence has an adverse effect on the morale of the people as they grapple with the more existential issue of self-preservation.

It is because of these reasons that public order in the country needs to be maintained at all the time. Public Order means absence of disturbance, riot, revolt and lawlessness and 'signifies that state of tranquillity which prevails among the members of a political society as a result of the internal regulations enforced by the government which they have established.'[2] Maintenance of public order is the fundamental function of the State because failure to discharge its fundamental duty would lead to its decay and disintegration.[3] Public Order requires a comprehensive approach that encompasses good governance, rule of law, effective law enforcement, a fair legal system and public participation. By prioritising public order, societies can ensure social harmony, protect individual rights, and create an environment conducive to progress and development.

Interestingly, 'public order', and 'law and order' are often understood as being similar. However, these two are not the same. Explaining the difference between 'public order' and 'law and order' as well as 'security of the state', the Supreme Court stated,

> Just as public order apprehends disorders of less gravity than those affecting the security of state, law and order also apprehends disorders of less gravity than those affecting public order. One has to imagine three concentric circles, the largest representing "law and order", the

> next representing "public order" and the smallest representing "security of State". An act may affect "law and order" but not "public order", just as an act may affect "public order" but not "security of the State".[4]

In other words, every situation or act threatening security of the state is a public order problem. Similarly, every situation or act affecting public order is a law and order problem. However, all law and order problem is not public order problem. Thus, clashes between two groups in a limited area, which does not affect the public in general is a law and order problem. On the other hand, widespread violent clashes involving two or more groups such as communal riots or ethnic clashes pose a threat to public order. Terror attacks involving bombings and large scale killings impinge on the security of the State.[5]

Internal Security is a vital sub-set of National Security. The Punchhi Committee defined it as:

> security against threats faced by a country within its national borders, either caused by inner political turmoil, or provoked, prompted or proxied by an enemy country, perpetrated even by such groups that use a failed, failing or weak state, causing insurgency, terrorism or any other subversive acts that target innocent citizens, cause animosity between and amongst groups of citizens and communities intended to cause or causing violence, destroy or attempt to destroy public and private establishment.[6]

In other words, Internal Security can be defined as any act threatening the existence of the state, and consequently, attracts emergency or extraordinary measures to tackle such threats. Based on this definition, Internal Security threats that India faces at present are classified into four categories: (a) Insurgency in the North Eastern States; (b) Left Wing Extremism (LWE) in certain areas; (c) Cross-border terrorism in J&K; and (d) Terrorism in the hinterland of the country.[7]

Internal Security: Institutional and Structural Arrangements

Under the Constitution of India, 'Public Order' and 'Police' are under the State List (List II) of the Seventh Schedule. Thus, maintaining public order primarily falls within the domain of the state governments. The state police forces are responsible for maintaining law and order, preventing and investigating crimes, and ensuring public safety. The state police machinery is not legally responsible or accountable to the Union government, except during emergency. However, the Constitution does allow the Union government to condition, influence, and interfere in policy formulation as well as the functioning of the state police.[8] Under Article 246 (2) and (3), the state governments have the power to make laws pertaining to public order, which are within their exclusive domain as well as in List III or the Concurrent List.[9] This Article also obligates the state as well as the union governments to ensure that the state executive power is so exercised as to ensure compliance of the laws made by the Parliament as well as the state legislatures.[10] In this respect, the responsibilities of the Union government include assisting the state governments to maintain public order and ensure the rule of law by providing armed forces and central police forces as well as the necessary legal framework whenever required.[11]

Significantly, the Union government can intervene directly in matters of public order if there is a breakdown of law and order in any state. Under Article 352 of the Constitution of India, the President can impose Emergency if he is satisfied that 'grave emergency exists whereby the security of India or of any part of the territory thereof is threatened, whether by war or external aggression or armed rebellion.'[12] The President, however, cannot issue a proclamation till such time he or she receives in writing the decision of the union cabinet that such a proclamation maybe issued.[13] Under such proclamation, the Union government's role is to issue directions to the state government, and the Parliament is responsible to make laws for the states concerned.

Further, Article 355 obligates the Union government to protect the states from external aggression and internal disturbance and ensure that the governance of the states is carried on in accordance to the provisions of the Constitution.[14] In such circumstances also the Union government performs the role of assisting the states by providing them with central armed police forces and armed forces, sharing intelligence, providing financial resources to strengthen the state security and intelligence apparatus, etc. For example, the Union government's security response to tackle the Maoist problem includes modernisation and strengthening of state police forces, long-term deployment of Central Armed Police Forces (CAPFs) and intensified intelligence-based well-coordinated anti-Naxal operations.[15] Towards this end, the Union government has constituted Inter-State Coordination Committees, Coordination Centres and Task Forces, and provides funds to the Maoist affected states under the Modernisation of Police Force (MPF) Scheme and reimburses Security Related Expenditure (SRE), deploys CAPFs in the affected states, etc.

Similarly Article 356 empowers the President to take control of the state government if he or she is satisfied that the government concerned is not able to function according to the provisions of the Constitution.[16] Under this provision, the state government is dismissed and the President's rule is proclaimed wherein the President assumes direct control of the state government and the Governor, as a representative of the President, exercises executive authority in the state. The proclamation can be initially imposed for six months, but it has to be approved by both houses of Parliament within two months.[17] Furthermore, Article 365 of the Constitution gives powers to the President of India to dismiss the state government if it is established that the state government failed to comply with the directions given by the Union government under any provisions of the Constitution.[18]

The security architecture for countering internal security threats comprises four prominent components – political, administrative, intelligence and enforcement.[19] Politically, the Union Cabinet and the Cabinet Committee on Security (CCS) are the apex political platforms dealing with matters of internal security in the Government. These two platforms not only provide the strategic guidance relating to matters of internal security but they also discuss and formulate policies on national security issues including internal security. The core members of the CCS comprise the prime minister, the home minister, the defence minister, the external affairs ministers, and the finance minister. At the state levels, the political decisions on internal security are taken by the state cabinet. While the states do not have an equivalence of the CCS, they may set up State Security Councils (SSC) or similar bodies to address security related matters.

Administratively, the Ministry of Home Affairs (MHA) is the nodal ministry at the apex level, which is responsible for ensuring internal security, maintaining law and order, and addressing various challenges related to national security and governance. The MHA formulates policies, plans and strategies to address various internal security threats to India. Besides managing various CAPFs and Central Police Organisations (CPOs), the Ministry also coordinates with various law enforcement agencies, intelligence agencies, and CAPFs and paramilitary forces to ensure effective responses to the security threats. This coordination takes place vertically between the Union and the state concerned or horizontally among states. At the state level, the state home ministry is responsible for public order and police, which plans and formulates policies and programmes with the approval of the state legislature.

For intelligence, Intelligence Bureau (IB), which functions under the MHA, is the premier agency for gathering domestic intelligence. Intelligence is also gathered by other agencies such as the Research & Analysis Wing (R&AW), the National Technical Research Organisation (NTRO), the Aviation Research Centre (ARC), Military Intelligence (MI), etc. For collecting financial intelligence for economic offences, Directorate of Revenue Intelligence (DRI), Directorate of Enforcement, Financial Intelligence Unit, etc. function under various authorities. For sharing of intelligence between different agencies to improve national security and counterterrorism efforts, the Multi Agency Centre (MAC) was instituted under the IB in 2001. The MAC collates intelligence from different agencies, conducts in-depth analysis of threats and facilitates real time communication and coordination among agencies during any crisis. The MAC has its subsidiaries at the state level called the State-MAC (S-MAC). In the states, the Special Branch of the Police is primarily responsible for gathering intelligence on various security related matters as well as analysing information pertaining to potential threats to law and order, public safety, and national security at the state level.

For enforcement purposes, there are several CAPFs and CPOs. The Central Reserve Police Force (CRPF) is the premier internal security force of the country. The CRPF are deployed to respond to internal security threats as well as maintain public order while assisting the state governments. For guarding the borders, four border guarding forces were raised, namely the Border Security Force (BSF), Indo-Tibetan Border Police Force (ITBP), the Sashastra Seema Bal (SSB), and the Assam Rifles (AR). More often than not, units from these border guarding forces are also deployed within the country to carry out internal security duties. The state police, both armed and civil, are responsible for law enforcement at the state level.

For investigating and prosecuting terrorism related cases including terror financing, the National Investigation Agency (NIA) was set up in 2008 following the Mumbai terror attack of 26 November 2008. It is the premier investigation agency at the Union level, which also functions as the Central Counter Terrorism Law Enforcement Agency in India. For investigating cases at the Union level, the Central Bureau of Investigation (CBI) was established. While the NIA functions under the MHA, the CBI functions under the Ministry of Personnel, Pension & Public Grievances. The Criminal Investigation Department (CID) focuses on criminal investigations and maintaining law and order at the state level.

Internal Security: Under the Union Government or the State Government?

It is an oft repeated demand in India that matters concerning internal security should be the sole responsibility of the Union government. This demand is built on the argument that while 'Police' and 'Public Order' are state subjects under the Constitution, internal security threats, especially terrorism and left wing extremism (LWE), are not only transcending state borders and becoming pan-Indian in character but are also acquiring a higher level of intensity. Given that the affected states cannot operate beyond its borders, and given that they lack the capacity and political will, these factors greatly constrain the ability of the state governments to effectively respond to these threats. In contrast, the Union government, with its superior coercive power, higher capacity, vast resources, and pan Indian jurisdiction, is better placed to handle internal security threats.

Such arguments, unfortunately, miss the point that state governments are democratically elected responsible governments and their sincerity in tackling internal security threats should not be doubted. In fact, state governments play an important role not only in crisis prevention, but also in conflict resolution and peace building at the local level. Bringing internal security under the sole purview of the Union government would not only lead to an encroachment on the legitimate jurisdiction of the states but also result in duality of responsibility, which could hamper effectiveness of the response.[20] This fact has been acknowledged by former prime minister Manmohan Singh in his address at a Conference of Chief Ministers when he said, '[I]ssues relating to our internal security (is) an area that requires utmost vigil, sustained and coordinated attention of both Central and State Governments...our success in large measure also depends on the response of the State Governments'.[21]

Some of the key efforts by state governments, for example, during counterinsurgency operations and peace building are: (a) assessment of overall security situation and recommendation/ pronouncement of disturbed area; (b) sharing of intelligence inputs with the CAPFs and the military and enhancing coordination among all the security forces; (c) building state capacity by strengthening the police and civil administration; (d) formulating policies and providing infrastructure for detention and rehabilitation of surrendered militants; (e) restoring the rule of law; (f) implementing confidence building measures; (g) formulating long term policies and plans to address grievances; (h) prioritising development programmes in targeted areas, and (i) initiating political processes such as strengthening of autonomous district councils, gram panchayats and village councils, etc. All these measures contribute towards the prevention of violence, reduction in fragility as a breeding ground for violence, and creation of opportunities for long-term peace and development.

Further, the UN Security Council and General Assembly also suggest that 'sustaining peace should be broadly understood as a goal and a process to build a common vision of a society, ensuring that the needs of all segments of the population are taken into account.' They also identify good governance as integral to the promotion of sustaining peace. The argument forwarded is that that delivery of basic amenities such as healthcare, education, sanitation, water, justice, etc. at the local level can sustain peace as the state governments are best positioned to respond to the needs and aspirations of the people at the ground. Failure to respond to people's needs has been a primary factor for discontentment and ensuing conflict.

By providing civic amenities efficiently and effectively the local administration increases the visibility and credibility of the government. This is important in conflict riddled areas where the insurgents/rebels attempt to undermine the legitimacy of the government by undermining the delivery system of the local administration. Local governments can also give voice to the marginalised sections of the people by bringing in appropriate legislations. Even the Punchhi Committee has highlighted that 'Areas which have seen the fruits of development, where infrastructure is good, where the local economy has been well integrated with the rest of the country, where people have participated in local governance and where their aspirations have been recognised and nurtured by the State administrations, have withstood the ideological onslaught.'[22]

In fact, the successes achieved by states such as Andhra Pradesh, Bihar and West Bengal in combating Naxal/Maoist violence as well as Punjab and Tripura in ending militancy and insurgency through proactive initiatives are cases in point. Apart from these states, some states such as Nagaland, Assam, and Meghalaya have been able to create a positive environment, which has brought down the incidents of violence and conflict tremendously. Mizoram, similarly, has remained peaceful for more than three decades after witnessing twenty years of insurgency. At the same time, states such as Chhattisgarh, Jharkhand, and Manipur are riddled with insurgency and conflict, and consequently witness persistence violence and poor governance.

Literature Review

Classic counterinsurgency literature articulates three principles for a successful counterinsurgency strategy: (a) the counterinsurgent regime should seek accommodation with the reconcilable armed opposition, (b) The counterinsurgent regime should use violence discriminately when targeting the irreconcilable opposition, and (c) The counterinsurgent regime should provide public goods to disaffected populations in order to ensure their loyalty and prevent their support of insurgent groups. The literature is based on the experiences of national governments. However, there is also a growing literature on how local or sub-national governance can contribute to sustaining peace in conflict areas by delivering services and promoting sustainable development more effectively and efficiently, giving people a voice in the management of their affairs in a representative and inclusive way, and nurturing political will to resolve conflict and sustain peace.[23] Scholars argue that this local perspective is important because policies that work in one region may not work in another region in the same country, since multiple conflicts and forms of governance can occur within the same state with limited geographical overlap. As a result, many governance interventions in conflict-affected countries have adopted a strong sub-national focus. Many have had positive results, while others have raised important challenges.[24]

In India, some policymakers and analysts have advocated a more centralised approach to conflict resolution, arguing that state governments do not have the institutional capacity and political sagacity to respond to high intensity internal conflicts. They argue that internal security threats are growing virulent with cross-state linkages, and therefore, a pan India threat requires a pan India response.[25] Providing a contrarian perspective, some scholars argue that the character of ethnic insurgency in the Northeast and LWE affected states especially Jharkhand has changed; these groups have developed close ties with organised crime, they obstruct normal politics, but their attacks against state targets have declined.[26]

Separatist groups in these areas operate by exploiting the gaps in the rule of law. In such an environment, counterinsurgency strategy of heavy deployment of military power will not succeed. What is required is building the rule of law by strengthening state governments. A number of scholars have highlighted the successes of various state governments in tackling insurgency and militancy with active cooperation from Union governments.[27]

Overview of the Book

The rationale of the study is to bring to the fore the important role state governments play in maintaining internal security of the country. The study will argue the necessity to consider state governments as an important component in conflict resolution and peace building, and incorporate them in the overall counterinsurgency-counterterrorism architecture.

The book includes six chapters besides introduction and conclusion. For the purposes of this study, six states are being selected based on their success and failure to deal with insurgency and establish sustainable peace. The selected states are Andhra Pradesh, Tripura, West Bengal, Punjab, Chhattisgarh and Manipur. Of these, four are success stories such as Andhra Pradesh, West Bengal, Tripura and Punjab. Here again, Andhra Pradesh and Tripura are two states that have been able to defeat insurgency convincingly because of the concerted efforts by the state governments. Punjab and West Bengal fought militancy and insurgency mostly with the active participation of the Union government as President's rule was imposed to restore law and order in these states. Even then, the state police and the civil administrations of the states concerned have been quite effective in combating insurgency through their own initiatives. However, in recent years, these two states have witnessed some kind of resurgence of conflicts instigated by the Sikh separatists and Maoist ideologues. Finally, states such as Chhattisgarh and Manipur are witnessing high levels of violence and have not been able to contain insurgency.

Each chapter is devoted to a particular state and first discusses the history of the conflict in the states. Then it goes on to assess the reasons behind the success or failure of the states in resolving the conflict, for which various political, constitutional/legal, security, and governance measures, which were implemented by the states are discussed in details.

NOTES

1. *Global Peace Index 2023: Measuring Peace in a Complex World*, Sydney: Institute for Economic and Peace, 2023, p. 91.
2. Public Order as defined by the Hon'ble Supreme Court in 'Romesh Thappar vs The State of Madras on 26 May, 1950', at https://indiankanoon.org/doc/456839/, accessed on 14 June 2023.
3. 'Public Order', Fifth Report, *Second Administrative Reforms Commission*, New Delhi: Government of India, June 2007, p. 5.
4. 'Dr. Ram Manohar Lohia vs State of Bihar and Others on 7 September, 1965', Supreme Court of India, New Delhi at https://indiankanoon.org/docfragment/1733535/?formInput=proclamation#:~:text= Dr.,Others%20on%207%20September%2C%201965&text=Article%20352%20of%20the%20 Constitution,inter %20alia%20by%20external%20 aggression., accessed on 27 June 2023.
5. n. 3, p. 6.
6. Madan Mohan Punchhi, 'Internal Security, Criminal Justice and Centre-State Cooperation', *Commission On Centre-State Relations Report Volume – V*, New Delhi: Government of India, March 2010, p. 5.
7. *Annual Report 2021-2022*, New Delhi: Ministry of Home Affairs, p. 6.
8. P.D. Sharma, *Police and Political Order in India*, Delhi: Research Publications, 1984, p. 168.
9. *Constitution of India*, New Delhi: Government of India, 2022, p. 211, at https://cdnbbsr.s3waas.gov.in/s380537a945c7aaa788ccfcdf1b99b5d8f/uploads/2023/05/2023050195.pdf, accessed on 28 June 2023.
10. Ibid.
11. 'Constitutional Issues and Special Laws', n. 3, p. 213.
12. 'Article 352 (1)', *Constitution of India*, New Delhi, Government of India, 2022, p. 208, at https://cdnbbsr.s3waas.gov.in/s380537a945c7aaa788ccfcdf1b99b5d8f/uploads/2023/05/2023050195.pdf, accessed on 28 June 2023.

13. Ibid. 'Article 352 (3)'.
14. n. 9.
15. *Annual Report 2003-04*, New Delhi: Ministry of Home Affairs, 2004, p. 3.
16. n. 9.
17. Ibid, p. 211-213.
18. Ibid, p. 222.
19. Amit Ahuja and Devesh Kapur (eds.), *Internal Security in India: Violence, Order and the State*, New York: Oxford University Press, 2023, p. 21.
20. n. 3, p. 214.
21. Prime Minister Manmohan Singh in his address to the Chief Ministers in the recent conference held on 7 February 2010 as quoted in *Commission on Centre-State Relations Report*, n. 6, pp. 140-141.
22. n. 6, p. 72.
23. 'The Role of Local Governance in Sustaining Peace', *International Peace Institute*, New York, February 2018, pp.1-6; Stephen Watts, et al, *Countering Others' Insurgencies: Understanding U.S. Small-Footprint Interventions in Local Context*, Santa Monica: RAND, 2014.
24. Patricia Justino, 'Governance Interventions in Fragile and Conflict-Affected Countries', IDS Working Paper 496, *Institute of Development Studies and Swiss Agency for Development and Cooperation*, October 2017.
25. K. Padmanabhaiah, *Committee on Restructuring Police*, New Delhi; Ministry of Home Affairs, 2000; V.S. Malimath, *Committee on Reforms of Criminal Justice System- Vol-1*, New Delhi; Ministry of Home Affairs, 2003; Prakash Singh's interview in *The Times of India*, February 11, 2019.
26. Bethany Lacina, 'The Problem of Political Stability in Northeast India, Local Ethnic Autocracy and the Rule of Law', *Asian Survey*, Vol. 49 (6), 2009, pp. 998-1020; Sanjay K Jha, 'Naxalite Movement in Bihar and Jharkhand', *Dialogue*, Vol. 6 (4), April-June, 2005.
27. K.P.S. Gill, 'Endgame in Punjab 1988-93', *Faultlines*, Vol. 1, May 1999; Ashoke Kumar Mukhopadhyay, 'Through the Eyes of the Police: Naxalites in Calcutta in 1970s', *Economic & Political weekly*, Vol. 41 (29), July 22-28, 2006, pp. 3227-3233; Shale Horowitz & Deepti Sharma, 'Democracies Fighting Ethnic Insurgencies: Evidence from India', *Studies in Conflict & Terrorism*, Vol. 31 (8), 2008, pp. 749-773; Rachel Kleinfeld and Rushda Majeed, 'Fighting Insurgency with Politics: The Case of Bihar', *Carnegie Endowment for International Peace*, May 2016; D.N Sahaya, 'How Tripura overcame insurgency', *The Hindu*, 9 November, 2016.

2

ANDHRA PRADESH

The First Communist Movement

The Maoist (Naxalite) movement in undivided Andhra Pradesh can be traced back to the early 1940s when the Communist Party of India (CPI) and the left cadres of the Andhra Mahasabha started organising villagers into *sanghams* (committees) around issues such as bonded and forced labour *(vetti)*, exploitation by landlords, grain levies, forcible eviction, etc.[1] Over the years these sanghams provided platforms for the villagers to express their grievances and start their resistance against the economically and politically dominant *jagirdars* and *deshmukhs* (large landlord) in rural Telangana. In the initial years, the peasant resistance against landlords was largely non-violent. It was only in October 1946, when the Nizam banned the Andhra Mahasabha and brutally suppressed the villagers that the peasants took up arms heralding the first phase of the Maoist movement in India. The movement was largely successful in ending vetti, illegal exaction, compulsory grain levies and reoccupying land seized from the landlords in rural Telangana.[2]

This peasant uprising received further impetus in June 1947, when the CPI and Andhra Mahasabha decided to joined hands with the Hyderabad State Congress Party after the Nizam declared that Hyderabad State will not merge with the Indian Union. This alliance was a tactical one aimed at overthrowing the Nizam and creating a new state of Vishalandhra by merging Telangana with the Telegu speaking part of the Madras Presidency. So when the Congress launched Satyagarha to merge Hyderabad into the Indian Union, the CPI cooperated with the Congress in holding meetings and conducting demonstrations.

However, unlike the Congress cadres who fled to the border areas in the face of largescale repression by the Nizam, the Communist cadres stayed back in the villages mobilising and arming the villagers. The mobilised villagers were divided into village squads with 10,000 members, and regular guerrilla squads with 2000 members. The guerrilla squad became the nucleus of peoples' armed forces. As the movement grew in strength, the squads attacked the landlords and forcibly took their land, forcing them to flee the villages. The flight of the rural elites created an administrative void, which was filled by the sanghams. The sanghams established gram rajyam (village republics) in around 3000 villages and enacted radical socioeconomic reforms.[3]

While the armed peasant uprising in rural Telangana was partially successful in ending generations of feudal oppression and exploitation, this Communist-led and Communist-inspired armed movement was short-lived. In the aftermath of the liberation of Hyderabad State in 1948, a debate had ensued within the CPI whether to continue the armed insurrection or employ peaceful means. While one section of the CPI decided to renounce violence for their struggle, the other section decided to keep their arms lest the gains hitherto accrued would be lost. It was this section of violent Communist insurgents who, following the successful 'police action', fled the plains and took refuge in the adjoining forested and hilly areas bordering Telangana and erstwhile Hyderabad state.

By late 1949 and early 1950, the movement had 'reorganised along strict lines of Maoist guerrilla warfare', and began to spread to new areas of Godavari forest and Bhadrachalam. The dense forest and rugged terrain provided ideal conditions for the rebels to launch raids into plains and retreat to these forested bases. Moreover, the indigenous inhabitants (*Koyas*) of this areas, who were highly discontent because of the exploitation by the money lenders, contractors, and forest and revenue officials, welcomed the rebels and protected them. In return, the communists reorganised the disparate Adivasi groups into village squads and village committees and channelled their diverse struggles into a common insurgency.[4] Thus despite differing ideologies and world view, a symbiotic relationship between the adivasis and the communist rebels was established.

The communist insurgency or the 'Telangana movement' in Andhra Pradesh, which began in 1946 came to an end after five years, when the CPI announced unconditional withdrawal of their armed struggle on 21 October 1951. The robust counterinsurgency operations mounted by the Hyderabad administration against the rebels was primarily responsible for the Communist to call off their struggle. The well trained military and police was more than a match for the tag-rag peasant army who were ill-trained and ill-equipped.

As their firepower and 'military skills' started decreasing, the squads started directing their attacks on individuals rather than on the military or police, thus degenerating into sporadic acts of terrorism. Decreasing participation of the masses in the communist 'struggle' and lack of solidarity with the Telangana movement in the rest of the country indicated the waning appeal of the communist insurgency. Sharp differences amongst its leaders, a realisation that continuation of an armed struggle against the Indian Union was not a sound decision and that instead a more flexible approach could have been adopted compelled Communist leadership to call off their 'armed struggle'.[5]

The Srikakulam Uprising

The communist insurgency in the state, however, did not end with the withdrawal of the armed struggle by the CPI in 1951, but resurfaced time and again as the factors which caused the rebellion to arise at first remained unresolved. The next episode of the Maoist-inspired armed insurrection to overthrow the state power, often referred to as the Girijan struggle, occurred in the district of Srikakulam. The Girijan or Hill tribes (*Savara* and *Jatapu*) inhabited the Agency area spread over 509 square miles in the Eastern Ghats and comprised 90 per cent of the population of the Sikakulam district. As was the case in rural Telangana, these hill tribes were exploited by the money lenders and the landlords who not only alienated them from their mortgaged land because of non-payment of loans but also forced them to work as bonded or low wage labourers. It was under these circumstances that the tribespeople organised themselves into mass organisations or Girijan Sanghams under the leadership of Vempatapu Satyanarayana and Adibhatla Kailashan belonging to the undivided CPI and launched their struggle in 1959.[6]

The main demands of the tribespeople were uplifting restrictions on their way of cultivation, increase in daily wages, and return of mortgaged land after the expiry of the mortgaged period. By 1967 when the Naxalbari movement started in West Bengal, the Girijan movement had already achieved remarkable success in getting most of its demands met. The movement also aimed at raising the political consciousness of the people and remained essentially non-violent and within the limits of the law.[7]

It, however, turned militant after an incident on 31 October 1967 in which two tribespeople were killed by the landlords during a protest march.[8] Instigated by Communist leaders to take revenge, the tribespeople organised themselves in guerrilla squads or *dalams*. The first phase of the insurgency was launched on 25 November 1968 when 250 of them attacked the house of a money lender in Parvathipuram and took away paddy and other grain worth over Rs 20,000. These incidents were followed by series of raids on the houses of landlords and moneylenders as well as attacks on the police. Between 20 December 1968 and 30 January 1969, 29 policemen were killed by the guerrilla squads.[9]

Meanwhile, the Srikakulam Communist leaders had joined the All India Coordination Committee of Communist Revolutionaries (AICCCR)[10] and received guidance from Charu Mazumdar to start guerrilla warfare by annihilating class enemies and destroying the police force.[11] Inspired by the new line of struggle, the insurgents launched the second phase of their movement from February 1969. The guerrilla squads adopted the strategy of 'annihilation of class enemy campaign' and killed several landlords and policemen. In all, 150 persons including policemen were killed by the Naxalites in this campaign, thus transforming a non-violent movement for better wages and improved living conditions into a struggle for seizure of state power. They also controlled 300 villages spread over an area of 500 to 700 sq. miles of area where the administration had collapsed as the revenue, forest and other officials fled the area.[12] The movement soon started spilling over into Orissa (Odisha) and undivided Madhya Pradesh. In March 1969, Charu visited Srikakulam and hoped that it would become the 'Yenan of India' from where armed struggle will spread to the rest of the country.

The Telangana Communist Insurrection

Even as the Girijan movement was continuing, the Communists were spreading their 'armed struggle' in the rest of undivided Andhra Pradesh. The Andhra

Pradesh Coordination Committee of Communist Revolutionaries (APCCCR) who had disaffiliated from the AICCCR in June 1968, abjured the call for annihilation of class enemies and stressed on building a mass support base before starting an insurgency.[13] In April 1969, the APCCCR adopted 'The Immediate Programme', which called upon the party workers to adopt the path of people's war and mobilise the people of the plains as well as the forests. The APCCCR leaders travelled to Coastal Andhra and Rayalaseema to propagate 'graduated and protracted struggle', but could not find any revolutionary potential. Instead, they observed that those areas were more useful for getting financial support.

The Telangana region because of its history of communist insurrection proved to be conducive for mass mobilisation. Accordingly, the APCCCR started insurgency in Karimnagar, Warrangal, and Khammam districts of Telangana. Strong mass support and a forested terrain for guerrilla warfare propelled the success of the communist insurgency. By mid-1970, the insurgents claimed that a total area covering '7,000 to 8,000 square miles with a population of nearly 500,000/600,000' came under their control.[14] The administration of the 'liberated area' was run by the *Ryotangna Sangram Samithi* – the mass front of the Naxalites.

However, relentless police actions through encounters and mass arrests as well as socio-economic measures aimed at weaning the masses away from the Naxalites turned the tide in favour of the state government. The imposition of Emergency by Prime Minister Indira Gandhi in 1975 provided the state government with extraordinary police powers to crush the Naxalite movement. While the state's counterinsurgency operations did damage the organisational capacity of the insurgents in northern Telangana, it yet again failed to defeat them altogether.[15]

The Resilience of the Telangana Naxalite Movement

The failure of the Naxalbari and Srikakulam insurgencies and the death of ideologue Charu Mazumdar in 1972 caused the Communist Party of India (Marxist- Leninist) [CPI (M-L)] to break into many factions. In undivided Andhra Pradesh, multiple splits occurred in the state CPI (M-L). The group that had the largest following was led by Kondapalli Seetharamaiah, which was pro-Charu Mazumdar and followed his ideological and tactical position.[16]

Despite the multiple splits, there was a broad consensus among the CPI (M-L) groups that the Indian State was semi-feudal and semi-colonial and the Indian capitalist, a comprador entity, is in active collaboration with the landlords and are dependent on the metropolitan bourgeoisie. According to the CPI (M-L) parties, the principal contradiction in Indian society is between feudalism and the mass of poor peasantry and landless agricultural labour. The principal task of the agrarian revolution, which it calls the 'New Democratic' stage, is to fight against and abolish the feudal class in the countryside and democratise the social relations therein. The strategy thus formulated by the CPI (M-L) emphasised on the unity of the poor peasantry and landless poor, constituting a majority of the agrarian population against the feudal class.[17]

After the lifting of the Emergency in 1977, the Andhra Pradesh State Committee of the CPI (M-L) became active and began expanding and consolidating the movement, especially in Karimnagar and Adilabad districts. Incidentally, these areas of Telangana had remained unaffected by the communist struggles of 1940s. The new class of landlords, which emerged post-Independence in this region had continued with the old feudal ways of oppression against the landless peasantry and lower castes. It was against this social backdrop that the CPI (M-L) started organising and mobilising the agrarian poor to fight against the feudal oppression, coercion, as well as the practice of vetti. The Communist cadres also formed *Ryuthu-Coolie Sangathans* (RCS) in various villages, which gained ample support from the educated but radicalised lower caste youths for whom exploitation was a lived experience.

The mass agitations organised by the RCS succeeded in forcing the landlords to yield to their demands without much resistance. A mere call for social boycott of landlords would result in all service castes refusing to provide services causing great inconvenience to the landlords. The RCS also conducted 'public hearings' of cases of atrocities by the landlords, forced them to pay huge amounts as compensation and forcibly redistributed land illegally held by the landlords to the landless.[18] However, soon the landlords responded with violence by beating up peasants, raiding their houses and unleashing terror. The peasants, on their part, organised resistance which resulted in further escalation of violence. These violent episodes brought them in frequent conflict with the police.[19] By October 1978, frictions between the police and the RCS became so intense that the state government was forced to declare Jagityal and

Siricilla taluqs of Karimnagar district as 'disturbed areas'.[20] Subsequently, the police, equipped with extraordinary power, successfully quelled the 'peasant struggle' in Karimnagar.

Meanwhile, owning to sharp differences on the issue of adopting a militant posture, Seetharamaiah broke away from the Central Organising Committee of the CPI (M-L) and formed the People's War (PW) on 22 April 1980, popularly known as the People's War Group (PWG). The PWG now planned to expand its activities into a wide contiguous zone and developed three guerrilla zones in Northern Telangana, Dandakarnya and Andhra-Odisha (erstwhile Orissa) border. In 1980, as part of efforts to build up the guerrilla zones in Karimnagar, Adilabad, Warrangal and Khammam, it sent seven armed guerrilla squads to the strategic area (Dandakaranya) on the borders of undivided Andhra Pradesh, undivided Madhya Pradesh and Maharashtra.[21] Gradually an extensive mass base was built among the tribespeople of Dandakaranya and in February 1987, five Forest Divisions comprising the forest regions of Adilabad and the East Division (Vishakhapatnam and East Godavari) in undivided Andhra Pradesh, Gadchiroli in Maharashtra, and Balaghat and Bastar in undivided Madhya Pradesh were formed.[22] The guerrilla squads gained the confidence of the tribespeople in this region and organised them as *Dandakaranya Adivasi Kisan Mazdoor Sangathans* (DAKMS) to lead struggles on issues concerning the tribespeople.

The PWG also created several front organisations to take up issues concerning the weak and marginalised sections of the society comprising peasants, industrial workers, women, artists, etc. Some of these organisations were the Radical Student Union (RSU), Radical Youth League (RYL), *Mahila Sravanthi, Singareni Karmika Samkhya* and *Jana Natya Manch*. These organisations helped the PWG mobilise the masses, raise funds for the party, and propagate the Maoist ideology of gaining power through protracted armed struggle. Thus strengthened, the PWG embarked upon a comprehensive course of action to win over the masses while at the same time challenging the legitimacy of the state government. Their activities included redistribution of land to the landless, enforcing payment of minimum wages to farm labour, imposing taxes and penalties, holding 'people's court', and enforcing social codes such as total ban on the consumption of liquor.[23] In fact, the PWG ran a 'parallel government' in its area of influence.

It also indulged in largescale violence by destroying government properties, kidnapping government functionaries, attacking policemen with an objective to weaken the administration and achieve its ultimate political goal of capturing political power. By 1988, the mass agitations and armed resistance movement gained intensity. With the acquisition of sophisticated weapons, mainly through raids on police arsenals, specialised squads and advanced guerrilla tactics, the PWG posed a formidable challenge to the Andhra government. While violence perpetrated by the PWG peaked in 1991, it was also the year when its founder Kondapalli Seetharamaiah was replaced by Mupalla Laxman Rao Ganapathy as the General Secretary of the party.

In the 1990s, the PWG gained strength, consolidated and expanded its activities from Telangana to not only Coastal and Rayalseema districts of Andhra Pradesh but also in adjoining areas of Odisha, undivided Madhya Pradesh, Maharashtra, as well as the virgin territories of Tamil Nadu and Karnataka. It also launched the People's Guerrilla Army (PGA) to counter the security forces offensive. At the launch of PGA [later renamed as People's Liberation Guerrilla Army (PLGA)], the *de facto* head of Maoist military arm, Nambala Keasava Rao alias Basava Raju, apparently claimed that the PGA was formed to 'smash the rule of imperialism, feudalism, comprador bureaucrat capitalism, and to seize political power by setting up a new democratic state as a first step in the path to socialism.'[24] The creation of PGA also indicated a shift in the focus of the Maoists as now the emphasis was more on taking the state head on militarily, rather than fighting for the socio-economic problems of the masses.[25]

On 14 October 2004, the PWG announced its merger with the Maoist Communist Centre-India (MCCI), and the creation of single outfit called the Communist Party of India (Maoist).[26] The creation of CPI (Maoist) added a new dimension to the Naxal problem as the PWG no longer remained a state entity but became a pan India group. In 2005, following its withdrawal from the peace talks, violence levels went up. The number of violent incidents in the state increased from 310 with 74 deaths in 2004 to 532 with 208 deaths in 2005.[27] However, since then violence perpetrated by the Maoists have come down gradually in the state. In 2008, the number of violent incidents were under 100 at 92 with 46 deaths while the corresponding figures for 2012 were 67 and 13 respectively.[28] On 2 June 2014, Andhra Pradesh was bifurcated into Andhra Pradesh and Telangana through the Andhra Pradesh Reorganisation Act.[29] The bifurcation, however, did not adversely affect counter-Maoist operations and consequently, Maoist related violence witnessed a sharp decline in both the states.

The State Government's Response

The response of the successive governments to the problem of left wing extremism in the Andhra Pradesh (and subsequently in Telangana) has been a mix of coercion and political conciliation towards the Maoist rebels. At the same time, it formulated various legislations to address land alienation, a primary source of public discontentment in the affected areas and therefore a support base and recruitment pool for communist insurgents. Several initiatives were also undertaken to provide for basic amenities to the people, especially tribespeople and bring about economic wellbeing to wean them away from the extremists' fold and support the local government. The following sections elaborate successive state governments' responses to tackle the Maoist problem in the state over the decades.

Constitutional/Legal Provisions

Legal Provisions for Security: In the face of growing Communist insurgency in the state in the late 1940s, one of the first steps that the Government did was to enact the 'Andhra Pradesh Suppression of Disturbances Act' in 1948. This Act derived its validity from the 'Madras Suppression of Disturbances Act', which had received the assent of the Governor-General on 7 April 1948.[30] The Act was enacted to enable police to supress the peasant rebellion which had spilled over from Telangana to the Andhra regions of the Madras Presidency. This Act allowed the state government to declare the whole state or parts of it to be disturbed. It also allowed certain offences committed or abetted under the Indian Penal Code (IPC) to be punished by death instead of the punishment he or she was liable to under the Code.

Section 5 of the Act bestowed upon any magistrate or police officer not below the rank of sub-Inspector the power to fire, use force or order fire upon any person, even causing his/ her death, to maintain public order in the disturbed area. The Act also stated that no legal proceedings could be initiated against any person discharging his duties under Section 5 without the previous sanction of the state government.[31] This Act enabled the state police to tackle the communist uprising effectively.

In the 1980s, the Andhra government also invoked the stringent central law, the Terrorist and Disruptive Activates (Prevention) Act (TADA), to empower the police to tackle the Maoist insurgency.[32] The Act defined an offence as a terrorist act that aimed at overawing the government or strike terror among people or alienate any section of people or adversely affect societal harmony by using lethal weapons causing death or injuries. If an individual is found committing or abetting such an offence, then he/she was liable to a punishment of not less than five years in jail and also liable to fine. The Act also made a confession before a police officer admissible as evidence. Further, the Courts could not release a person arrested under this Act by issuing a habeas corpus.[33] The Act was allowed to lapse in 1995 because of its rampant misuse.

Legislations to Protect Poor Peasants and Tribals: The communist movement while challenging the state government legitimacy had also forced it to recognise the genuine hardship of the girijans. The government recognised that one of the factors responsible for the girijans to actively support the Naxalite is the fact that they lost their land to the non-tribals. Here, it is important to note that the state of Andhra Pradesh was formed on 1 November 1956 by merging the Andhra state (formed in 1953, on separation from Madras Presidency) and Telangana region of the erstwhile Hyderabad state, which was under the Nizam's rule. Being under different sets of regimes before 1956, the two regions experienced different land tenures in agrarian and land relations.

For the Telangana region, the Hyderabad Tenancy and Agricultural Lands Act of 1950 was promulgated with an objective to improve conditions in the *ryotwari* areas. The Act provided for the determination of area of family holdings as well as persons deemed as tenants.[34] The Act also laid down the maximum rent payable by the tenant as '1/4th of the gross produce for irrigated lands, other than well irrigated lands, and 1/5th in other cases or 3 to 5 times the land revenue (according to class of soil), whichever is less.'[35] At the same time, it prohibited receiving rent in form of labour. The Act eliminated intermediaries by abolishing tenancy as an institution in three to five years. It prevented the accumulation of land in the hands of a few by allowing the protected tenants to retain some portion of the land in case the landlord decides to resume cultivation personally. The protected tenants also had the option of purchasing the ownership of non-resumable lands under some conditions.[36] The Act prohibited land alienation and land fragmentation, and encouraged cooperative farming.

In the Andhra region, the Andhra Tenancy Act, which was temporary in nature was in force. It provided for stay of ejectments and fixation of rent at 50 per cent of the gross produce for irrigated lands, 28.1/3 per cent for lands irrigated by baling and 45 per cent for dry lands.[37] After its formation in 1956, the Andhra government enacted the first comprehensive land reforms legislation called the Andhra Pradesh Scheduled Areas Land Transfer Regulation (APSALTR of 1959 or Regulation 1 of 1959) Act in 1959 for the protection of tribal land. The Act prohibited the transfer of land in the Scheduled Areas by the tribals to non-tribals without permission, and if such transfers had taken place, then the land had to be returned to the tribal people.[38]

This Act, however, was not extended to the Telangana region. As a result, land alienation was very high among the girijans in the districts of Telangana and the offenders were not prosecuted at all. Finally in 1963, the Act was enforced in the Telangana region as well. But again, it remained ineffective because the rules could be framed only ten years later. Meanwhile, alienation of land among the tribals continued unabated. The need of the hour therefore was to enact protective laws, formulate rules for the laws and enforce them through special enforcement machinery.

Keeping this issue in perspective, the Andhra government passed the Andhra Pradesh Muttas (Abolition and Conversion into Ryotwari) Regulation in 1969 (Regulation II of 1969). Under this Regulation, the Muttadari system or 'mini-zamindari' system was abolished in the Scheduled Areas and facilitated the conferment of *patta* rights for the tribal ryots over the land held by them for a continuous period of not less than twelve months before the notified date.[39] This Regulation, however, benefitted only a third of the girijans who had access to the land and were cultivating it, rest of them languished as landless peasants.

The state government also attempted to restore land alienated from the girijans by the non-tribal moneylenders through coercive or illegal methods by constituting the Andhra (Scheduled Areas) Land Transfer (Amendment) Regulation of 1970 by amending the Andhra Pradesh (Scheduled Area) Land Transfer Regulation of 1959. The amended Regulation imposed absolute prohibition on transfer of immovable property in the Agency Tracts. It further stated that possession of any immovable property by a non-tribal will be presumed as being mortgaged to him by a Scheduled Tribe, until the contrary is proven.[40]

A sincere effort was made by district officials to enforce the Legislation by conducting surveys, writing out court applications for restoration of land to the girijans and serving eviction notices to the landlords.[41] All these efforts, however, did not achieve the objective of restoration of alienated land to the girijans because of the cumbersome and protracted judicial procedures. One of the reasons for the delays was the fact that the courts granted 'endless stays' to the landlords who were trying to perpetuate their possession of land by filing innumerable writ petitions.[42]

Moreover, in 1971 the Andhra Pradesh High Court ruled that the amendment is not retrospective, thus dealing a blow to the government's much delayed but sincere attempts at restoring land to the landless tribespeople. The state government tried to salvage the situation by distributing government owned waste lands to the landless girijans. So by 1971, the Andhra government had distributed between eight and nine thousand acres of land to the landless tribespeople.[43]

Further to addressing the issue of indebtedness of the tribespeople, which was the main reason for them to forfeit their land to the moneylenders, the state government enacted the Andhra Pradesh Scheduled Tribe Debt Relief Regulation (Regulation III of 1970). This Regulation strengthened the 1960 Moneylenders Regulation and provided relief to the tribespeople by scaling down their outstanding debts in two ways – first, all interests outstanding as on 1 January 1957 were deemed to have been discharged and only the principal amount alone was payable. In case the debts were incurred after 1 January 1957, the amount was calculated up to the commencement of the Regulation on 5 per cent simple interest per annum. Second, where twice the amount of principal was paid, the entire debt was deemed to have been discharged.[44] Further, legal proceedings initiated by the moneylenders to recover their loan amount were barred for a period of two years.

However, slow judicial process ensured that during 1971-72, out of 2015 cases, only in 153 cases debts were scaled down.[45] Thus, these measures although commendable, did not succeed in restoring alienated land because of legal loopholes, non-retrospective land regulations, powerful outsiders and a continuing lack of political commitment to protect tribal rights. Most non-tribals managed to hold on to their land by obtaining stay orders or producing false documents, which were further facilitated by rampant rent-seeking among officials.[46]

Security Response

After the Nizam was ousted by the Indian army, General J.N. Choudhuri established a new administration in the Hyderabad State on 18 September 1948. The newly formed government viewed the Communist led peasant uprising in rural Telangana as a rebellion against it. General Chaudhuri confidently announced that he would liquidate the Communists in all of Hyderabad in six weeks.[47] Subsequently, the government launched a massive counter insurgency offensive against the Communist rebels. This counterinsurgency operation was a combined police and military action involving two brigades of the Indian army and over nine thousand armed policemen along with a few battalions of the Hyderabad Army and two squadrons of cavalry.[48]

The counterinsurgency operations launched against the rebels by the military administration typically involved 'encirclement raid' in which the army would encircle anywhere from five to twenty villages at a time, gathering all the inhabitants at one place, and then conducting house to house searches. Since the guerrillas usually hid in the fields, the circle would slowly be closed until they were discovered.[49] Ironically, the villagers, who were earlier pro Sangham, helped the government identify communist sympathisers, guerrilla squads and their hiding places, as well as testify against them in court.[50] By the latter part of 1948 and early 1949, thousands of rebel leaders and cadres were either killed or imprisoned. Once the army took control of the villages, the administration dismantled the village republics propped up by the Communists, re-established village administration, and returned land and properties to the landlords, which had been forcibly taken away from them by the rebels.[51]

The strong military response against the communist rebels, however, only dispersed them into the forested areas of the state from where they reorganised and relaunched their rebellion. Alarmed by the spread of the communist movement, the Hyderabad administration urgently took steps to counter the insurgents. In effect, it employed a two pronged strategy of security and development targeting the insurgents and the population respectively. Under the security approach, joint police and military actions were directed against the insurgents. The police action was further bolstered by organising villagers and adivasis into civil defence groups variously named as Home Guards, Village Defence Squads and Gram Raksha Dal.

While the leadership for these groups were provided by local Congress politicians or local landlords, the foot soldiers were recruited by the police.[52] These vigilante groups were armed with firearms as well as spears and axes. Incentives were also offered to these groups for killing suspected insurgents. For instance, three hundred persons belonging to the Koya tribe were organised into 'tiger squads' and sent inside the forests to target communist *dalams* (armed squads).[53] Furthermore, to prevent the villagers and adivasis from providing logistical support to the insurgents, the administration employed the classic strategy of isolating the population from the insurgent or the 'Briggs Plan'. Accordingly, villagers and adivasis from thousands of villages and scattered hamlets in the forested areas were evacuated and settled near police and military camps.[54]

The Briggs Plan was a strategy developed by General Sir Harold Briggs, the Director Operations, who was fighting communist insurgency in Malaya. His plan was based on the principle that the best way to defeat the insurgency was to cut off the insurgents' access to logistical supplies and intelligence from their supporters amongst the population.[55] The plan essentially involved forced relocation of the population into guarded camps called the New Villages. In all, close to 500,000 villagers including 400,000 Chinese squatters from the fringes of the forests were shifted to these New Villages. Most of the so called New Villages were surrounded by wire fences, were floodlit and had police posts. The idea was to keep the population in and the insurgents out.[56] The site of the New Villages were chosen more for their defensibility rather than agricultural or other economic considerations.

After a lull of two decades, the Naxalite challenge which resurfaced in

1968 was met with a coercive state response. The Andhra government deployed the District Reserve Police (DRP) and Special Armed Police (SAP) in Srikakulam. Between December 1968 and February 1969, nine additional platoons of SAP was sanctioned and three police stations and a police outpost were setup with the border with Odisha.[57] Initially, the capabilities of the state police proved to be inadequate in tackling the insurgency, inviting criticism that the Andhra government was not serious about tackling the communist insurgency in the state.

To address the issue and to respond effectively to the insurgency, the state government declared the Agency areas in Parvathipuram, Palakonda and Pathapatnam Taluks of Srikakulam district as 'disturbed areas' under the Andhra Pradesh Suppression of Disturbances Act of 1948 on 7 June 1969. The Act bestowed enormous discretionary powers upon the police to use lethal violence against suspected insurgents. The Act also enabled the state government to strengthen its counterinsurgency operations by bringing in two battalions of the CRPF in the district.[58] The CRPF were joined by three battalions of the SAP and six platoons of DRP in addition to the regular district police. Besides, 80 armed outposts were also set up in the district.[59]

By August 1969 almost all of Srikakulam district was declared 'disturbed area' and an emergency police headquarter was established in the district to coordinate the governmental efforts. The Andhra government also reached out to the Odisha and the undivided Madhya Pradesh governments to coordinate police response against the Naxalites in the bordering areas. Further, the state government reemployed the programme of regrouping of villages. This programme was an iteration of Briggs Plan known as the 'strategic hamlets programme', which was implemented in South Vietnam in 1961-1963.

Like in the Malaya under the Briggs Plan, the American troops fighting the Viet Cong (Communist rebels) would round up South Vietnamese villagers in the insurgency affected areas and relocate them in newly built strategic hamlets. The programme, however, had dual objectives. The first was to deny the communist rebels food, shelter, intelligence as well as recruits from the local population. The second objective was to pacify the villagers and mobilise them politically to support the Government of Vietnam by providing them with basic amenities and infrastructure.[60]

In Andhra Pradesh, the government established new villages in the plains and brought the girijans from the hills and forested areas to resettle there. Six such villages with a population of five to six thousand were established.[61] The regrouping of the villages were ostensibly done to protect the tribespeople from the communist rebels on one hand, and on the other hand to promote tribal welfare by providing them with amenities such as health, education and drinking water.[62] The real motive of the government, however, was to deprive the Naxalites any support from the tribespeople by keeping the girijans under their constant watch. For example, the girijans were escorted to the field by the policemen and were instructed to return to the regrouped villages by evening. They were not allowed to carry food when they went out to their old villages to cultivate the fields. They were also instructed not to build any shelters in their fields and rest during the daytime.

As discussed, the state government provided these villages with basic necessities such as food and clothing, but by 1971, this support ceased as it was believed that the villagers should work for their own economic welfare by cultivating their land and collecting forests products for sustenance. As the government withdrew its support, the tribal people in these villages started to farm on their own. However, because of restrictions on their movement, they could not take care of their crop in the night from wild beasts and lost whatever they cultivated.[63] Thus, by 1974, these villages started witnessing famine-like situations and the tribespeople pleaded with the authorities to let them go back to their old villages.

Meanwhile, the police had resorted to largescale arrests as well as extrajudicial killings. Between May and December 1969, prominent leaders of the communist movement were killed. In May 1970, Panchadi Krishnamurthy, one of the most important Srikakulam naxalite leader was killed along with six others. In July 1970, Vempatapu Satyanarayana and Adibhatla Kailashan were killed and, by August 1970, 1641 insurgents were arrested by the police.[64] The killing of the two prominent leaders effectively brought an end to the Girijan Movement in Srikakulam.

It was in the early 1980s when the PWG was formed that communist insurgency resurfaced, and the state, once again, witnessed a gradual increase in violence perpetrated by the PWG. Stung by the increased targeting and killing of policemen by the PWG cadres, the state government resorted to coercive measures. By 1985, special anti-extremist wings of the police were created,[65] which established armed camps in the worst affected districts. The Andhra government also banned the PWG along with other Maoist groups in 1987 and invoked TADA, which gave power to the police to arrest suspected Naxalites and keep them in jail without trial for long periods of time.[66] Two years later in 1989, an elite police force called the Greyhounds was created to tackle the Naxal problem head on. The Greyhound consisted of 800 specially trained anti-guerrilla personnel 'that lives and operates as the Naxalite's armed squad'.[67]

When the Chandrababu Naidu government came to power in 1995, his government allocated resources to strengthen and modernise the police force as well as the state intelligence bureau.[68] Accordingly, the Greyhound training schools were revamped and new courses and methodologies were introduced. Most of the armed reserved battalions were converted into commando units and attached to the Greyhounds. All Greyhound personnel serving in Maoist areas were given additional 50 per cent salary as incentive.[69] The new personnel inducted into the police force had to serve their first four years in the Greyhounds and meritorious service in Greyhounds was mandatory to get accelerated promotions. Similarly, the State Police Intelligence wing was separated from Police HQs and strengthened with competent manpower, ample resources and improved technical back up.[70]

By 1999, ten years after its formation, the Greyhounds started getting an upper hand.[71] The counterinsurgency operations became more effective resulting in successfully 'neutralising' Naxal squads. Between 1996 and 2001, the Andhra police killed, on an average, 200 PWG cadres per year in 'encounters', which included three top PWG leaders – Nalla Adi Reddy, Erramreddy Santosh Reddy and Sheelam Naresh.[72]

The Y.S. Reddy government, which came to power in 2004, restarted counter-insurgency operations against the Maoists after the failure of the peace talks in 2005. While the peace talks provided some breather to the Maoists and allowed them to ensure recruitment and political mobilisation, it also provided the state police and intelligence agencies time to train continuously, consolidate their strengths and augment their capacities. The state government built upon the efforts of previous government and beefed up the coercive capabilities of the state. The Greyhounds were further strengthened with well-trained manpower, sophisticated weaponry, high tech surveillance and communication systems, monetary incentives and operational freedom.

The district police force was also simultaneously made more effective. Police personnel were trained to carry out police work such as profiling, investigation and prosecution of criminal cases against Maoist cadres, which not only resulted in their conviction but also succeeded in unearthing valuable information regarding the Maoist cadres and the organisation.[73] Police stations, especially in the rural areas, were adequately fortified so that the PLGA and the *Jan militia* do not run over them and carry away the weapons, as was happening in other Maoist affected states. The police also conducted mass contact programmes to identify and resolve people's problems as well as inculcate a sense of confidence in the local administration machinery.[74]

Likewise, the state intelligence bureau was provided with manpower, resources and infrastructure. For example in July 2006, the Y.S. Reddy government decided to recruit 100 personnel each in State Intelligence Bureau (SIB) and Counter Intelligence.[75] This helped them establish a reliable information network in the Maoist affected areas as well as penetrate the Maoist organisation successfully. In fact, when top Maoist leaders came out of hiding to participate in the peace talks, the state SIB entered the Nallamala Forest and gathered information about the leaders, their style of functioning and their networks.[76] Thus, when counterinsurgency operation resumed after the breakdown of the peace talks, the SIB was able to gather, collate, and analysis both technical and human intelligence and provide actionable intelligence to the counterinsurgency units.[77] The SIB provided intelligence about top Maoist leaders not only to Andhra Pradesh but also to others states, which resulted in the decimation of top leaders and resultant weakening of the CPI (Maoist).[78]

In addition, a generous surrender and rehabilitation policy weaved into the counterinsurgency strategy played an important role in facilitating a large number of cadres to surrender, which dealt a big blow to the Maoist movement in the state. The cash reward lured many Maoist cadres and leaders, some of whom have been in the forests for long years, to come out, surrender and start a new life. Some of the surrendered Maoist cadres also provided information about the organisations and its cadres, which were used by the authorities to undertake precise operations. In December 2012, the state government updated its surrender policy and offered a cash reward of Rs 10 lakhs to 25 lakhs depending upon the rank of the surrendered Maoist cadre. These rewards could also be given to the police force and informants if Maoist cadres are killed during operations.

These preparations enabled the Greyhounds to launch a successful operation against the Maoists in the Nallamala Forest spanning approximately 13,000 square kilometres across parts of five districts in central undivided Andhra Pradesh: Kurnool, Mahbubnagar, Nalgonda, Guntur, and Prakasam.[79] As a result of sustained pressure put by the Greyhounds, approximately 9,000 CPI (Maoist) cadres were either arrested or surrendered in the state between 2005 and 2008.[80] By 2007, the top leadership of CPI (Maoist) were forced to relocate outside the state, particularly in the Andhra-Odisha Border (AOB) and the Bastar Region of neighbouring Chhattisgarh.[81]

Political Response

That the Communists were a force to reckon with in Andhra Pradesh was not lost on the Congress Party post-independence. The earliest elections in which the Communists not only won legislative seats but also considerable voter's share indicated that the Communists had a strong support base, especially among the poor peasants and landless labourers. In a bid to increase its support base and to eliminate the popular support for the Communists, the Congress co-opted the leftist agenda and initiated land reforms. Several legislations to abolish intermediaries and to bestow tenancy rights to the landless peasants were enacted to project a progressive image of Congress and endear it to the peasantry. Importantly, it also politically co-opted the Reddys, Khammas and the Kapus, who were the landed gentries in the countryside, and some of who held leadership positions in the dalams.[82]

The Congress Party also introduced the Panchayati Raj system in Andhra Pradesh in 1957 and successive elections to the *Zilla Parishads* and *Panchayati Samitis* saw the dominance of the peasant castes. Thus, by accommodating large sections of rich peasant elites in political positions, the Congress was able to consolidate its grassroot leadership base in the state.[83] With the support of prominent castes firmly behind it, the state governments dominated by the Congress party, in the initial decades, viewed the communist insurrection essentially as a law and order problem and treated it as such by deploying police and enacting the Disturbed Areas Act to give special powers to the police to deal with the armed extremists.[84]

It was only in the 1980s and afterwards that the political parties termed Naxalism as a political problem and tried to find a solution through conciliations and negotiations. For example, during the run up to the state elections, N.T. Rama Rao (NTR) had referred to the PWG cadres as *desabhaktalu* (patriots) and *annalu* (elder brother) in an effort to win them over.[85] Once in power in 1983, Rao announced a lucrative Surrender and Rehabilitation Policy of Rs 1 Lakh cash award to each of the cadres and offered peace negotiations to the PWG.[86]

This lenient approach of the NTR government towards the PWG, instead of bringing it to the negotiating table, emboldened its leaders to defy the state leadership and continue with their violent activities.[87] In fact, much of the PWG's expansion and consolidation in the eighties can also be attributed to the benign and friendly approach of the Telegu Desam government. Critics of NTR's policies towards Naxalites pointed out that the government considered Naxalism only as a political problem instead of a socio-economic problem. Therefore, his efforts to end the Naxal problem was a total failure because his government focused on buying off the Naxal cadres instead of implementing land reforms and other measures to improve the socio-economic conditions of the poor.[88]

Be that as it may, the NTR government could not overlook the mindless killings of police personnel and civilians by the PWG for long. Slowly but surely, the government was forced to harden its stance against the PWG and impose a ban on it besides strengthening the police to deal with the Naxal menace in the state.[89]

The N T Rama Rao government was followed by the Marri Chenna Reddy government, who also employed a conciliatory attitude towards the Naxalites. Rumours were rife that the reason behind Chenna Reddy's soft approach was the fact that, like NTR, he also came to power with the help and support of the PWG.[90] Not surprisingly, the ban imposed on the PWG and other groups was lifted in December 1989. Reddy's government also released all Naxalite prisoners held without trial. It permitted the Naxalites to come over ground, hold legal activities such as protests/demonstrations as well as conduct dispute resolutions in villages.[91]

The conciliatory approach of the state government once again allowed the PWG to recruit, rearm and energize itself. The release of 190 hard-core Naxalites provided the much needed leadership and cadres as well as helped in reinvigorating the movement at the grassroots.[92] Consequently, Naxalite violence increased forcing the Janardhan Reddy government to re-impose ban on the PWG and its seven front organisations in May 1992.[93] The state government also brought in the CRPF to reinforce the efforts of the state police, established informant networks and announced a lucrative Surrender and Rehabilitation Policy in 1993 to lure the Naxalites out of insurgency. The ban on the PWG accompanied by police operations resulted in the surrender of nearly 2500 militants and activists.[94] The ban on the PWG was, however, briefly lifted when N.T. Rama Rao returned to power in May 1995.

The vacillating approach of successive governments in Andhra Pradesh in the 1980s and early 1990s towards the PWG allowed it to gain in strength and expand its activities beyond Telangana into adjoining states. This trend of a conciliatory approach towards the PWG was reversed when Chandrababu Naidu formed his government in September 1995. His government re-enforced the ban on the PWG and its front organizations in July 1996 and reverted to the policy of confronting Naxalism with force.[95] In addition to coercive force, the Chandrababu Naidu's government also continued with the lucrative surrender and rehabilitation policy. Some of the salient features of the policy were:

(a) on the spot disbursal of Rs 5000 to meet the immediate expenses of the surrendering Naxalite;
(b) financial assistance equivalent to the reward money declared by the government if the Naxalite is arrested by the police and a loan of a maximum of Rs 4 lakh;
(c) additional financial assistance if the Naxalite surrenders with weapons, etc.

Thus between 1998 and 2002, 2481 Naxalites surrendered, which peaked in 2003 with 890 cadres surrendering before the Andhra government.[96]

Surrenders are encouraged by the state governments because 'it shatters the myth of Naxalism'.[97] Surrenders are seen as a rejection of the Maoist ideology and therefore demoralising for the cadres. Besides, highlighting the sufferings of the families of cadres still in the insurgency folds, surrenders also reveal how a life is wasted chasing an elusive dream when the surrendered person is unable to integrate in the society. These factors deter potential recruits from joining the folds of the Maoist insurgency.[98]

Interestingly, the Naidu government also entered into peace talks, albeit, reluctantly in an effort to find a political solution to the Naxal problem. The atmosphere for peace talks was created when the PWG was compelled to declare ceasefire in May 2002 because of relentless counterinsurgency operations and a concomitant loss of influence in its traditional stronghold. The peace negotiations, however, collapsed within three months resulting in the re-imposing of the ban.[99] The breakdown of talks led to the increase in violence and counter violence by the PWG and the police forces.

Incidents of violence in the state started increasing from 18 in 2001 to 26 in 2005.[100] As a matter of fact, the PWG made an unsuccessful attempt on the life of Chandrababu Naidu in October 2003. Following the attack, the state government intensified security operations against the Naxalites. It also embarked on rapid modernisation of police force and invested in augmenting its technical intelligence arm. The 'intelligence driven' counter insurgency operations were successful in breaking the Naxalites forcing them to move back on 'strategic defensive phase'.[101]

Significantly, all efforts to tackle the naxal insurgency through coercive actions came to a halt when the Y. Shekhar Reddy came to power in May 2004 promising to tackle the problem through negotiations with PWG. Accordingly, the ban on the PWG was lifted and police action against them was suspended on the understanding that the PWG will also stop armed action.[102] Preliminary process of the peace talks started with discussing the terms of the draft of the ceasefire agreement between the state government and the PWG. While an unofficial ceasefire was implemented in July 2004, it was poorly observed given that the PWG cadres continued to wield weapons in public gatherings despite the state government's strong reservations.[103]

Interestingly, just a day before formal talks were to start, the PWG announced on 14 October 2004, creation of the Communist Party of India (Maoist).[104] This announcement acted as a dampener because the creation of CPI (Maoist) added a new dimension to the Naxal problem as the PWG no longer remained a state entity but became a pan India group.

Nevertheless, during the second rounds of talks, the Maoists raised issues such as extra-judicial killings, state patronage to vigilante groups, right to freedom of expression, etc., but more specifically, the Maoist interlocutors raised the issue of non-implementation of land reforms. The Maoists asserted that though land reform legislations had been enacted in 1972, only 5 per cent of the cultivable land had been redistributed till 2004.[105]

To which the state government responded that in the absence of land records, land reform measures could not be implemented.[106] At the same time, it promised that a comprehensive land inventory would be compiled and a commission will be set up to look into the matters of land reforms. The CPI (Maoist), however, pulled out of the peace talks in January 2005 before the third round of talks could start. It accused the state government of letting loose repression by the state police and cited specific incidents in which Maoists cadres were killed.[107]

The withdrawal of the Maoists from the peace talks saw an increase in the incidents of violence in the state. Many observers argued that the offer for talks by the CPI (Maoist) was a ruse to get respite from police action and consolidate their strength in the interregnum. In reality, the Maoists were never interested in peace talks. They did so because of immense pressure exerted by the CCC (Committee of Concerned Citizens) who wanted an end to the cycle of violence in the state[108] and also because the PWG had lost considerable ground in their area of domination, the North Telangana Special Zone.[109] In fact, a senior CPI (Maoist) leader had stated that talks are for solving the problems of the masses, but their ultimate aim is to establish Communism through armed struggle.[110]

Following the withdrawal of the CPI (Maoist) from peace talks, and the brutal killing of Congress Party's MLA along with six others by the Maoists on 15 August 2005, the Andhra government re-imposed the ban on the CPI (Maoist) and its front organisations two days later.

Governance

One of the first acts of the military administration was the incorporation of *Serf-e-Khas* (Crown) lands into the diwani (government) area. Except personal lands, all the territory held by the Nizam was taken over and merged into government lands. [111] At the same time, in an effort to co-opt peasants' support, the military administration abolished the jagirs of the erstwhile Hyderabad State under the Jagir Abolition Regulation in August 1949.[112] For the administration of the jagirs, pending their assimilation with the diwani, a jagir administrator (and assistant jagir administrators) were appointed by the military governor, who were empowered to determine the size of the farmland. Civil courts replaced the *Atiyat* authority. The military administration also set up an Agrarian Enquiry Committee to recommend comprehensive land reform legislation in Telangana.

The administration also undertook a development approach to win the hearts and minds of the people. Under this approach, it created the 'Telangana Special Area' in early 1950 and appointed a Special Commissioner to undertake developmental works in the region. These developmental works included construction and repair of irrigation tanks, sinking of wells, provision of medical aid, opening of schools, distribution of food and other essential commodities, and most importantly, agrarian reform legislation. To what extent these developmental initiatives brought about positive changes in the rural life remains debatable.

These measures, however, did help the counter-insurgency operations as they enabled the military and police to reach far flung areas and stay put. For example, the rural roads were primarily used by the counter-insurgents to travel rapidly to remote villages and forested areas. Similarly, the 268 'civil centres' which were built to act as 'centres of rural uplift' were converted into police out posts where landlords and government officials could reside and visit their villages with police protection.[113] Furthermore, the land reform Act of 1950 resulted in more landless peasants as the landlord evicted cultivators in a bid to prevent them from acquiring tenancy rights under the Act.

Beginning in 1968 when Naxalism resurfaced in undivided Andhra Pradesh, the state government posted 'young and dedicated' district officials in the tribal dominated areas. It also created a new post, the 'Special Deputy Collector for Tribal Welfare', as a clear recognition that the incumbent officials' unresponsiveness to tribal needs were responsible for the growth of Naxalite problem in the state.[114] The new officials were directed to initiate development works such as roads, irrigation as well as vigorously implement the protective legislation that already existed. In 1970-71, the state government allocated an additional Rs 32.74 lakhs to the Srikakulam District 'with a view to accelerate the development of the Scheduled Tribes'.[115] However, half of allocated amounts were for improving transportation meant for speedy deployment of police forces.

During the 1980 and 1990s, in order to tackle the communist rebellion spearheaded by the PWG, successive governments took into consideration the socio-economic aspect of the extremist movement and initiated an economic development scheme called the Remote and Interior Areas Development Programme (RIAD).[116] The RIAD was started with the realisation that some parts of the state continue to be underdeveloped because of 'their remoteness, inaccessibility and years of neglect.'[117] The programme started in May 1990 with an outlay of Rs 86 crores and had schemes ranging from building roads, to minor irrigation wells, drinking water facilities, credit facilities for Girijans, training programmes, and so on and so forth.[118] The programme was implemented in nine 'naxalite districts', which were predominantly inhabited by tribal people. Interestingly, the implementation of the schemes under the RIAD programme was entrusted to the local people, especially tribals and youths, who were perceived to be more vulnerable to the Naxalite influences. Given the enormity of poverty in the state and given that land reforms were not implemented effectively, the developmental programme could not make a meaningful difference in the socio-economic well-being of the peasants and tribal people.

In the mid-2000s, the Y.S. Reddy government focused on the rural economy with the understanding that the Maoist problem was a manifestation of socio-economic grievances. His government launched several agrarian and welfare programmes for the rapid development of the rural areas. For the farmers, the state government waived off agricultural loans, provided free electricity and input subsidies. It also launched a massive irrigation project-cum-drinking water programme called Jalayagnam with an outlay of Rs 46,000 crores to irrigate 87.32 lakh acres of fallow land in the backward tribal and drought prone areas and generate 2,115 MW of power, besides providing drinking water.[119]

Several schemes such as low cost health insurance (*Rajiv Arogyasri*), free emergency ambulance, low cost housing (INDIRAMMA), subsidised rice for the poor, loans for women and pensions for old and destitute, rural and urban employment, reimbursement of fee for higher education from low income families, etc. were also initiated and implemented.[120] Besides, a number of roads, health centres schools, etc. were constructed in the rural areas, with special focus on Maoist affected areas in Telangana. The state government also effectively implemented various centrally sponsored schemes such Backward Districts Initiative (BDI), Backward Regions Grant Fund (BRGF), the National Rural Employment Guarantee Scheme (NREGS), the Prime Minister's Gram Sadak Yojna, the National Rural Health Mission Scheme (NRHM) and Sarva Siksha Abhiyan (SSA).[121]

While critiques have questioned the desired benefits accrued to the poor and tribespeople of the state by these welfare and developmental scheme,[122] there is no denying that these measure did ameliorate the material condition of the villagers and tribespeople albeit incrementally. More significantly, effective implementation of these developmental measures robbed the Maoists of issues to mobilise the masses against the government.[123] This argument can be corroborated by the fact that the number of violent incidents witnessed by Andhra Pradesh also saw a steady decline from a high of 535 in 2005 to 92 incidents in 2008 and 28 in 2013.[124] A total of 1608 Maoist leaders and cadres surrendered between 2005 and 2013.[125]

Summary

The Andhra Pradesh government defeated the Communist (Naxal/Maoist) insurgency predominantly through a force centric counterinsurgency strategy. A coercive counterinsurgency strategy of raising special elite police force backed by an effective and sophisticated intelligence apparatus to take the Maoist rebels head-on was substantially responsible for uprooting of Maoist insurgency in the state. This strategy resulted in either killing or arrest of a number of top Maoist leaders, forcing rest of the leadership to flee the state and take shelter in neighbouring states.

A lucrative surrender and rehabilitation policy also lured a large number of middle and lower rung cadres to surrender and join the mainstream. Socio-political engineering by state political leaders of empowering the middle and lower castes through grass-root institutions and developmental programmes, which addressed the political and economic aspirations of the people in the rural and tribal areas of the state also robbed the Maoists the opportunity of exploiting the genuine and perceived grievances of the poor, thereby decreasing their allure among the people.

NOTES

1. P. Saundaryya, *Telangana People's Struggle and its Lessons*, Communist Party of India: Calcutta, 1972, p. 28.
2. Ibid, pp. 54-55.
3. Ibid, p. 60.
4. Ibid, pp. 246-247. Jonathan Kennedy and Sunil Purushotham, 'Beyond Naxalbari: A Comparative Analysis of Maoist Insurgency and Counterinsurgency in Independent India', *Comparative Studies in Society and History*, Vol. 54 (4), October 2012, p. 841.
5. Ibid, pp. 423-427.
6. Biplab Dasgupta, 'Naxalite Armed Struggles and the Annihilation Campaign in Rural Areas', *Economic and Political Weekly*, Vol. 8 (4/6), Feb., 1973, p. 177.
7. Ibid.
8. Prakash Singh, *The Naxalite Movement in India*, New Delhi: Rupa, 2016, p. 37.
9. n. 6, pp. 177-178.
10. The AICCR was formed in November 1967 and formally became the CPI (Marxist-Leninist) on Mayday 1969.
11. n. 6.
12. Ibid, p. 178.
13. Jonathan Kennedy and Sunil Purushotham, n. 4, p. 889.
14. C. Chandra Sekhara Rao, 'What to do?', in Samar Sen, Debabrata Panda, and Ashish Lahiri (Eds.), *Naxalbari and After, A Frontier Anthology*, Vol. 1, Kolkata: Kothashilpa, 1978, p. 101.
15. Jonathan Kennedy and Sunil Purushotham, n. 4, p. 889.
16. n. 8, p. 113.
17. K. Srinivasulu, 'Caste, Class and Social Articulation in Andhra Pradesh: Mapping Differential Regional Trajectories', Working Paper No. 179, New Delhi: Overseas Development Institute, September 2002, p. 16.
18. Ibid, p. 22.
19. Ibid.
20. Giridhari Nayak, *Neo-Naxal Challenge, Issues & Options*, New Delhi: Pentagon Press, 2011, p. 10.
21. Ibid.
22. Rajeshwari Ravikant, *"People's War" and State Response: The Naxalite Movement in Telangana, India (1970-1993)*, Ph. D Thesis, Vancouver: University of British Columbia, September 1995, p. 65.
23. n. 8, p. 113.
24. The PGA was later renamed as the People's Liberation Guerrilla Army (PLGA) following the merger of PWG with the Maoist Communist Centre of India (MCCI) on 21 September 2004. P.V. Ramana, 'Maoist People's Liberation Guerrilla Army', *IDSA Comment*, 12 December 2011, at https://www.idsa.in/idsacomments/MaoistPeoplesLiberationGuerrillaArmy_pvramana_121211, accessed on 30 December 2021.
25. K. Balagopal, 'Maoist Movement in Andhra Pradesh', *Economic and Political Weekly*, Vol. 41(29), 22-28 July 2006, p. 3185.
26. *Annual Report 2008-09*, New Delhi: Ministry of Home Affairs, 2009, p. 3.
27. *Annual Report 2004-05*, New Delhi: Ministry of Home Affairs, 2005, p. 171.
28. *Annual Report 2019-20*, New Delhi: Ministry of Home Affairs, 2020, p. 10.
29. *The Andhra Pradesh Reorganisation Act, 2014 (Act No. 6 of 2014)*, at https://www.aplegislature.org/documents/12524/17895/APRegACT2014.pdf/8505fe86-f67b-41a7-

ac8f-571f58090586, accessed on 17 October 2022.

30. *The Tamil Nadu Suppression of Disturbances Act, 1948 Act 3 of 1948*, 1948, at https://prsindia.org/files/bills_acts/acts_states/tamil-nadu/1948/1948TN3.pdf, accessed on 13 October 2022.
31. Ibid.
32. (The) *Terrorist and Disruptive Activities (Prevention) Act,* 1987, at https://www.indiacode.nic.in/bitstream/123456789/15340/1/terrorist_and_disruptive.pdf, accessed on 19 October 2022.
33. Ibid.
34. *The Telangana Tenancy and Agricultural Lands Act,* 1950. *(Act No. XXI of 1950)*, pp. 7-8, at https://law.telangana.gov.in/pdf/Act%20XXI%20of%201950_13012023_113416.pdf, accessed on 13 October 2022.
35. *Implementation of Land Reforms: A Review by the Land Reforms Implementation Committee of the National Development Council*, New Delhi, Planning Commission, 1966, p. 1.
36. Ibid, p. 2.
37. Ibid.
38. S. Laxman Rao, Priya Deshingkar and John Farrington, 'Tribal Land Alienation in Andhra Pradesh Processes, Impacts and Policy Concerns', *The Economic and Political Weekly*, Vol. 41 (52), 30 December 2006, p. 5401.
39. The British had adopted the system of indirect rule over these areas through feudal intermediaries like Muttadars, Mahaldars, Jagirdars and Zamindars. The estate holders divided the tribal areas into groups of villages called Muttas, or Mahals and entrusted their management to influential individuals called Muttadars or Mahaldars. In course of time, the Muttadars and Mahaldars became all powerful and oppressive. They collected rents far in excess of the prescribed rates and extracted free labour from the tenants. The tribal tenants had no security of tenure under them. For details see, D. Ramachandra Raju, 'Protective Laws in Scheduled Areas of Andhra Pradesh', *Cochin University Law Review*, Vol. IX, 1985, p. 150, 155.
40. Ibid, p. 153.
41. n. 14, p. 101.
42. Ibid. Leslie J. Calman, *Protest in Democratic India, Authority's Response to Challenge*, London: Westview Press, 1985, pp. 105-106.
43. Ibid, p. 106.
44. n. 39, p. 155.
45. Ibid, p. 108.
46. n. 38, p. 5406.
47. n. 1, p. 178.
48. n. 4, p. 842.
49. n. 1, p. 196.
50. Ibid
51. Ibid, p. 195
52. n. 4, p. 843.
53. Ibid.
54. n. 1, p. 290.
55. Sir Michael Burton, 'The Malayan Emergency: A Subaltern's view', *Asian Affairs*, Vol. 42 (2), 2011, p. 254.
56. Ibid.
57. n. 42, p. 75.
58. N. Subba Reddy, 'Crisis of Confidence among the Tribal People and the Naxalite Movement in Srikakulam District', *Human Organization*, Vol. 36 (2), Summer 1977, p. 148.

59. n. 42, pp.78-79.
60. Philip E. Catton, 'Counter-Insurgency and Nation Building: The Strategic Hamlet Programme in South Vietnam, 1961-1963', *The International History Review*, Vol. 21 (4), December 1999, p. 919.
61. Amrita Rangaswami, 'Making a Village: An Andhra Experiment', *Economic and Political Weekly*, Vol. 9 (36), 7 September, 1974, p. 1524.
62. Ibid. 1525-1526.
63. Ibid, p. 1524.
64. n. 6, p. 179.
65. K. Balagopal, 'People's War and the Government: Did the Police Have the Last Laugh?', *Economic and Political Weekly* , Vol. 38 (6), 8-14 February 2003, p. 514.
66. Jennifer L. Oetken, 'Counterinsurgency against Naxalites in India', in Sumit Ganguly, David P. Fidler (eds.), *India and Counterinsurgency: Lessons Learned*, Oxon: Routledge, 2009, p. 137. Also see, n. 22, p. 90.
67. n. 25.
68. Arijit Mazumdar, 'Left-Wing Extremism and Counterinsurgency in India: The "Andhra Model"', *Strategic Analysis*, Vol. 37 (4), 2013, pp. 450-451.
69. Col. J. K. Achuthan (Retd.), 'Tackling Maoists: the Andhra paradigm', *India Defence Review*, Vol. 25, Apr-June 2010 at http://www.indiandefencereview.com/news/tackling-maoists-the-andhra-paradigm/, accessed on 3 January 2022.
70. Ibid.
71. G.S. Radha Krishna, 'Malkangiri encounter: Ill-fated peace talks in 2004 with Andhra govt reason behind recent bloodbath', *FirstPost*, 7 November 2016 at https://www.firstpost.com/india/malkangiri-encounter-ill-fated-peace-talks-in-2004-with-andhra-govt-reason-behind-recent-bloodbath-3091790.html, accessed on 3 January 2021.
72. n. 65, p. 516.
73. n. 68, p. 452.
74. P.V. Ramana, 'A Critical Evaluation of the Union Government's Response to the Maoist Challenge', *Strategic Analysis*, Vol. 33 (5), September 2009, p. 747. Also see, n. 26, pp. 18-19.
75. 'AP govt to strengthen SPF, SIB, Counter Intelligence', *One India*, 18 July 2006 at https://www.oneindia.com/2006/07/18/ap-govt-to-strengthen-spf-sib-counter-intelligence-1153222954.html, accessed on 4 January 2022.
76. Madhavi Tata, 'Lessons From Andhra', *Outlook*, 19 April 2010 at https://www.outlookindia.com/magazine/story/lessons-from-andhra/265014, accessed on 4 January 2022.
77. Ajai Sahni, 'The State Advances, the Maoists Retreat', *South Asia Intelligence Review*, Vol. 6 (10), 17 September 2007.
78. n. 68, p. 453.
79. n. 77.
80. n. 68, p. 452.
81. n. 76.
82. n. 17, p. 8.
83. Ibid, p. 9.
84. M. Shashidhar Reddy, 'A Political Approach to Naxalite Problem: Viability and Prerequisites for Success', in P. V. Ramana (ed.), *The Naxal Challenge: Causes, Linkages, and Policy Options*, Delhi: Pearson Longman, 2008, p. 42.
85. n. 22, p. 84.
86. Ibid, p. 84.

87. For details of the violence perpetrated by the Naxals see, n. 8, pp. 117-119.
88. n. 22, p. 85.
89. Ajai Sahni, ''Naxalism' The Retreat of Civil Governance', *Faultline*, Vol. 5, May 2000, at https://www.satp.org/satporgtp/publication/faultlines/volume5/fault5-7asahni.htm, accessed on 10 October 2022.
90. n. 66, p. 137. Also see, n. 25, p. 3185.
91. n. 8, p. 121.
92. Ajai Sahni, 'Delusion of peace', *Frontline*, 21 October 2005 at https://frontline.thehindu.com/cover-story/article30206860.ece, accessed on 30 December 2021.
93. The seven organizations were: Radical Youth League, Rythu Coolie Sangham, Radical Students' Union, Singareni Karmika Samakhya, Viplava Karmika Samakhya, All-India Revolutionary Students' Federation and the Revolutionary Writers' Association or Virasam. These were banned under the Andhra Pradesh Public Security Act, 1992. Saji Cherian, 'The States Of Denial', *Outlook India*, 23 August 2005 at https://www.outlookindia.com/website/story/the-states-of-denial/228369, accessed on 30 December 2021.
94. Amarnath K Menon, 'Andhra Pradesh: People's War Group operations curbed, but still deadly', *India Today*, 15 October 1992 at https://www.indiatoday.in/magazine/indiascope/story/19921015-andhra-pradesh-peoples-war-group-operations-curbed-but-still-deadly-766978-2012-12-26, accessed on 31 December 2021.
95. n. 92.
96. Data from P.V. Ramana, 'Taming India's Maoists: Surrender and Rehabilitation', *Strategic Analysis*, Vol. 37 (6), 2013, p. 723.
97. P.V. Ramana, 'Taming India's Maoists: Surrender and Rehabilitation', *Strategic Analysis*, Vol. 37 (6), 2013, p. 722.
98. K. Srinivas Reddy, 'Maoist Movement in Andhra Pradesh: The Now and Why', Paper presented at the National Conference on Non-State Armed Groups and India's Security, 2007 as quoted in n. 124.
99. n. 65, p. 519.
100. Data Sheet Andhra Pradesh, Major Incidents at https://www.satp.org/datasheet-terrorist-attack/major-incidents/india-maoistinsurgency-andhrapradesh, accessed on 31 December 2021.
101. K. Srinivas Reddy, 'The Maoist challenge', *Seminar*, Vol. 569, 2007 at https://www.india-seminar.com/2007/569/569_k_srinivas_reddy.htm, accessed on 31 December 2021.
102. K. Srinivas Reddy, 'Revolutionary and Counter Revolutionary Strategies of the Naxalites and the State', in P. V. Raman (ed.), *The Naxal Challenge, Causes, Linkages, and Policy Options*, New Delhi, Pearson, 2008, p. 98.
103. Tanweer Fazal, 'Peace Talks' as Strategic Deployment: the State, Maoists and Political Violence in India', *Irish Studies in International Affairs*, Vol. 26, Special focus: Conflict Resolution in South Asia, 2015, pp. 47-48.
104. *Annual Report 2004-05*, New Delhi: Ministry of Home Affairs, 2005, p. 3.
105. Sreenivas Janyala, 'When they talked – and failed', *The Indian Express*, 14 March 2010 at https://indianexpress.com/article/news-archive/print/when-they-talked-and-failed/, accessed on 3 January 2022.
106. n. 103, p. 48.
107. Sanjay K. Jha, 'Political Bases and dimensions of the Naxalite Movement', in P.V. Ramana (ed.), *The Naxal Challenge: Causes, Linkages, and Policy Options*, Delhi: Pearson Longman, 2008, p. 67.
108. n. 65, p. 513.
109. P.V. Ramana, 'Peace with PWG Naxals: A wishful exercise?', New Delhi: Observer Research

Foundation, 2 July 2004 at https://www.orfonline.org/research/peace-with-pwg-naxals-a-wishful-exercise/, accessed on 3 January 2022.

110. CPI (Maoist) leader, Prakash, as quoted in n. 107, p. 68.
111. S. Kesava Iyenger, 'Land Reforms in the Hyderabad State', *The Indian Journal of Agricultural Economics*, Vol. 8 (1), March 1953, p. 114.
112. Rohan D. Mathew, 'The Telengana Movement: Peasant Protests in India, 1946-51', *ritimo*, 1 July 2021 at https://www.ritimo.org/The-Telengana-Movement-Peasant-Protests-in-India-1946-51, accessed on 12 October 2021.
113. n. 4, p. 842.
114. n. 42. 102-103.
115. Ibid, pp. 104-105.
116. n. 84, p. 43; n. 22, pp. 85-86.
117. n. 84, p. 44.
118. Ibid, pp. 46-48.
119. n. 94.
120. 'Major schemes initiated by YSR', *The New Indian Express*, 4 September 2009 at https://www.newindianexpress.com/states/andhra-pradesh/2009/sep/04/major-schemes-initiated-by-ysr-83265.html, accessed on 4 January 2022.
121. n. 26, p. 16.
122. K. Srinivasulu, 'Y S Rajasekhara Reddy: A Political Appraisal', *Economic and Political Weekly*, Vol. 44(38), 19-25 September 2009, pp. 8-10.
123. n. 69. n. 68, p. 453-454.
124. n. 28.
125. Total number of surrenders from 2005 to 2013. South Asia Terrorism Portal.

3

TRIPURA

Tripura is a classic case where simmering ethnic tensions between the indigenous people and migrant Bengalis gradually morphed into a raging insurgency. During the colonial period, the promotional migration policy of the Rajas of Tripura had led to largescale migration into Tripura from undivided Bengal. By virtue of their long and close association with Bengal, the Rajas of Tripura were impressed with the intellectual and economic development of Bengal and desired to replicate the same system in Tripura. So, they invited educated Bengalis to help modernise their principality by organising the administration. They also encouraged East Bengali agriculturists to cultivate the forested tracts of Tripura to boost revenue generation in the state for which they doled out land on easy terms under the 'junglabadi' system.[1] Thus, lured by a respected and brighter future in Tripura, educated youths as well as uneducated peasants started arriving in Tripura by the turn of twentieth century.

The number of immigrants from Bengal was a little over 40,000 in 1901, but in the subsequent decades, the trend of migrants settling in Tripura started increasingly and by 1931 it rose to more than 1 lakh.[2] Due to massive immigration, Tripura registered a population increase of 195.28 per cent as against the national average of 33.67 per cent between 1901 and 1941.[3] The partition of the Indian subcontinent and subsequent Independence further fuelled this trend of migration as persecuted Hindu population from East Pakistan started taking refuge in Tripura. As a result, in the first decade after independence, the state's population increased from 6.39 lakhs to 11.42 lakhs, registering a growth of 78.71 per cent, which was highest in the country. In the subsequent three decades the population growth rate continued to hover around 30 to 35 per cent. Consequently, the share of indigenous population in the state decreased from 53.16 per cent in 1941 to 31.50 per cent in 1961, which further decreased to 28 per cent in 1981.[4]

Besides being reduced to a demographic minority, the indigenous people or the tribals (as popularly called) were also alienated from their land. In 1943, the Tripura monarch had earmarked 1950 sq. miles of land as Tribal Reserve, but in 1948, 300 sq. miles were thrown open for the settlement of the refugees pouring in from East Bengal. Throughout the 1950s and 1960s, successive governments in Tripura de-reserved tribal land for establishing refugee settlements.[5] There were also widespread encroachments by Bengali migrants of the tribal land as well as land alienation of the tribals as the debt ridden tribals had to sell their land to non-tribal money lenders.

Communist Insurgency

For the tribal people, their dwindling majority, loss of their land to the outsiders and a sense of being economically, politically and culturally overwhelmed by the non-tribal people induced an acute sense of insecurity. Furthermore, an unsympathetic administration dominated by Bengalis fuelled their indignation against the migrants all the more. The CPI, which was establishing a base in Tripura during that time, exploited the insecurity of the tribespeople and organised them to form the Tripura Rajya Mukti Parishad (TRMP) in 1948.[6] The TRMP (renamed as Gana Mukti Parishad in 1950 and Upajati Gana Mukti Parishad later) joined the CPI in 1949, which further consolidated the Communist base in Tripura. The Gana Mukti Parishad (GMP) also raised a voluntary military arm, called the Shanti Sena, which was populated by hundreds of disbanded World War II soldiers from the Tripura Rifles.[7] Between 1949 and 1951, the rebels carried out an armed movement and established 'liberated areas' and ran parallel governments in the tribal belts of Tripura.[8] Efforts by the government to combat communist insurgency in the state did not achieve much success. It was only in 1952 when the CPI renounced 'armed struggle' and entered into electoral politics that the armed struggle in the state ended.

Eruption of Ethnic Insurgency

However, throughout the 1950s and 1960s, the Seng-krak (clenched fist), an anti-Bengali and anti-refugee political group formed in 1947, [9] along the Tripura Upajati Juba Samiti (TUJS) formed in 1967, carried out a large number of violent protests against the Bengali settler; at the same time, asserting Tripuri identity and demanding land rights for the tribals and recognition of Kokborok as the official language.[10] The Seng-krak was eventually crushed by the Tripura Police by infiltrating its ranks and killing its leaders.[11] Be that as it may, it was the formation of the Tripura/Tribal National Volunteers (TNV) in 1978 that transformed the political agitations of the tribals into an insurgent movement.[12]

The TNV rebels intensified their attacks against the Bengalis, which brought them in direct conflict with Amra Bangali, a radical organisation formed by the Bengalis to counter the violence perpetrated against them by the tribal militants. Clashes between these two organisations resulted in widespread violence in the state throughout the 1980s. The brand of politics propagated by the TNV and the TUJS was, however, not acceptable to the Communists, as they could not afford to lose Bengali votes.[13]

While Amra Bangali was suppressed by the state government, it could not effectively put down the TNV. Several factors hamstrung the state government's efforts. First, the imperative to guard the Bengali settlements engaged a large number of police force in static duties. Since Tripura had only two battalions of armed police force, it left very little or no force in the hands of the state government to conduct counter-insurgency operations. Further, the Tripura police was highly politicised, undisciplined and demotivated.[14] Second, the international boundary with Bangladesh was porous, which allowed the insurgents to cross over with ease when chased by security forces. Third, a hostile Bangladeshi dispensation allowed the insurgents to build safe havens in its territory, where the rebels could rest, recoup, train and escape to after carrying out terror acts in Tripura. Last but not least, the government did not succeed in weaning the tribals away from the folds of insurgency through various incentives.[15]

Nonetheless, in 1988, the TNV reached a political settlement with the Union and the state governments for ending its decade old insurgency. The memorandum of settlement (MoU) signed between the parties did not address major concerns of the tribals such as land alienation raising suspicions about a possible nexus between the TNV and the Congress. These suspicions were reinforced as the Congress government generously rehabilitated the TNV chief, Bijoy Hrangkawl, by making him the Chairman of the Tripura Rehabilitation Plantation Corporation (TRPC) besides granting him a loan from the Gramin Bank.[16] The TNV cadres likewise were provided with proper rehabilitation package.

Resurgence of Ethnic Insurgency

Although the TNV signed the peace agreement, militancy did not subside in Tripura because the core issues of discontentment amongst the tribals were not addressed. In fact, the signing of the peace accord was immediately followed by the formation of two new militant organisations: the National Liberation Front of Twipra (NLFT) and the All Twipra Tiger Force (ATTF),[17] in 1989 and 1990 respectively. From 1989 onwards, 28 insurgent organisations were formed in the state, some of which were splinter organisations. Personal ambitions of the insurgent leaders, intra-tribal rivalries and religious differences between the Hindu and Christian cadres of the insurgent groups are some of the reasons for factions to split from their parent organisation. For example in 2001, Nayanbasi Jamatiya and Biswamohan Debbarma split from the NLTF and formed their own factions.[18] Be that as it may, the NLFT and ATTF emerged as the two most powerful faces of insurgency in Tripura during the 1990s and the 2000s.

Analysts have argued that both the insurgent groups did not have any concrete idea of Tripuri nationalism and that they were propelled by fear psychosis of being dominated by outsiders and motivated by their anger and hatred towards the Bengali settlers.[19] Many scholars have also argued that these insurgent groups have strong links with political parties, with few claiming that some of the insurgent organisations were in fact established by political parties. For example, the NLFT has links with the Indigenous People's Front of Tripura (IPFT) and the Congress,[20] while the ATTF was floated by the CPI (M) to protect its tribal base.[21]

Thus bereft of any ideology, insurgent groups resorted to widespread terrorism and unleashed a spate of violence against the Bengalis in the state. During peak of insurgency between 1993 and 2003, 2312 civilians were killed, besides widespread extortion and rampant kidnapping.[22] In fact, abduction for money was so rampant that Tripura figured as one of the most violent states in the Northeast during that period. Between January 1997 and December 2000, 1617 persons were abducted for ransoms.[23] The terror perpetrated by the insurgents forced civilians to flee their houses and villages and 19,468 families were displaced between March 1998 and February 2003.[24]

Fortunately, from 2004 onwards, the insurgency scenario in Tripura came under control. The violent incidents started declining from 394 in 2003 to only 8 in 2014. There was also a corresponding decline in number of casualties. In 2003, 654 extremists and 207 civilians were killed, whereas in 2014 no extremist or civilian was killed.[25] Even violence during elections, which had become a regular feature in Tripura was rare in 2013 as compared to 2003 and 2008. The turnaround in the insurgency situation in Tripura was because of a holistic strategy crafted by the Tripura government over a period of years. This strategy had a fair mix of security, politics, economics and governance components.

The State Government's Response

The Security Component

As insurgency resurfaced in Tripura in the early 1990s and went beyond control, the state government on 16 February 1997 declared the entire state 'disturbed area' and invoked the Armed Forces Special Powers Act (AFSPA).[26] The AFSPA was in force fully in 34 police station areas and partially in six police station areas. The Act gave the security forces special legal protections to act against the insurgents. The ATTF and the NLFT were banned under the Unlawful Activities (Prevention) Act (UAPA), 1967. The Tripura government also requested the Union government to deploy the CRPF and the Assam Rifles, besides the BSF, which was deployed along the international boundary with Bangladesh. Over the next four years, 18 battalions of CRPF, four battalions of AR and nine battalions of BSF were operational in Tripura.[27]

The Tripura government also raised additional battalions of the Tripura State Rifles (TSR) and by 2001, six new battalions were raised and deployed for counter insurgency operations. Despite the deployment of so many armed police forces, insurgency raged unabated in the state. Factors such as poor coordination between the central armed forces and the state police, absence of intelligence regarding the insurgents and their hideouts, demoralised police force, lack of manpower and resources to fight insurgency, a hostile neighbouring country, etc. contributed to the failure of the state government in tackling insurgency in the 1990s.

The turnaround in Tripura's fight against insurgency came about in the beginning of 2000, when the Tripura police got two successive chiefs of high calibre and efficiency. The police chiefs focused on improving the fighting capabilities of the force under their commands by introducing measures such as intensive training, manpower augmentation, modernisation, and restructuring of field police stations.[28] For example, the TSR which was raised in 1984 with a focused responsibility for conducting counter insurgency operations, started training in the Counter-Insurgency and Jungle Warfare School (CIJWS) at Vairangte in 2002. This training enabled the force to live off the land for days on end. This capability allowed the TSR to effectively dominate the insurgency affected area, thereby countering the insurgents by denying them food and shelter from the local population.[29] Gaining from this experience, a small Jungle Warfare and Counter Insurgency (JWCI) school was set up in Tripura to impart continuous training to the TSR battalions, police and central armed police force.[30] The JWCI was upgraded into a Counter-Insurgency and Anti-Terrorism (CIAT) school in 2013.

Further, the manpower of the police was increased to over 25,000 by raising ten new armed battalions for the TSR. In 2013, three more battalions were raised thereby bringing the total number of TSR battalion to 15. All the TSR battalions thus raised were India Reserve Battalions (IRBs). The availability of 10-15 armed battalions facilitated the government to deploy the police force in an offensive position, thus, bringing the anti-insurgency offensive right at the doorstep of the insurgents. The fighting capabilities of the police was further augmented by the induction of several sophisticated weapons and high tech communication systems and modern transport. For example, the TSR was provided with AK-47 rifles, INSAS rifles and self-loading rifles (SLRs), light machines guns, mortars, armoured vehicles, bullet proof jackets and vehicles. The Police Modernisation scheme initiated by the Union government was utilised for procuring these equipment and between 2000 and 2014, a total of Rs 39.40 crores were spent for this purpose.[31]

Similarly, 28 new police stations and 15 outposts were added since 2000 as against only one police station and two outposts in the previous decade.[32] Besides, 300 police camps staffed by one or two platoon outposts were set up in hill ranges and remote areas to effectively dominate the rural hinterland. In fact, the Tripura government, disregarding logistics problems, established the headquarters of TSR units in the interior areas, which ensured permanent presence of armed police in these affected areas. This move not only helped in dominating the interior and inaccessible areas, but also put pressure on militants as the reaction time of the security forces was drastically reduced. The permanent presence of security forces consolidated the hold of security forces and civil administration in the remote areas.

In 2003, a zonal policing system was introduced under which a TSR Commandant in conjunction with the district superintendent of police was responsible for launching operations within his jurisdiction. Special Operations Groups (SOG) were also created within the TSR battalions to carry out covert operations. These SOGs mostly comprised tribal recruits as they were considered to be hardy and able to sustain themselves in deep remote jungles where most of the counter insurgent operations were conducted.[33]

In addition, 100 special police pickets manned by 30 armed civilian Special Police Officers (SPOs) under the command of regular police and village resistance parties were also set up to guard villages, markets and other government establishments in thickly populated areas.[34] In fact, active public participation against the insurgents freed the police from static duties of guarding the settlements, etc. and allowed it to concentrate on intensive counter-insurgency operations.

Intelligence is most essential for fighting insurgency. For this purposes, the generation of intelligence, especially at the local levels, was accorded high priority. The TSR developed its own system of intelligence gathering. Special training was imparted to the troops to gather intelligence through meticulous data collection about missing youths as well as scanning the surroundings during patrolling in the affected areas. The TSR also selected few tribal personnel, briefed them, and sent them to their villages to gather information regarding the insurgents from their families and friends.[35] The intelligence thus collected resulted in some successful counterinsurgency operations because not only was the information accurate but the tribal personnel also acted as guides for rest of the troops in the remote and hilly terrain. The TSR also generated intelligence by carefully studying their own counter insurgency operations and improvised their strategies and tactics.

Another source of intelligence for the TSR was the local people. The force, through various civic action programmes such as helping build schools, dispensaries, bridges, etc., in the affected areas steadily gained the confidence of the local people who in turn provided relevant information about the insurgents and their over ground networks. The arrested and surrendered militants were also valuable sources of intelligence for the police, especially regarding the location of the insurgent hideouts, their strategy and tactics. Besides human intelligence, the TSR also utilised technical intelligence gathered through the interception of wireless communication of insurgents. In fact, investments were made for procuring state-of- the-art communication monitoring equipment to intercept and monitor insurgent communication.[36]

To overcome the problem of coordination among various armed police and paramilitary forces, the state government constituted a multilayer institutional mechanism. At the state level, the State Level Coordination Committee (SLCC) was set up, which is headed by the Chief Secretary. The SLCC comprises senior officers of central armed police force, paramilitary force, state police, intelligence, and other organisations concerned.[37] Besides the issues of coordination, policies relating to counterinsurgency were formulated and discussed in the Committee. Similar coordination committees were set up at the district level headed by the district magistrate and at the sub-divisional level by the sub-divisional magistrate. These multi-layered platforms contributed in enhancing coordination as well as decision making abilities at various levels, which were crucial to defeat insurgency at the grass-root.

For ensuring operational synergies between various security forces, the State Level Operations and Intelligence Group (SLOG) headed by the Director General of Police with representatives from security and intelligence organisations was constituted.[38] Similar groups were also constituted at the district and sub-divisional levels. These committees and groups not only ensured proper coordination among the security forces but also provided platforms to the officers to interact and develop rapport, which proved useful during crisis times. The chief minister also held weekly meetings with the state police chief and chief secretary as well as district officials to regularly review the law and order situation of the state.

Further, for effective conduct of countering insurgency operations, a counter insurgency manual was prepared by the SLOG and circulated in August 2000. The manual outlined the 'concepts' and strategy of conducting counter insurgency operations. Some of the salient features of the manual are: Establish a grid of Company Operated Bases (COBs) and ensure availability of a Quick Reaction Team (QRT) at each COB and battalion headquarters; planning and execution of operations at the company level; generation of local intelligence; conducting aggressive patrolling, ambushes and 'cordon and search' operations.[39] Besides, all security forces were instructed to conduct 'synergised operations' based on hard intelligence to disrupt insurgent network and operational capabilities. The security forces were also instructed to ensure safety of their camps and troops at all times as well as provide assistance to police and administration in the interior areas.[40]

The CPI (M) government which had lost a number of their cadres to targeted assassination by the militant groups gave a free hand to the police to deal with the insurgency with a caveat that human rights violations should be avoided.[41] As the police took the lead, the CRPF and the AR provided ample assistance and the BSF ensured that the borders were properly secured to deny the insurgents an easy access to their bases in Bangladesh. The strategy adopted by the police was area domination especially in the remote and rural areas and small company level frequent counter-insurgency operations based on correct intelligence. The construction of fences and roads along the international border with Bangladesh created physical hurdles for the insurgent groups to cross the borders freely and provided rapid mobility for the BSF to intercept fleeing insurgents.

The police and other security forces also conducted cross-border covert operations against the NLFT and ATTF bases as well as safe houses in Bangladesh. Between 2003 and 2006, as many as 17 such operations were conducted on the bases of the NLFT and the ATTF in Bangladesh.[42] Attacks on the bases of the militants forced them to build bases further deep inside Bangladesh and the leaders and their families hid themselves in safe houses in Dhaka. More often than not, surrendered militants and Bangladeshi mafias were utilised to conduct such cross-border operations on the promise of higher payments.[43]

Besides domestic counterinsurgency efforts, diplomatic engagements with Bangladesh contributed tremendously in breaking the back of insurgency in the state. The return of Sheikh Hasina to power in January 2009 and her statement that Bangladesh territory will not be allowed to be exploited for anti-India activities sent a strong signal to the Indian insurgents holed up in the country. Bangladesh not only shut down all permanent bases of Indian insurgent groups on its territory but also arrested several top insurgent leaders including Biswamohan Deb Burman of NLFT and Ranjit Debbarma of ATTF and handed them over to the Indian security forces. Today, according to the BSF, there are no permanent camps of Indian insurgent groups in Bangladesh.[44]

As a result of the robust counter insurgency operations, between 2000 and 2013, approximately 280 hard core insurgents were killed and around 1000 were arrested by the Tripura police.[45] In addition, around 2600 over-ground workers and sympathisers were also arrested. The fighting strength of the ATTF has also been diminished substantially with the arrest of the outfit's chief Ranjit Debbarma in 2013 and it's 'Chief of Army' Chitta Debbarma in 2012.

Political Measures

Successive state governments had been nudging the militants to give up militancy and start a new peaceful and productive life. For this, it implemented the Surrender-cum-Rehabilitation Scheme, which was first launched by the Union government in April 1998. The scheme was revised in April 2018 in which the stipend of the surrendered militants was increased from Rs 3500/- p.m. to Rs 6000/- p.m. and the one time grant from Rs 1.5 lakh to Rs 4 lakh. There are also revised incentives for the weapons surrendered by the insurgents.[46] The most important aspect of the policy is that unlike other northeastern states affected by insurgency, Tripura does not have any Surrendered, Ceasefire and Suspension of Operation camps, which houses militants awaiting rehabilitation for years. The surrendered militants are housed in rehabilitation camps and their stay do not exceed more than three years. Militants are rehabilitated within three years.[47] Tripura has the best record for rehabilitating surrendered militants, which can be corroborated by the fact that between April 2014 and March 2018, Tripura had spent 138.28 crores in the rehabilitation of militants.[48]

The state government has also been keen on arriving at a negotiated political settlement with the militants. In fact, the state governments has been working closely with the Union government by holding talks with major militant groups and concluding peace settlements. In fact, a number of peace settlements have been negotiated with militant groups since 1980s. The signing of a MoU with TNV in 12 August 1988 to end the decade long insurgency is a case in point. The MoU led to the TNV abjuring violence and surrender of 445 cadres. This was followed by signing of another MoU with Lalit Debbarma on 23 August 1993, in which 1663 cadres of the ATTF surrendered.[49] In 1997, Dhanonjoy Reang who was the chief of the NLFT and later the founder of the Tripura Resurrection Army (TRA) after being expelled from the NLFT also surrendered.

In 2001, Nayanbasi Jamatiya expressed his desire to renounce violence and surrendered with 137 cadres. In 2004, he signed a tripartite MoU with the union and state governments in which a special economic package was sanctioned by the Union government for taking up projects for the welfare of the tribal communities. For this purpose, the state government utilised Rs 13.5 crores released by the Union government.[50] Similarly, in 2003 Mantu Koloi who was heading the NLFT after Nayanbasi also surrendered with 80 rebels.[51] All these militants were rehabilitated under the generous surrender and rehabilitation policy of the state. Furthermore, peace talks are on with the NLFT's Biswamohan faction since 2015. And on 10 August 2019, the Shabbir Kumar Debbarma faction of the NLFT signed a Memorandum of Settlement (MoS) with the union and state governments, and three days later its 88 cadres surrendered with weapons.[52]

As the security situation in Tripura improved, the state government took the decision to withdraw the AFSPA. This decision was taken after a number of local tribal political groups such as the IPFT and the Indigenous Nationalist Party of Tripura (INPT) as well as other civil rights groups demanded the withdrawal of the Act. Listening to the popular sentiments, the state government withdrew the Disturbed Area Act as well as the AFSPA from the entire state on 28 May 2015.[53]

Constitutional Provisions

The Tripura government also established and strengthened local self-governance institutions such as autonomous tribal districts and Panchayati Raj Institutions (PRIs). Being overwhelmed by the non-tribal Bengali population, the tribespeople of Tripura have been demanding active participation in administration, self-management and adequate control over their own affairs. The TUJS, in particular, had been demanding the establishment of an Autonomous District Council in the state.[54] So, when the CPI (M) government came to power in 1978, it established the Tripura Tribal Areas Autonomous District Council (TTAADC) with an aim 'to provide internal autonomy in compact areas inhabited overwhelmingly by tribal people; to protect the social, economic and cultural interests of the tribal population; and to promote the all-round socio-economic development of the territory covered by the TTAADC.'[55] Initially, the TTAADC was set up under the Seventh Schedule of the Indian Constitution when the Tripura Tribal Areas Autonomous District Council Bill was unanimously passed in the Assembly in March 1979.[56]

The TTAADC, however, could not be constituted immediately because violence broke out in June 1980. It was only in January 1982 that the District Council was operationalised by electing members through secret ballots. However, the Tribals of the state were not satisfied with the provisions of the TTAADC and therefore in 1985, the TTAADC was brought under the Sixth Schedule of the Constitution through the 49th Amendment Bill in the Parliament. The TTAADC covers almost two third of the area of the state, and has a population of 121,600.[57] The TTAADC is a three tiered structure with a District Council at the district level, Block Advisory Council at the block level and the Village Council at the village level. Unlike in other northeastern state, the TTAADC in Tripura is not for a specific tribe but for all tribes, and is intended to address the problems of all tribal people.

The Left Front led by CPI (M) has been winning the TTAADC elections since its inception, only exceptions being in 1990-95 when the TUJS backed by the Congress won, and in 2000-05 when the IPFT backed by the NLFT emerged victorious in the elections. The fact that the same party was in power in state and in the District Council had resulted in better flow of funds from the state to the District Council as well as better coordination in the formulation and implementation of developmental schemes. In fact, the TTAADC is often touted as the model District Council to be emulated by others in the northeastern states. In November 2019, the state government decided to elevate the TTAADC to a 'Territorial Council' to provide greater autonomy and financial grants. In 2020, the Tripura Assembly passed a resolution to increase the number of seats in the TTAADC from 30 to 50.[58] The local bodies have a strong presence in rural areas and play an active oversight-cum-supportive role in the implementation of most development programmes of the state.

Economic Development and Effective Governance

Recognising that one of the factors that fuelled and sustained insurgency in the state is the socio-economic disparities among the population as well as regions of the state, successive Tripura governments, attempted to implement a holistic policy aimed at addressing insurgency and raise the standard of living of its people. The initiatives undertaken by the state governments include:

> ...attempts to restore alienated lands to tribals; rehabilitation of the jhumias through different schemes; measures for poverty alleviation; the decentralisation of administration and devolution of powers to local bodies; providing employment for tribal youth in the State sector (for instance, by filling reserved quotas); working to protect tribal languages and cultures; strengthening friendly relations with people on the other side of the border; and attempting to convince youth that legitimate socio-political grievances can be resolved through dialogue and within the framework of the Constitution of India.[59]

One of the major factors for the outburst of insurgency in the state was land alienation of the indigenous people. As stated above, the large scale in-migration of Bengali refugees and their subsequent settlement robbed the tribals' rights over their land. This, in turn, induced strong resentment against the outsiders and propelled them to demand restoration of land to them. In response, in 1960 the Government of India enacted the Tripura Land Revenue and Land Reforms (TLR & LR) Act.

The TLR & LR Act was based on the understanding that unless the land ownership of the tribals is ensured and protected by law, illegal transfer of their land to non-tribals would not be stopped. Inter alia, the Act dealt with abolition of Zamindari, rights to the cultivating tenants, land ceiling and acquisition of excess land, proper maintenance of land records and prevention of land alienation.[60] Thus, the Act not only provisioned for bestowing land rights to the tribals but also barred transfer of land from a tribal owner. While the Act was well-meaning, unfortunately it could not effectively prevent land alienation among the indigenous people because 'benami' transfers of land to non-tribals could not be checked.[61]

Further, in 1974 the government amended the Land Reforms Act, which was ostensibly to restore the tribal land but the amendment ended up invalidating all tribal land alienated before 1 January 1969.[62] The Congress government ruled the state till 1977 and supported the Bengali migrants. It was therefore reluctant to implement the land reforms fearing the loss of its vote bank. It was only after the Left Front government led by the CPI (M) came to power in 1978 that the process of restoration of land to the tribals began gradually. The establishment and functioning of the TTAADC in 1982 also helped the process. By 2011, the tribal population owned 44 per cent of the land which is higher than their population share of 32 per cent.[63]

Another major policy initiative taken for the well-being of the tribal people by the state government was the rehabilitation of the Jhumias. The tribals of the state practice slash and burn agriculture *(Jhum)*. Since Jhum cultivation has serious repercussions on the forest cover, efforts were made to induce the tribals to take up plough cultivation since long. Such efforts taken during the Maharaja's time as well as Congress rule in the state, unfortunately, did not succeed. By 1980, around 1 lakh hectares in the reserve forest and protected forests were used for Jhum cultivation by the tribals. Since land for rehabilitation for the Jhumias was scarce outside forested areas, the state government realised that non-agricultural forest-based options for livelihood had to be pursued. It is in this context that the Nripen Chakraborty government introduced horticultural and plantation crops, especially rubber plantation and pineapple in the state in early 1980s.

The state set up the TRPC in 1983 and rubber plantation started in 1985. As per the records of the Directorate of Welfare for Scheduled Tribes, Government of Tripura, the number of families that benefitted from rubber plantation scheme was 26,129 for the period of 1992-2015 involving 26,129 hectares of land. The number of Jhumia families that benefitted economically from horticulture plantation scheme was 49,325 for the period of 1955-2015 involving 49,326 hectares of land.[64] The state government has empowered the rubber growers by forming societies of their own and transferring benefits directly to these societies. This has generated a great deal of goodwill between the government and the tribals. The plantation schemes have also met the livelihood needs of the Jhumias to a great extent, which has undermined the roots of tribal insurgency in the state. This is because the poor Jhumias who were the major source of recruitment for the insurgent groups are no longer turning to insurgency.[65]

One of the fallouts of insurgency in the state was the displacement of people because of violence perpetrated by the militants. According to a statement by the state revenue minister in 2004, around 25,000 families were displaced in seven sub-divisions of the state.[66] Such attacks by militants on the tribals as well as other communities showed an increasing trends during the elections to the state assembly and the TTAADC. With an aim to protect the tribal people from the insurgent groups and insulate them from the militants' propaganda and attacks, the Tripura government established forest villages based on the concept of cluster villages of Mizoram. These forest villages are provided with all the basic and infrastructural facilities such as drinking water, sanitation, electricity, education, and employment under poverty alleviation programmes.[67] Since, these villages are inhabited by persons who were displaced by militant violence rather than by forcibly evicting villagers, there has been no condemnation of the move. In fact, the tribal and other displaced communities welcomed the efforts made by the government.

The state government has also undertaken special programmes to protect and promote tribal culture and language. In this respect, an All India Radio channel broadcasting in Kokborok, the main tribal language, was inaugurated. Kokborok is also taught as a language in the tribal areas at the school level. In August 2012, the state government also constituted a separate Directorate of Kokborok and other minority languages. The State Council of Education Research and Training (SCERT) has published textbooks in seven tribal languages for the academic year 2015.

The Tripura government has also provided focused attention on the development of basic infrastructure such as schools, health centres, village roads, electricity, etc. in the rural and tribal areas. The overall literacy rate of Tripura stood at 88 per cent in 2011. The fact that there is very little spatial and inter group differences in literacy points to the inclusivity of the educational opportunities that are offered to all by the state government. The Gross Enrolment Ratio (GER) at primary level has been hovering around 135 to 141 in recent years and the Net Enrolment Ratio (NER) at 98.5 at the primary level confirms that not only almost all children attend primary school in the state, they do so at the appropriate age.[68]

In fact, education in Tripura is predominantly provided by the state with 91 per cent of total children enrolled in state run schools. In 2014-15, Tripura had 4818 schools, out of which 94.5 per cent was government schools. Majority of these schools are run either by the School Education Department (56.7 per cent) or by the TTAADC (37.7 per cent).[69] Another factor that has ensured greater literacy in the state is the availability of teachers, especially at the elementary levels. Against a requirement of 20,785, Tripura has 36,817 – 77 percent over and above the minimum requirement.[70] However, shortage of teacher is observed at the higher levels.

Similarly, Tripura has improved its health system tremendously. Tripura has 1001 health sub centre, 115 primary health centre and 23 community health centre. These three categories of health centres are of most importance as they cater to the rural and tribal population.[71] Tripura had also implemented the NRHM to provide effective health care to the rural people. As a result, the state have improved its health care indices such as infant mortality rate, etc. tremendously. As regards the road ways, Tripura had 11734 km of village roads, 461 km of other district roads and 1057 km of state highways in 2020.

The state government has also implemented various centrally sponsored self-employment programmes such as the Pradhan Mantri Employment Generation Programme (PMEGP) and Swabalamban through incentives and supportive financial measures to offset limitations for first generation entrepreneurs and promotion of self-employment. The Work Participation Rate (WPR) of Tripura has improved from 36.29 per cent in 2001 and 40 per cent in 2011.

Summary

Political marginalisation and socio-economic exploitation of the tribal people in the state were the primary factors for insurgency in Tripura. Successive state governments addressed the problem of insurgency by carrying out measures which were people centric rather than insurgent centric. This was done by eliminating the causes which implanted a sense of disenchantment in the tribal community and induced some of them to take up arms against the state. First, since land alienation was a crucial issue among the tribal people, the government effectively implemented land reforms which provided a sense of security to them. Second, the government ensured that the tribal people became economically self-sufficient, which reduced the pool for recruitment for the insurgents. Third, the issue of political alienation was addressed by providing the tribal people with self-governance through the territorial council. The state governments also provided good and effective governance which ensured that the socio-cultural requirements of the tribal people are taken care of. Once the basic causes of disenchantment and alienation were addressed, the state government could tackle insurgency effectively.

NOTES

1. Subir Bhaumik, 'Disaster in Tripura', *Seminar*, Vol. 510, 2005, https://www.india-seminar.com/2002/510/510%20subir%20bhaumik.htm, accessed on 13 January 2022.
2. Nilanjan De, 'Bengali Immigration and Renovation of the Administrative Structure of Tripura: An Analytical Study', *IJRSS*, Vol. 2(3), August 2012, pp. 130-131.
3. Jogesh Ch. Bhuyan, 'Illegal Migration from Bangladesh and the Demographic Change in the North-East Region', in B B Kumar (ed.), *Illegal Migration from Bangladesh*, Delhi: Asthabharati, 2006, p. 79.
4. Subir Bhaumik, *Insurgent Crossfire, Northeast India*, New Delhi: Lancer Publishers, 1996, p. 78.
5. Anindita Ghoshal, 'Tripura: A Chronicle of Politicisation of the Refugees and Ethnic Tribals', *Social Change and Development*, Vol. 16, July 2017, p. 32.
6. Biswajit Ghosh, 'Ethnicity and Insurgency in Tripura', *Sociological Bulletin*, Vol. 52 (2), September 2003, p. 225.
7. n. 5, p. 33.
8. Subir Bhaumik, 'Tripura: ethnic Conflict, Militancy & Counterinsurgency', *Politics and Practices*, Vol. 52, 2012, p. 8.
9. The Seng-krak was banned in 1948, but it was revived in 1967. Willem Van Schendel, *The Bengal Borderland, Beyond State and Nation in South Asia*, London: Anthem Press, 2005, p. 195.
10. n. 4, p. 86.
11. n. 8.
12. Subir Bhaumik, 'Ethnicity, Ideology and Religion: Separatist Movements in India's Northeast', in Satu Limaye, et al., (eds.), *Religious Radicalism and Security in South Asia*, Honolulu, Hawaii: Asia Pacific Center for Security Studies, 2004, p. 231.
13. n. 6, p. 228.
14. Kuldeep Kumar, *Police and Counter Insurgency, The untold story of Tripura's COIN Campaign*, New Delhi: Sage, 2016, p. 191.
15. n. 8, p. 10.
16. n. 6, p. 234. Also see, n. 8, p. 12.

17. The ATTF was formed as All Tripura Tribal Force. It was rechristened as All Tripura Tiger Force in 1993 after Ranjit Debbarma took over as its chief.
18. *National Liberation Front of Tripura* at https://www.satp.org/satporgtp/countries/india/states/tripura/terrorist_outfits/nlft., accessed on 18 January 2022. Also see, n. 14, pp. 168-169. n. 8, p. 12.
19. Mahadev Chakravarti, 'Insurgency in Tripura: Some Trends', *Economic and Political Weekly*, Vol. 36 (25), 23- 29 June 23-29, 2001, pp. 2229. n. 6, p. 235. n. 8, p. 13.
20. n. 8. pp. 15-16.
21. Ajai Sahni, 'Tripura: The Politics of Ethnic Terror', *South Asia Intelligence Review,* Vol. 1 (6), 2002 at https://www.satp.org/south-asia-intelligence-review-Volume-1-No-6, accessed on 18 January 2022. n. 14, p. 162.
22. Bibhu Prasad Routray, 'Tripura: Creating an Unenviable Record', *South Asia Intelligence Review*, Vol. 2 (14), 20 October 2003 at https://www.satp.org/south-asia-intelligence-review-Volume-2-No-14, accessed on 17 January 2022.
23. n. 8, p. 15.
24. n. 22.
25. *Annual Report 2007-08*, New Delhi: Ministry of Home Affairs, 2008, p. 139, *and Annual Report 2014-15*, New Delhi: Ministry of Home Affairs, 2015, p. 264.
26. Anshu Lal, 'AFSPA removed in Tripura after 18 years: Here's why it was enforced and why it's gone now', *First Post*, 29 May, 2015 at https://www.firstpost.com/india/afspa-removed-in-tripura-after-18-years-heres-why-it-was-enforced-and-why-its-gone-now-2266770.html accessed on 19 January 2022.
27. n. 14, p. 227.
28. n. 8, p. 16.
29. Ibid, p. 17.
30. n. 14, p. 194.
31. Ibid, p. 199.
32. Ibid, p. 189.
33. Ibid, p. 203.
34. Ibid, p. 189.
35. Ibid, p. 197.
36. Ibid.
37. Ibid, p. 214.
38. Ibid.
39. Ibid, pp. 186-187.
40. Ibid, pp. 187-188.
41. Bibhu Prasad Routray, 'India: Fleeting Attachment to the Counterinsurgency Grand Strategy', *Small Wars & Insurgencies*, Vol. 28 (1), 2017, pp. 64-65.
42. n. 8, p. 17.
43. Ibid.
44. PTI, 'India Bangladesh border: First time: Insurgent camps on Bangladesh soil reduced to zero, says BSF', *The Economic Times*, New Delhi, 14 July 2018, https://economictimes.indiatimes.com/news/defence/first-time-insurgent-camps-on-bangladesh-soil-reduced-to-zero-says-bsf/articleshow/62105460.cms?from=mdr, accessed on 20 January 2022.
45. n. 14, p. 165.
46. *Annual Report 2018-19*, New Delhi: Ministry of Home Affairs, 2019, pp. 25-26.
47. Tripura Police, 'Counter Insurgency Strategy', *Government of Tripura* at https://tripurapolice.gov.in/CounterInsurgency, accessed on 20 January 2022.

48. Ministry of Home Affairs, 'Surrender Cum Rehabilitation of Militants', *Press Information of India,* New Delhi, 20 March 2018 at https://pib.gov.in/Pressreleaseshare.aspx?PRID=1519502#:~:text=The%20 Government%20of%20India%20has,monthly% 20stipend %20not%20exceeding%20Rs., accessed on 20 January 2022.
49. Tripura Police, 'Present Phase Of Insurgency', *Government of Tripura* at https://tripurapolice.gov.in/PresentPhaseInsurgency, accessed on 20 January 2022.
50. *Annual Report 2008-2009*, New Delhi: Ministry of Home Affair, 2009, p. 15.
51. Subir Bhaumik, 'Tripura rebels surrenders', *The BBC News*, Calcutta, 6 May 2004 at http://news.bbc.co.uk/2/hi/south_asia/3689925.stm, accessed on 20 January 2022.
52. Priyanka Deb Barman, '"No regrets": 88 NLFT militants surrender in Tripura after PM Modi's peace call', *The Hindustan Times*, Agartala, 14 August 2019 at https://www.hindustantimes.com/india-news/no-regrets-88-nlft-militants-surrender-in-tripura-after-pm-modi-s-peace-call/story-U8lXxB7mN7vzdeHcbb5qmO.html, accessed on 20 January 2022.
53. Syed Sajjad Ali, 'Tripura withdraws AFSPA, says insurgency on the wane', *The Hindu*, 28 May 2015 at https://www.thehindu.com/news/national/other-states/Tripura-withdraws-AFSPA-says-insurgency-on-the-wane/article60487657.ece, accessed on 20 January 2022.
54. n. 5, p. 39.
55. *Tripura-Human Development Report 2007*, New Delhi: Government of Tripura, 2007, p. 121.
56. Law Department, *The Tripura Tribal Areas Autonomous District Council Act, 1979*, Extraordinary Issue of Tripura Gazette, Government of Tripura, 8 August 1979, accessed on 20 January 2022.
57. Ibid.
58. PTI, 'Tripura Tribal Areas Autonomous District Council : TTAADC seats to increase from 30 to 50', *The Financial Express*, 18 January 2020 at https://www.financialexpress.com/india-news/tripura-tribal-areas-autonomous-district-council-ttaadc-seats-to-increase-from-30-to-50/1827396/, accessed on 20 January 2022.
59. n. 55, p. 114.
60. *The Tripura land Revenue and Land Reforms Act, 1960* at https://jami.tripura.gov.in/download/TLR_ACT.pdf, accessed on 17 January 2022.
61. n. 5, p. 38.
62. n. 14, pp. 168-169.
63. Manabi Majumdar, et al, *Tripura Human Development Report II*, Kolkata: Pratichi Institute, 2018, p. 20.
64. Ibid, p. 51.
65. n. 8, pp. 11-12.
66. n. 55, p. 109.
67. Ibid, p. 114.
68. n. 63, pp. 21-22.
69. n. 55, p. 112.
70. n. 63, p. 22.
71. 'Health and Family Welfare Department', *Government of Tripura* at https://health.tripura.gov.in/, accessed on 24 January 2022.

4

WEST BENGAL

West Bengal has a history of peasants' uprising organised by the Communists. The first such movement was the Tebhaga movement in 1946-47 started by the Kisan Sabha, the peasant organisation of the CPI. It was an agrarian struggle by the share croppers (*bargadars*) in Bengal[1] to retain two-third of the crops cultivated by them and give away only one third (*tebhaga*) to the landlords as rents.[2] While there had been several peasant movements in the country, but almost all of them aimed at bringing secular agrarian reforms were 'passive' and 'non-violent'. The Tebhaga movement, which started in the backdrop of the Independence movement was the first expression of revolt by rural masses mobilised by the Communists.[3] The worsening condition of the poor peasants coupled with famine, high inflation and incoming refugees from East Bengal who took up sharecropping provided[4] an ideal condition to start an uprising with demands for an end to 'eviction, two third share, right to stock harvested crop in the bargadar's farmyard, and reduction in the exorbitant interest rates on advance and elimination of all illegal exactions (*abwabs*).'[5]

The Tebhaga Movement

Although the peasant movement was launched in September 1946, it gained momentum in November 1946 in Jalpaiguri, Dinajpur and Rangpur districts of North Bengal and then spread to the southern districts.[6] While peasants and landless labourers (*Rajbonshis, Namasundras* and Muslims) took active part, it was the adivasis (*Santhals* and *Hajongs*) who were at the forefront of the movement in North Bengal. The movement first started in Atwari village of Dinajpur, where the peasants harvested the crops and brought to their thrashing floor (*Khamar)* instead of the landlord's Khamar.[7] Since the uprising was spontaneous, the landlords and the administration were taken aback and could not respond, which provided a free run to the peasants. However, when they were resisted by the landlords' private army and the police, the peasants resorted to violence such as burning government buildings, landlord's houses, etc.[8]

In order to bring the situation under control, the Muslim League government in Bengal, on 22 January 1947, accepted most of the demands of the peasants led by the Kisan Sabha, circulated the 'Bargadar Bill of 1947' and published it in the Gazette. Once the Kisan Sabha pulled out from the movement, the Bill was promptly withdrawn and it never became an Act. Besides conciliatory approach, scholars argue that the Surahwardy government also used coercive tactics as well as the Hindu-Muslim tensions to divide the peasantry and weaken the movement.[9] The fact that the Kishan Sabha was also not clear about the aim, strategy and continuation of the movement added to the ending of the movement quite abruptly without bringing in concrete changes in the material conditions of the sharecroppers and landless peasants. So, by March 1947 the Tebhaga movement fizzled out in the state.

The Communist Movement, 1948-52

Post-independence, the CPI extended its cooperation to the Congress governments at the Centre and the state so that the governments at both the levels are better positioned to manage the grim situation arising out of the riots caused by partition of the Bengal province. The Communists, however, withdrew their cooperation once the riots stopped and the situation normalised in late 1947. The withdrawal of support to the government was triggered by the realisation that they were 'losing the political initiative to organise mass movement in order to seize political power from an independent India.'[10] The Communists soon started organising the peasants against the landlords demanding abolition of the zamindari system. The ongoing Telangana movement provided a model for the Communists to follow in Bengal. In addition, several such Communist movements in other parts of Asia also provided the required impetus for them to revive their activities in India.

In fact, in February-March 1948, the Communists organised its 'Second

Congress' wherein it adopted its 'Political Thesis' in which it argued that the National Government established on 15 August 1947 was indeed an enemy of freedom and democracy for the Indian people and therefore needed to be overthrown by what they called the 'People's Democratic Revolution'.[11] In its place, a People's Democratic Republic – a republic of workers, peasants and oppressed middle classes would be installed.[12] Incidentally, within weeks of the Second Congress, the CPI was banned by the state government in March 1948 and all its leaders were arrested.

Despite the ban, the Communists were able to carry out their activities, especially in the countryside. Between 1948 and 1949, they mobilised the sharecroppers with the demand for abolition of zamindari system without compensation and bestowing the land to the tillers. The peasant movement was effective in inaccessible places in rural Bengal such as Kakdwip in 24 Paraganas, Domjur and Jagatballavpur in Howrah, Borakamalpur and Chanditala areas in Hooghly, Jaypur and Vishnupur police stations in Bankura, Agradwip and Raina areas in Burdwan and the Tamluk, Ghatal and Sadar sub-divisions in Midnapore district.[13] In the tribal dominated regions of the state, the Communists organised the adivasis and raised the demand for raising daily wages and fixing working hours for the labourers. There were close to 170 incidents of demonstrations, rioting, looting, attacks on landlords, clashes with police, etc. reported between 1949 and 1950 in various districts of the state.

The Communists' efforts to overthrow the state government, however, did not find any perches among the peasants and the tribal people because this section of the population was driven against the government by their own grievances rather than the ideas of installing a People's Republic. In fact, the peasants and the tribespeople did not understand the ideas of the Communists. Moreover, the peasant uprisings remained highly localised and therefore, could not threaten the state government. The increased incidents of violence also proved to be a turn off for the people, especially in the urban areas, and they started distancing themselves from the Communists. In fact, between 1948 and 1950, the membership of the Communist Party had fallen from 90,000 to 20,000.[14] The loss of popular support coupled with arrests of its leaders forced the CPI to rethink its strategy which now refrained from terrorist attacks and focussed on anti-communalism. The ouster of B.T. Ranadive and the decision of the party to fight the first general election effectively brought the communist movement in the state to a close.

The Naxalbari Movement

The second phase of communist movement in the state began in late 1960s as the situation in the countryside continued to be fraught. Despite the enactment of legal provisions for safeguarding the land of the poor peasants, the landlords exploited the loopholes and refused to surrender their excess land. It was against this backdrop that the Kisan Sabha started mobilising peasants in the rural areas, including Naxalbari where some land was recovered from the landlords and incidents of eviction of sharecroppers were reduced. This movement, however, received a set-back because of internal dissensions within the party and the eventual spilt in the CPI. Intense debates within the CPI broke out whether to support the Congress Party's policies and bring socialism peacefully or through radical means.[15]

Furthermore, following the India-China border war, a number of Kishan Sabha leaders either were arrested or went underground. The Sino-Soviet split also led to a pro-Chinese group to break away from the CPI and form the CPI (M) in 1964. After the breakup, most of the party cells in the North Bengal were captured by the CPI (M) who advocated a moderate line. Such a line of action was not acceptable to the extremist elements in the party namely Charu Mazumdar, Kanu Sanyal and Jangal Santhal. Inspired by the ideology propounded by Mao Tse Tung, Charu Mazumdar became the ideologue and propagated a violent revolution to establish the authority of the peasants in the countryside. Kanu Sanyal spread the organisation's network and Jangal Santhal mobilised the adivasis.[16]

Thus, on 3 March 1967, 'a group of peasants surrounded a plot of land in Naxalbari, marked the boundaries with red flags, and began harvesting the crop',[17] thus sowing the seeds of future Maoist insurgency, twenty years after the end of the first major peasant uprising in Bengal. In the next couple of months, the peasants organised themselves into Krishak Samiti (peasant committees) under the leadership of the extremist faction of the CPI (M). These committees together with the adivasi militia seized lands of the landlords and forcibly cultivated them to establish their ownership, burnt land records, looted weapons of the landlords, established people's courts and passed death sentences on landlords.

The areas upon which the peasant committees had established their stronghold were Naxalbari, Kharibari and Phansidewa in Siliguri Sub-division.[18] Matters went to the head on 25 May 1967, when the police fired on the crowd, which had gathered to protest against the killing of a peasant the previous day. The police firing led to the death of 11 persons including seven women and two infants. This incident further infuriated the peasants and they intensified their violent activities. The bows and arrows of the adivasis were also replaced by firearms. As incidents of loot, arson and murder increased, people started clamouring for state intervention. The state government finally responded (discussed later) and successfully suppressed the Naxalbari movement.

The leaders of the peasant movement in Naxalbari attributed four reasons for its failure: a) lack of strong party organisation, b) failure to build a powerful mass base, c) ignorance of military affairs, and d) a formal attitude towards land reforms.[19] It is in this context, Kanu Sanyal suggested in his 'Report' that 'in the next phase of struggle the revolutionaries would set up party units which would be fully armed.' Consequently, on 13 November 1967, the extremists expelled from the CPI (M) formed the All India Co-ordination Committee of Revolutionaries (AICCR). The AICCR issued a Declaration which stated that the party will develop and coordinate militant and revolutionary struggles of the peasants and working class, and popularise the thought of Mao Tse-tung, which is Marxism-Leninism.[20]

On 14 May 1968, the AICCR transformed itself into the AICCCR, which was subsequently dissolved, and a new party the CPI (M-L) was formed on 22 April 1969 with Charu Mazumdar as its chairman.

The Debra-Gopiballavpur Uprising

While the Naxalbari rebellion was successfully doused by the state government, the fire kindled by the peasant uprising spread to rest of the states of India such as Andhra Pradesh, Bihar, Punjab, Odisha, Tripura, Uttar Pradesh and other parts of West Bengal. In West Bengal, after Naxalbari, the Debra-Gopiballavpur belt in Medinipur district was the second place where the CPI (M-L) carried out rural guerrilla warfare. The belt bordered Bihar and Odisha, was forested and substantially inhabited by tribal people. The peasant uprising in Gopiballavpur and Debra began in September and October 1969 respectively. The CPI (M-L) leadership had exhorted educated students and professionals to leave their studies and professions and go to the countryside, integrate themselves with the peasant masses and impart political awareness to the villagers. Responding to the call, thousands of students and professionals from Kolkata and other urban areas left their studies and careers and went to the villages to indoctrinate the peasants and lead the movement.[21]

This time around, however, the peasant armed revolution apparently represented a higher stage of class struggle as it was based on the campaign of 'annihilation of class enemy' and establishment of peasants' authority in the 'red bases', instead of mass mobilisation.[22] The aim of 'annihilation of class enemy' was to spread 'red terror' in the rural areas so that the wanton killings would break the morale of the enemy. Accordingly, the guerrilla squads organised armed raids on the houses of the landlords and money lenders, seized their crops and set up people's court to try the 'oppressors', most of whom were given death sentences.

The movement picked up by November of 1969 when thousands of armed peasants under the leadership of CPI (M-L) attacked landlords, killed them, distributed the food grains to the poor and landless people, returned mortgaged property, fixed wages of the landless labourers and establish peasants' political power in rural areas. This strategy was immensely successful because as some of the feudal lords were killed, many fled the villages and those who stayed behind extended their support to the CPI (M-L) and became 'revolutionaries' overnight.[23] Thus, by late 1969, the CPI (M-L) consolidated its position in about 200 square miles of 'liberated zone' of the Debra-Gopiballavpur area where the writ of the state government did not run at all.[24]

The state government responded by initiating police action, which was bolstered by the deployment of the CRPF against the Communist rebels and in matter of months the guerrilla movement was contained. Inability of the 'revolutionaries' to expand their activities and support outside the encircled areas, brought them in conflict with the party leadership. Most on-ground activists favoured mobilisation of the masses by organising peasant committees instead of the annihilation policy, but their suggestions were dismissed.[25]

Interestingly, instead of inspiring the rural masses to join the 'revolutionaries' as envisaged by Charu Mazumdar, the policy of 'annihilation of class enemy' especially in the non-tribal areas instilled a sense of fear in the poor and landless peasants and alienated them from the movement. In the absence of political propaganda and mass organisation, the politically unlettered villagers could not identify with the political aims of the movement and saw the movement as nothing but the murder of their co-inhabitants by the town folks. Slogans like 'China's Chairman is Our Chairman' were lost on them.[26]

Furthermore, in a bid to shore up the morale of the cadres, Charu Mazumdar had exhorted the cadres to intensify terror attacks on individual landlords and leave the area quickly to save themselves from police action. While this tactic helped the cadres to some extent, it left the poor villagers to face the brunt of police suppression, which highly disillusioned them. In fact, such was their disillusionment that the peasantry refused shelter to the guerrilla squads, provided information about suspected Naxalites when asked and willingly handed over the insurgents to the police. Another factor that weakened the movement was a conflict between the tribal people and the non-tribal peasants. The fact that the Naxalites were not interested in redistribution of the confiscated land to the tribals alienated them from the movement. There were also clashes between the tribals and the students who were accused of trying to dominate the tribals.[27]

The Urban Movement

While the peasant uprising was being crushed in the rural areas, Kolkata and the adjoining towns and cities started witnessing an 'urban movement' as the CPI (M-L) ideologues and cadres started returning to the cities and towns from the countryside.[28] The 'urban movement' of the CPI (M-L) had three main components: destroy the cultural heritage of Bengal, particularly the Bengali middle class by profaning their cultural symbols; carry out an 'annihilation of class enemy' campaign against police personnel, informers and political rivals; and build-up an arsenal by large scale snatching of arms.[29] Incidentally, the towns and cities of West Bengal were quite ripe for such an uprising because while higher education had expanded in response to the demands of the middle class post-independence, a concomitant increase in economic growth was missing, resulting in largescale unemployment of educated youths. The industrial recession of 1966-67 further contributed in dampening the employment prospects for thousands of engineers who had graduated from various engineering colleges.

Between March-April 1970 and June-July 1971, Kolkata and its suburbs were in the grips of unprecedented urban violence. The 'urban movement' began by the CPI (M-L) cadres indulged in iconoclasm and incendiary activities. The students destroyed statues of social reformers and political leaders such Ram Mohan Roy, Ishwar Chandra Vidyasagar, Mahatma Gandhi, Swami Vivekananda, etc. and set on fire educational institutions. Students and youths also formed Red Guard groups (a group of five to six youths) and attacked traffic constables, plainclothes policemen, police officers and personnel of the BSF and the CRPF. In addition, the urban guerrilla squads also snatched weapons from the armed policemen after attacking them. Significantly, the police did not have a public friendly appearance and it was looked down upon as a corrupt and brutal force. Such was the public hostility against the police that when an attack on a policeman happened in broad day light, the city people and townsfolk neither protected the policeman nor caught the assailant.[30]

The state police force was highly politicised and divided because the ruling CPI (M) had successfully infiltrated the police ranks and co-opted several of them. The comprised policemen formed the Calcutta Police Association (CPA) and pledged their allegiance to the Party instead of the state government.[31] Resultantly, the efficiency and morale of the police were low making them ineffective against the CPI (M-L) urban guerrillas who between 1 April and 12 November 1970, killed 36 policemen and injured 400 others.[32] Incidentally, most of the policemen killed belonged to the lower echelons such as constables, sergeants and sub-inspectors; police officers were rarely targeted. This was done primarily to break the morale of the constabulary, which comprised the main component of the police force.[33] Taking advantage of the disarray in the police force, the CPI (M-L) even reminded the lower echelons about their origins in peasantry, workers and petty bourgeois class, and urged them to turn against their bosses.

The Kolkata Police had estimated that by November 1970, around 10,000 to 20,000 CPI (M-L) cadres were operating in the state and half of whom focussed on Kolkata and adjoining areas. An interesting aspect of the 'urban movement' was that a substantial portion of the cadre comprised criminals and goons who were attracted by the annihilation policy of Charu Mazumdar and exploited the movement to settle scores and expand their areas of influence in the cities. In fact, when the student and youth leaders returned from the countryside to Kolkata they realised that the vacuum left by them was filled by anti-social elements and bad characters.[34] In rest of the industrial centres of the state such as Durgapur, Asansol and Burdwan, the CPI (M-L) mobilised the workers who formed squads and attacked the police, snatched weapons and raised Communist flags atop factories.[35] Such attacks on the police became rampant by the end of 1970 and beginning of 1971.

Of all the 'urban movements' in the state, the one in Birbhum is of significance because it showcased a close coordination between the urban and rural tactics. The Naxalite activities in this district first started in the towns such as Bolpur, Hetampur, Suri, etc. in May-June 1970 where the students and youths were radicalised. Once radicalised, the youths indulged in arson, snatching guns from the police and killing them. The rural areas, which surrounded these towns, soon came under the spell of the CPI (M-L) and the peasants started snatching weapons from landlords and the police to unleash the annihilation campaign.[36] In fact, Birbhum witnessed the largest number of arms-snatching incidents. The location of the district close to Jharkhand and a heavily forested tract provided the Naxalites ideal shelter. Furthermore, the police in the district became completely ineffective because of sheer panic induced by the terror activities of the Naxalites and also because several of the relatives of the policemen were directly or indirectly involved with the CPI (M-L).[37]

The 'urban movements' and the terror campaign of the Naxalites were brought to an end by the state government through police action and other political measures by mid-1970s (discussed later).

Maoist Resurgence in Junglemahal

After a lull of two decades, Maoists became active in West Bengal once again in the 1990s when they started organising the people, especially, the adivasis to demand basic rights such as drinking water, healthcare, irrigation facilities, decent wages, etc. One of the major factors responsible for the resurgence of Maoist activities in the tribal dominated districts of West Bengal is the 'break down of party-society' edifice.[38] The CPI (M) which ruled the state for two decades till then, had systematically dismantled all traditional grievance redressal and dispute resolution institutions such as the landlords' houses, caste councils, religious assemblies, etc. In their place, it had empowered the village panchayats dominated by the CPI (M) as well as the district magistrates and block development officers to distribute governmental benefits to the local people. These two structures were successful in managing the rural discontentment in the 1980s when land reforms resulted in record agricultural productivity and the state government could afford to distribute the economic benefits among the people.

However, agricultural productivity started falling in 1990s and revenue generated through agriculture also fell. Consequently, the largesse distributed by the party through the state government among the people spread thin.[39] Moreover, large-scale industrialisation, which could have otherwise absorbed the growing work force, especially agricultural labourers, had gradually declined in the state, forcing the labourers to migrate to other states in search of employment.[40] Falling revenues with concomitant rise in fiscal debt made the state government led by the CPI (M) unable to meet the rising aspirations of the people, especially the rural poor.

The tribal dominated belt of the state was the hardest hit because of deindustrialisation and falling agricultural productivity. The region itself was in dire state because the land was mono-cropped with little provision for irrigation. Pervasive underdevelopment characterised the region with lack or absence of basic amenities such as health, education, drinking water, etc. The inability of the CPI (M) to meet the basic requirements of the tribal people led to the gradual erosion of its legitimacy as the sole arbitrator in the tribal dominated region.

The vacuum was gradually filled up by the Maoists who had been entering the tribal dominated region from adjoining Jharkhand. Over a period of time, they started mobilising the adivasis around certain basic grievances and issues such as lack of basic amenities and employment, end to the harassment by forest guards and police, and so and so forth. The articulation of these grievances became the agenda of the Maoist movement, and intensified when faced with repressive actions of the state government.[41] The Maoists even demanded autonomy for the districts of Purulia, Bankura and West Midnapore on the lines of the Darjeeling Gorkha Hill Council.[42]

In the beginning, the Maoists employed peaceful means such as protest march to the divisional office and petitioning, but as the state government started suppressing the protesters, the Maoists became violent and started targeting the CPI (M) cadres and sympathizers.[43] Matters came to the head when on 2 November 2008, the Maoists targeted the convoy of the union ministers Jitin Prasada and Ram Vilas Paswan, chief minister Buddhadeb Bhattacharjee and state industries minister Nirupam Sen at Salboni in Midnapore District. Fortunately no one was killed in the incident.[44] Following the attack, the police carried out investigations and arrested a number of villagers in the Lalgarh area. The adivasis were indignant about the way the police had handled the investigation and viewed the police action as an affront to their tribal culture and tradition. In response to the police brazenness, the adivasis started a protest, which quickly spread to the adjoining areas. The tribal protests were organised and led by the People's Committee against Police Atrocities (PCPA), which was backed by the Maoists as well as other political parties opposed to the CPI (M).

The protesters began blockading the area, thereby effectively denying entry to the police and prevented the administration to function. Such was the success of the blockade that many observers believed that the Maoists had hijacked the movement and had established a 'liberated zone' in Lalgarh.[45] Once the 'liberated zone' was established, the Maoists expanded their area of influence by burning down police stations and offices of the CPI (M) in Dharampur, Belatikri, Koima and Ramgarh. They also killed a large number of local CPI (M) leaders and cadres.[46] The Maoists tried to portray the Lalgarh unrest as a social uprising against the state government. The unrest also had a separatist underpinning as the Aditya group of the Jharkhand Party, which was supporting the 'movement' was doing so on the understanding that the tribal dominated areas of Purulia, Bankura and West Medinipur will be merged with Jharkhand.[47]

The Maoists had found a similar opportunity to register their presence in the state earlier in 2006-07 when the state government decided to acquire 22,000 acres of land in Nandigram for establishing a chemical Special Economic Zone (SEZ). The people of Nandigram were not enthusiastic about the government's proposed setting up of SEZ given that earlier attempts at industrialisation in their area had failed. They were also suspicious of the government's plan to acquire land and therefore, demanded more information and transparency.[48] The government and the CPI (M), however, were not forthcoming with the information desired by the villagers. In response to state apathy, the people of Nandigram started a protest on 3 January 2007 against land acquisition and fortified villages which were to be acquired for setting up of the SEZ.[49] The villagers, in fact, dug up roads, established camps and organised night vigils to prevent the police as well as the CPI (M) cadres from accessing their area, thereby effectively creating a 'liberated zone' (*muktanchal*).

The movement against land acquisition in Nandigram and adjoining areas was spearheaded by the Bhoomi Uchched Protirodh Committee – Committee Against Land Dispossession (BUPC) – composed of 22 organisations. While political parties such as the Trinamool Congress (TMC), Congress, and Jamiat Ulema-e-Hind were part of the BUPC, it was suspected that Maoists were actively involved in the movement. In fact, such suspicions were proven true when the Maoist leader Ganapathy in an interview said, 'Kalinga Nagar, Singur and Nandigram, in particular, have become important symbols in this struggle. As for our role in such movements we shall definitely make all efforts to be in the forefront and lead the movement in the correct direction.'[50]

As mentioned, the protesters did not allow a single 'outsider' including police personnel or CPI (M) cadres to enter Nandigram. After two months, on 14 March 2007, the police along with CPI (M) armed cadres attempted to enter Nandigram. However, this attempt was met with violence and in the ensuing police firing 14 people were killed.[51] Following the incident, the state government declared that the proposal for setting up a SEZ in Nandigram has been postponed and no land shall be acquired forcefully from the villagers. Despite the assurance from the government, the people of Nandigram continued with the blockade. It was only after ten months in November 2007 that the blockade could be broken by the combined might of the CRPF, the police and the armed CPI (M) militia.[52]

West Bengal was badly hit by Maoist violence between 2006 and 2011. In 2006 there were 23 violent incidents in which 17 people lost their lives. The number of violent incidents rose to 32 in the subsequent year.[53] Maoist related violence escalated from 2009 onwards when 255 violent incidents were recorded in which 158 persons lost their lives. In 2010, violence peaked to 355 violent incidents with 258 deaths. In fact, between 2009 and 2011, the Maoist had established a 'liberated zone' in Junglemahal comprising three districts of West Medinipur, Purulia and Bankura. However, from 2011 onwards Maoists insurgency in the state saw a drastic decline. In that year 90 incidents and 41 deaths were recorded, in 2012 only 6 incident were reported.[54] Since 2014 there were no reports of any Maoist related violence in the state.

Counteroffensive Strategies by the State Government

Legislations

In the wake of Communist movement in the state, the West Bengal government introduced the 'West Bengal Security Bill' in November 1947. The Bill was intended to legalise an ordinance brought by the previous Muslim League government to crush the peasant uprising. The Bill proposed to detain rebels without trial for up to six months. Under this bill 1,486 people were arrested between March and November 1947.[55] The Bill finally became the West Bengal Security Act and came into force on 26 January 1950. The Act makes 'special provision for the maintenance of public order by the prevention of illegal acquisition, possession or use of arms, the suppression of subversive movements endangering communal, harmony or the safety or stability of the State and the suppression of goondas and for maintaining supplies and services essential to the life of the community.'[56]

Compelled by peasant movements led by the CPI between 1948 and 1952, the West Bengal government tried to provide security to sharecroppers and landless peasants. Accordingly, it enacted the Bargadar Act in 1950, which after a few modifications, was incorporated in the West Bengal Land Reform Act of 1955.[57] This Act of 1950 'provide[s] for the regulation of certain rights inter se of bargadars and owners of land and for the establishment of Bhag Chas Conciliation Boards for the settlement of disputes relating to certain matters between bargadars and owners of land.'[58] Three years later, a more comprehensive and important Act known as the West Bengal Estates Acquisition Act of 1953 was passed. This Act aimed at eliminating the intermediaries (Zamindars and *Jotedars*) on all lands except which they 'self-cultivated' by hiring labourers.[59]

The Act divided all landlords and holders of interest in land into two categories – intermediaries and *Raiyats* (fixed-rent tenants). It allowed the intermediaries possession of 25 acres of their agricultural *(khas)* land, 15 acres for non-agricultural land and 5 acres for homestead land, a total of 45 acres per head.[60] For the *Raiyats*, who were cultivating the rest of the intermediaries' land were brought directly under the state government. [61] Two years later, the Land Reforms Act of 1955 was passed. The Act aimed at limiting the land owners' ability to transfer land in order to prevent them from circumventing the land holding ceiling and providing better rights to the sharecroppers.[62] The Act 'covers a range of land-related topics, but most significantly it: (1) defines the rights and obligations of landowners and bargadars; (2) prohibits fixed-rent leasing of land; (3) places a ceiling on the size of landholdings; (4) defines how land taken by the government should be distributed; and (5) limits the transferability of land held by Scheduled Tribe members as well as much of the land obtained through redistribution.'[63]

While these two land reform Acts were successful to some extent in abolishing intermediaries and providing greater land rights to the actual cultivators, both the laws were flagrantly violated by the landlords by deliberately suppressing the amount of land owned by them, mala fide transfers including *benami* (fictious) transfers and *Mitakshara* law of inheritance. In fact, many landlords evicted the labourers cultivating their land leading to an increase in landless agricultural labourers in the state. The landlords also filed a large number of suits claiming Fundamental Right to property as vested in the Constitution.[64] These factors that resulted in poor implementation of the Land Reform Acts generated lot of anger and frustrations among the poor peasantry and consequently they rose up against the corrupt and cruel landlords in 1967.

It was only after the CPI (M) came to power in 1977 that a comprehensive and successful implementation of the land reform legislations were initiated and achieved. The state government laid emphasis on safeguarding the interests and rights of the bargadars. For this purpose, it acted more proactively to take over land that exceeded the ceiling limits as well as amended the Land Reforms Act of 1955 in order to plug the loopholes in earlier legislations, which allowed exemptions to the ceilings for religious and charitable trusts, plantations and fisheries.[65] The amendment, for the first time, defined 'personal cultivation' as the actual physical cultivation of the land in order to remove absentee landlordism and improve the status of sharecroppers vis-à-vis the landlords so that the landlords are compelled to give them their due share of the produce.[66]

Political Response

For the ruling United Front government headed by the CPI (M), the violent movement in March 1967 caused great dilemma because on one hand, the violence was against the norms of democratic centralism to which the Marxist party adhere. On the other hand, the movement was undertaken by the poor peasants and tribespeople under the leadership of their own local unit.[67] Faced with the dilemma, the state government tried unsuccessfully to talk to the rebels by sending a Cabinet Mission consisting of six ministers on 12 June 1967. As the violence continued relentlessly, the Cabinet Mission suggested police patrolling in disturbed villages, sealing of the state borders with Nepal and Pakistan and providing police protection on receiving complaints.[68] The West Bengal State Committee of the CPI (M) also expelled 19 leaders including Charu Mazumdar and Kanu Sanyal along with 400 members. Alongside, the Darjeeling District Committee of the CPI (M), which spearheaded the entire movement was also disbanded.[69]

After a lull of two years when the peasant uprising led by the CPI (M-L) spread to the Debra-Gopiballavpur belt, the CPI (M) government, which came to power in February 1969, ignored the activities of the CPI (M-L) for political expediency. During the elections, the CPI (M) leaders had promised that no action would be taken to stall 'democratic movements' by taking action against the activists. So once in power, the state government released all the prisoners arrested during the Naxalbari police action.[70] The CPI (M) government supported controlled violence as they wanted to send out the message to the masses as well as the Union government that they were the ones carrying the flag of revolution within the limits of the Constitution.[71] However, the increase in the lawlessness created by the CPI (M-L) in the rural areas forced the state political leaders to reassess their perspective towards the CPI (M-L) and its activities. Finally in December 1969, the state government launched an all-out attack on the Naxalites.[72]

Despite police action initiated by the state government, the guerrilla squads continued with indiscriminate killings of landlords, money lenders and 'informers' and most of its leaders also escaped the police dragnet. The reason behind this was the fact that the CPI (M) leadership considered the CPI (M-L) as a group of adventurists and ideological dissidents who could be taken care of by the party cadres. It, therefore, did not give clear directives to the police to emphatically put down the revolt.[73] In absence of any clear orders, police action did not go beyond containing the activities of the CPI (M-L) cadres and throwing a cordon around the affected villages.[74]

The beginning of the 1971 saw a renewal of hostility between the CPI (M) and the CPI (M-L) as the state elections were announced. While the CPI (M) considered the CPI (M-L) as renegades, the CPI (M-L) regarded the CPI (M) as neo-revisionists misdirecting the people's struggle. The CPI (M-L), like in 1969, gave a call for boycott of the elections and went on to terrorise the voters. The CPI (M) and the CPI (M-L) marked out localities of Kolkata as their areas of influence and any trespassing by either party was punished with death. What ensued was a cycle of torture and murder between the two left parties. In fact, the CPI (M-L) armed squads and the CPI (M) cadres killed a number of leaders, workers and sympathisers of each other's party.[75] In this messy mix, the Congress cadres initially allied with the CPI (M-L) hoodlums in order to target their rival, the CPI (M), but once they came to power in 1972, they started killing the CPI (M-L) cadres, thus sounding a death knell to the 'urban movement'.[76]

One of the main reasons for the failure of the 'urban movement' was the absence of guidance from the CPI (M-L) leadership. Charu Mazumdar neither planned nor crafted any strategy for the 'urban movement'. Even for his policy of annihilation of class enemy there were no specific targets in the urban areas except for the police (a natural enemy for the lumpen proletariat) and the CPI (M) cadres (a natural enemy of the CPI (M-L).[77] It has been argued that the 'urban movement', in effect, was started by the youths and students. The CPI (M-L) leadership and his associates merely accepted it as *fait accompli*. Significantly, because the educated youths and students could not get over their class inhibitions, they could not join the anti-socials wholeheartedly in killing people in cold blood.[78] In fact, by end of 1970, Charu Mazumdar started doubting the sustainability of the urban movement and its dependence on the petty bourgeoisie youths.[79]

The CPI (M-L) in West Bengal also suffered because of multiple splits. In fact, at one point of time, there were around five to six Maoist groups proclaiming to be propagating the correct thoughts of Mao Tse-Tung.[80] There was also intense criticism of Charu Mazumdar for arrogating all powers to himself as well as his policy of annihilation. The spilt within the CPI (M-L) together with intense police action deprived the CPI (M-L) of dedicated cadres essential for carrying out the revolution.

Once the CPI (M) came back to power in 1977, it deftly suppressed any dissent, especially among the Adivasis. In fact, the party appointed aspirational Adivasi groups such as the Santhals and Mahatos as local party leaders and provided resources to the poorer Lodhas. However, as discussed earlier, lack of developmental activities in the tribal dominated areas combined with dwindling financial resources of the state, which constrained the CPI (M) in distributing state largesse to the people, robbed the party and its cadres of its legitimacy to rule. This political vacuum was exploited by the Maoists, who started a reign of violence in the garb of fighting for the rights of the tribal people.

To counter the Maoists, the CPI (M) established camps in the affected districts of Bankura, Purulia and West Medinipur districts, which were manned by its armed cadres called the *Hamrad Bahini* and vigilante groups such as the *Gana Pratirodh Manch* (People's Resistance Force) and *Maoist Daman Sena* (Maoist Repression Force).[81] Fierce struggle often broke out between the CPI (M) *militia* and the Maoist rebels resulting in a number deaths on both sides.

Another organisation that filled up the political vacuum in the tribal dominated areas was the TMC. In fact, during the Lalgrah unrest, TMC leader Mamata Banerjee even visited Lalgarh to show her solidarity with the tribal people. In the run up to the 2011 state elections, Mamata Banerjee had promised to remove all union and state armed police force, release all political prisoners without condition and start a dialogue with the Maoists.[82] The result of these overtures was that the people of Junglemahal, with the alleged tacit support of the Maoists, voted overwhelming for the TMC. So, in 2011 when the TMC came to power after defeating the CPI (M), allegations were rife that she had won the elections with the help of the Maoists.[83] However, many commentators also argued that the people of Junglemahal voted for the TMC because they were disillusioned by the CPI (M) as well as repelled by the

Maoists for their indiscriminate killings of people who they claimed were informers of the government.[84]

Be that as it may, the fact remains that the Maoists were 'defeated' in the state within a year of Mamata Banerjee coming to power, who employed the dual strategy of coercion and development. Continuing with the stance against the Maoists of the Left government who had imprisoned a large number of Maoists, Mamata Banerjee set up crack teams of police officers to deal with armed Maoists.[85] She set up anti-Maoist armed vigilante groups (*Bhairab Bahini*) led by TMC members to pass on information about the Maoists to the Police and the CRPF.[86] She also reached out to the rebels and asked them to surrender and join the mainstream. She announced a lucrative Surrender and Rehabilitation package in which Rs 1.5 lakh was offered as fixed deposit for each rebel who surrendered with arms, which can be encashed after three years. Each surrendered Maoist also received Rs 2000 per month as allowance for three years till he/she was gainfully employed. Maoist rebels also received Rs 25,000 to Rs 2 lakhs (depending upon the quality) for surrendering arms.[87]

The TMC government also tried to win the people affected by Maoist violence by announcing compensation package for civilians killed in Maoists attacks. Under the package, the state government would provide Rs 2 lakh and the Union government would give Rs 3 lakh to the families of the civilians who fall victims to such attacks.[88] She also announced that in the fresh recruitments in police force in the Junglemahal area, local youths will be given preference. Furthermore, the Mamata Banerjee government in July 2011 tried to start a peace negotiation with the Maoists. She appointed six eminent persons as interlocutors for the peace dialogues. The talks took place between July and October 2011.[89] During the negotiations, the Maoists and state government agreed to halt fighting. However, the killing of Maoist Politburo member Mallojula Koteswara Rao alias Kishenji, who had spearheaded Maoist operations in West Bengal's Jangalmahal region, in an encounter in November 2011 brought the peace negotiations to an end.[90]

The Security Response

In the aftermath of the Naxalbari uprising, the failure to restrain the rebels and incessant pressure put by the Union government to bring the situation under control compelled the state government to order police action on 5

July 1967. The police action was codenamed 'Operation Crossbow' and launched on 12 July 1967. Close of 1500 policemen were deployed in the affected areas, who set up police camps in almost all the villages. The police conducted door to door cordon and search operations and carried out constant raids on the Naxalite hideouts. In the process, the police arrested close to 562 rebels including several top leaders such as Jangal Santhal on 20 July 1967.[91] Subsequently, several followers of the Naxalbari movement also surrendered. Surprisingly, the police did not face any stiff resistance from the peasants and adivasis, and by the end of July 1967, the entire uprising in Naxalbari and adjoining areas was put down.

In response to the terror unleashed by the CPI (M-L) cadres in the second phase of peasant uprising in Debra-Gopiballavpur belt, initially, the police set up camps in the affected villages, but an ill-equipped local police were ineffective in face of the violence unleashed by the CPI (M-L) cadres. Such was the terror of the Naxalites that no one in the affected villages dared lodge complaints against the 'revolutionaries', not even the wives and sons of the landlords who were killed by the Naxalites. In absence of any cooperation from the locals, the police also refused to enter the villages without armed protection. Summing the advantage of establishing the 'liberated area', Charu Mazumdar had said,

> Once an area is liberated from the clutches of class enemies (some are annihilated while some others flee) the repressive state machinery is deprived of its eyes and ear making it impossible for the police to know who is a guerrilla and who is not, and who is tilling his own land and who tills that of the jotedars.[92]

As situation started deteriorating, the state government brought in the Eastern Frontier Rifles (EFR), which is the armed police force of the state, in order to strengthen the local police in the affected areas. According to newspaper reports, about 1200 EPR personnel were stationed in Gopiballavpur and 700 were stationed in Debra. Since the Gopiballavpur and Debra belt was also proximate to the Bihar border and Baharagora in Singhbhum district of Bihar was also affected, a coordinated police action of the two states was undertaken. The Bihar government posted around 400 Bihar Armed Police Force in Baharagora to block the flight of the Naxalites and 'neutralise' them.[93]

The state government also asked the Union government for the deployment of the CRPF. Thus strengthened, the police started counter-insurgency operations. The strategy employed was 'encirclement and suppression',[94] wherein the police along with the EFR and the CRPF encircled a village and conducted door to door search to nab suspected Naxalites. In fact, the police was reportedly authorised to shoot to kill and use light machine guns and hand grenades, if necessary. Chased by the police, the guerrilla squads dispersed to wider areas where they carried out annihilation campaigns and political propaganda.[95]

Meanwhile, the second United Front government led by the CPI (M) government fell in March 1970 and President's rule was imposed in the state. This provided the Union government to crack down upon the CPI (M-L) insurgents in Debra and Gopiballavpur with the help of the local police, the EFR and the CRPF. The police raided the villages where the CPI (M-L) cadres had established 'bases' and arrested scores of cadres and sympathisers. The 'encirclement and suppression' strategy was successful in breaking the will of the insurgents. The Maoist leadership also admitted that 'the police encirclement was responsible for our guerrilla squads' absolute loss of initiative. Our aggressive tactics of launching offensives steadily degenerated into an escapist mood of passive defence.'[96]

The counterinsurgency operation against the CPI (M-L) in the urban areas begun in September 1970 with the imposing of the Bengal Suppression of Terrorist Outrages Act of 1936. Under the Act, the police was empowered to detain persons on grounds of suspicion for a period of 24 hours. In November 1970, the West Bengal Prevention of Violent Activities Act was imposed which gave the police greater power including arrest without warrant.[97] The first important component for launching a counteroffensive against the urban guerrilla was to develop an efficient and effective counterinsurgency force. This was done by reorganising the Kolkata police force, providing the police personnel with adequate training as well as arms and ammunition, and ensuring their personal safety as well as safety of their families against Naxalite attacks.[98]

The heavily compromised Calcutta Police Association was dissolved by enforcing the Police Forces (Restriction of Rights) Act of 1966, on 1 November 1970.[99] Alongside, a series of directives were also issued to make the policemen more alert against attacks. The police personnel on duty with arms were even directed to tie their rifles/revolvers to 'the web or leather belt on the right side' to prevent snatching of arms.[100] The policemen were, in fact, warned against any loss of arm or ammunition.

The second component for an effective counterinsurgency strategy is to have precise intelligence. In this regard, the city police faced problems initially, especially in profiling the CPI (M-L) leaders and cadres because the CPI (M-L) did not develop any mass based organisations to mobilise sympathisers and recruit cadres. In absence of a front organisation, the police did not have any member to extract relevant information about the identities of the members of the CPI (M-L). The police, however, suspected that the Naxalites who were retreating from the rural areas and were operating in the urban areas had formed an alliance with the criminals and anti-socials. This suspicion was corroborated by the post mortem reports of persons allegedly killed by the Naxalites. Upon examining the cut marks, the police concluded that the knife thrusts were made by experienced criminals rather than by amateur cadres.[101] Armed with this evidence, the police zeroed upon the criminals and anti-socials and arrested them. More often than not, these arrests provided the police with further information about the Naxalites in the city.

Based on the information, the Kolkata police categorised the CPI (M-L) cadres under three groups. The first comprising the criminals; the second group, the non-political students, who willy-nilly got dragged into the movement; and third, the dedicated students.[102] Since the police had to mainly deal with anti-socials, the detective and Special Branch of the police were strengthened to gather intelligence.[103] While persons belonging to first and the third categories were either arrested or killed, the persons in the second category were dealt softly. In most cases, the youths were let off after a warning in lieu of information about their hard-core compatriots.

Furthermore, to understand the extent of urban terrorism, the police reorganised their field stations. Accordingly, smaller and manageable police divisions were carved out of existing unwieldy police stations. The officer-in-charge of these police stations were given the responsibility of tackling Naxalite terror in their areas of jurisdiction. This was based on the understanding that the police stations have the required ground level intelligence to identify the perpetrator given that most of them were criminals and anti-social elements.[104] Moreover, the police also selectively recruited several of the criminals as Home Guards to work as informers in lieu of daily payment.[105] Being locals, the criminals knew their locality well and could correctly identify the ideologues from the student and youth cadres. Apparently, these Home Guards were presented as 'people's resistance to the Naxalite depredations.'[106]

Besides, the police also carried out 'cordon and search' operations also known as combing operations. In such operations, the Army or the CRPF threw a cordon around a colony, and then the police entered and searched each and every house for suspected Naxalites. Such 'cordon and search' operations became frequent after the successful holding of the state elections in March 1971. For the operations, the police took the assistance of the Army, the BSF and the CRPF to avoid leakage of information as the soldiery did not have any contact with the locals. Moreover, the armed forces were disciplined and efficient in stopping people inside the cordoned areas.

During the 'cordon and search' operations, more often than not, youths of the colony were rounded up and forced to explain their presence in the place. If someone failed to explain, then that person was immediately arrested.[107] There were many tales of police high-handedness during and after the 'cordon and search' operations. It has been alleged that the police would arrest the youths (some being innocent), torture them for information and then kill them in cold blood.[108] There were also several stories of encounter killings by the Kolkata police during the anti-naxal operations in the city.[109] Between March 1970 and August 1971, 1783 CPI (M-L) cadres were killed by the police in Kolkata and its suburbs, but unofficial figures were reportedly double the number.[110] Charu Mazumdar was arrested from his hideout on 16 July 1972. With his arrest and arrest of a large number of CPI (M-L) cadres, the 'urban movement' in Kolkata and adjoining cities was effectively put down. The remaining urban Naxalites were a spent force indulging in sporadic incidents of terror for the next two years.

History shows that guerrilla warfare cannot be sustained in the urban areas. The CPI (M-L) youth and student activists had carved out 'liberated zones' in Kolkata and its adjoining areas, similar to the 'base areas' in the rural areas. They failed to realise that terrain plays an important role in sustenance of base areas. A forested or hilly area is ideal for guerrilla warfare because the terrain is remote and inaccessible to the counter insurgents. The administration also does not have its reach in these areas, allowing the insurgents to win over the population by providing them with basic needs and instant justice through kangaroo courts. In return, they demand food and shelter from the people.

In the cities and town, administrative reach is all pervasive and every area is well connected with roads enabling the police or the army to move quickly and smash the hideouts of the insurgents. This pattern was discerned in Kolkata. Moreover, the city dwellers, especially the middle class, was repelled by the mindless killings by the CPI (M-L) cadres. They had also voted for peace as well as against the CPI (M) ideology in the elections in 1972. Moreover, the pressure exerted by the police compelled them not only to refuse food and shelter to the urban guerrillas but also to provide information about them to the police.

While the 'urban movement' in Kolkata and its suburbs were brought down by effective police action, ably assisted by the Indian army and the central armed police forces, in the rural areas the Maoist movement was crushed through a joint action of the Indian army, the CRPF, the BSF, and the district police. The preparations for the Bangladesh liberation war in 1971 saw the induction of additional units of the CRPF and the Army in the state. So when the state government was dismissed and President's Rule was imposed in West Bengal, the Union government deployed the central forces to tackle the Naxal insurgency, especially in the countryside. Accordingly, 'Operation Steeple Chase' was launched between 1 July and 15 August 1971.

This Operation was a coordinated action by the Indian army, the CRPF, and local police across contiguous districts in West Bengal, Bihar, and Odisha that were affected by Naxalite violence.[111] During this operation, a corps of the Indian army with about 45,000 troops was deployed in the Midnapore, Purulia, Burdwan and Birbhum districts of West Bengal as well as in the districts of Singhbhum, Dhanbad, Santhal Parganas of Bihar (now Jharkhand), and in Mayurbhanj district of Orissa.[112] The Army carried out area dominance exercise in which it surrounded the Maoist affected villages sealing the entry and exit routes. While the army formed the outer cordon, the CRPF formed the inner ring which allowed the police along with the district magistrate to enter and search every house. Suspected Maoist cadres were arrested, and weapons and documents were seized. [113]

In the initial phase the Army, however, faced few setbacks because the local police were not able to provide precise information about the rebel hideouts.[114] There were also reports of turf wars between the three organisations. Subsequently, the Indian army was successful in effectively cordoning the villages forcing the cadres to flee to the forests and hilly terrain, where during combing operations the cadres were easily surrounded and either captured or killed.[115] Once the rebels fled the villages, the peasantry could not offer any resistance to the Indian army and the armed police. Absence of people militias or revolutionary committees and lack of sophisticated weapons were main reason for the peasants to capitulate in front of the superior might of the state.

As discussed earlier, West Bengal witnessed a resurgence of Maoist violence in the mid-2000s. Initially, the state government was reluctant to act against the Maoists, but targeting of the chief minister's convoy in 2008 changed its attitude towards the rebels. In June 2009, the West Bengal government banned the CPI (Maoist) under the Criminal Law Amendment Act of 1908 and not the UAPA. However, the Maoists who were arrested were booked under the UAPA, thus sending a clear signal about the government's intention of tackling the Maoists problem effectively.[116] Further, in March 2010, it decided to raise Special Forces on the lines of *Greyhounds* specialised in anti-Maoist operations.[117]

While the state government deployed the police to counter the Maoists, much of the anti-Maoist operations were conducted by the CRPF including the elite CoBRA (Commando Battalion for Resolute Action) battalion. For instance, to recapture Lalgarh in June 2009, five companies of the CRPF were deployed. They were assisted by two companies of State Armed Police (SAP) and one company of the BSF.[118] The strategy employed was: the police would first push back the villagers to separate them from the Maoists and minimise collateral damage and then the CRPF would target the Maoist camps located deep inside. The armed cadres of the CPI (M) also participated in the fight against the Maoists in the tribal belts of the state.

The anti-Maoist operation in Lalgarh was a long drawn battle because the CRPF were first, hamstrung by the decision of the political leadership not to open fire during attacks on the Maoist camps. Second, the CRPF did not have adequate information regarding the terrain and the movement of the Maoist rebels. Much of their information about the Maoist rebels and their camps were taken from second hand sources such as video footages, etc. The Maoists not only had a good knowledge about the terrain, they were also forewarned about the movements of the CRPF and the SAP companies by the villagers.[119] Last but not least, the Maoists also deployed women and children in the front to act as a shield against any action by the armed police forces.

Despite these constraints, the joint forces through sustained anti-Naxal operations could re-establish the writ of the government in the affected regions incrementally. Lalgarh itself was freed from the clutches of the Maoists by June 2009 after an intense battle spanning a couple of days. These anti-naxal operations were, however, not restricted to Lalgarh and adjoining areas only, but were carried out in all the 18 districts affected by Maoist violence. Thus by 2011, through sustained and politically backed anti-naxal operations, the Maoist menace in the state was tackled successfully. In fact, the killing of Kishenji effectively brought an end to the Maoist movement in the state. Kishenji was killed in an encounter by a joint operation of the Police, the CRPF and the CoBRA in the Kushbani forest in Paschim Medinipur district on 24 November 2011.[120]

Governance

In the first phase of Communist movement between 1948 and 1952, the state government employed its bureaucracy to launch anti-Communist campaign and manage public perception. The local and sub-divisional officials were dispatched in the rural areas where they denounced Communists ideology and methods, and highlighted the developmental work implemented by the government. The officials also distributed small national flags and photos of national leaders to the villagers free of cost which could be pinned to the shirts. The bureaucracy managed the media by supplying information about the arrests of Communist leaders on one hand, and on the other hand they planted news about various developmental initiatives launched by the state government.[121]

During the second phase of Communist movement, realising that the poor implementation of the land reforms was one of the single most important reasons for the peasant uprising, the first United Front government in 1967 once again galvanised its administrative machinery as well as mobilised the peasantry to implement the land reforms. The objective was to take over the land legally vested upon it but were still in the possession of the landlords, and redistribute them to the landless peasants. It is estimated that around

2.5 lakh acres of land were redistributed to an equal number of peasants during this period.[122]

For example, following the Naxalbari incident, the state government set up the Thana Land Reform Committees in each of the police stations in Siliguri, Phansidewa, Naxalbari and Kharibari to expedite the implementation of the land reforms with an aim to isolate the extremists. The Committee had to look into matters inter alia, action against mala fide transfer of land, prosecution for cases of eviction of bargadars, and educate all sections of the society about their rights and obligations under the law.[123] Interestingly, the land settlement records of Siliguri compiled after the Naxalbari peasant uprising revealed that all the leaders of the movement owned substantial landholdings, few in excess of the ceiling.[124] In fact, Charu Mazumdar had stated in his writing that the Naxalbari struggle was 'not for land or crop but for political power.'[125]

Nevertheless, the government took upon itself to redistribute land to as many landless peasants as possible even if the amount of land given to each peasant was less[126] so that the discontentment among the peasants could be minimised. The coming to power of the second United Front government in 1969 saw the intensification of the drive to detect and cancel mala fide transfers of land. Thus, between 1967 and 1970, close to 600,000 acres of ceiling-surplus land was redistributed by the state government. Incidentally, much of the redistributed land had been forcibly taken over by the sharecroppers during the uprisings. However, when the Congress government came to power in 1972, it stated that peasant uprisings will not be tolerated and therefore the land that were occupied by the peasants during the United Front governments were evicted and given back to the landlords from whom they were snatched before.[127]

That the land reform legislations did not succeed in bringing in equitable distribution of land in the state was revealed in a Study conducted by the state Directorate of Land Records and Surveys in 1971. It stated:

> that the amount of land vested in the state upto June, 1971 (by which time the implementation of WBEA Act, 1953 was supposed to have been completed in all respects) was 1,373,284 acres of arable land (including culturable waste) out of 14,377,572 acres of arable land

> (including culturable waste) in the state, that is, only 9.5 percent of total arable land actually vested under the WBEA Act as against an ideal target of 37.3 percent, or the achievement was only about one-fourth of the target; a poor performance by any standards.[128]

So, when the CPI (M) government came to power in 1977 it resolved to implement the land reforms in all earnestness. Accordingly, the government launched Operation Barga on September 1978 under which it started recording the names of the bargadars who still remained unrecorded in the records-of-rights. Once again the government involved the peasant organisations and rural poor in the operation. The government set up reorientation camps, especially in areas with large concentration of bargadars to educate the peasants about their rights and spread awareness about the importance of recording their names in the record-of-rights. These camps were also meant to sensitise the local officials to the plight of the rural poor and landless labourers.[129]

Furthermore, the state government directed the local revenue officers and junior Land Reforms Officers to collect the information about *benami* land from the peasant organisations. The government also directed the officials to ascertain if any land is cultivated by hired labourers and if they were paid a portion of the produce as wages. If so, then such labourers were to be recorded as bargadars. For the successful implementation of the land reforms, the government also carried out three changes in its administrative structure. First, the land management and land settlement branches were partially integrated. Second, the position of Land Reforms Commissioner was re-implemented. Third, the post of Additional Advocate General was created to follow land reform cases in the High Court.[130]

Operation Barga was successful in recording the bargadars and by 1981 it had recorded 12 lakh bargadars. Furthermore, a total of 11.94 beneficiaries received vested agricultural land from the government during the same period.[131] The state government also initiated a pilot project in 1978 wherein agricultural credits were given to the recorded bargadars and beneficiaries of vested land in 23 selected clusters in 12 districts. By 1979, 79,837 sharecroppers and beneficiaries of vested lands were given loan by 11 public sector and cooperative banks.[132] The agricultural loans not only freed the cultivators from the clutches of the moneylenders but also encouraged them to increase production of their agricultural land. In fact, agricultural production of West

Bengal during the 1980s was 5.5 per cent, which was much above than the national average.[133]

However, as discussed earlier, the land reforms could bring about only limited economic gains to the state. Lack of additional agricultural inputs such as proper irrigation, fertilisers, etc. to increase output as well as the absence of industrialisation pushed the state towards a dire economic situation. Shrinking of resources and general apathy of the administration towards the welfare of the people, especially the tribal people, provided a fertile ground for the Maoists to spread their influence in Junglemahal. Recognising the lack of development as a key factor for the resurgence of Maoist violence in the tribal dominated belt in the state, the Mamata Banerjee government implemented the 'Chief Minister's special package for Junglemahal'.

The package includes several development initiatives such as providing basic amenities, infrastructure, economic opportunities, etc. The package was implemented in conjunction with other centrally sponsored projects such as the Integrated Action Plan (IAP), a centrally sponsored developmental scheme for the Maoist affected districts, Mahatma Gandhi National Rural Employment Guarantee Scheme (henceforth MGNREGS), Indira Awas Yojna (IAY), etc. For the effective implementation of all the union and state governments sponsored packages, Mamata Banerjee ensured speedy inflow of resources in the region. At the same time, she made the local bureaucracy solely responsible instead of the local panchayats.[134] In fact, Mamata Banerjee personally supervised the implementation of these projects in Junglemahal. The state government also gave priority to teaching in Santhali language in 900 government schools in the region.[135]

Summary

Exploitation of the landless peasants and tribal people by landlords and money lenders in Bengal provided ideal issues for the Communists to exploit and stage rebellions against the government over a period of time. Faced with the Communist challenge, successive state governments employed multi-pronged strategies to deal with the problem. So, when the *Tebhaga* movement broke out, the Bengal government primarily employed repressive measures to come down heavily on the fledgling communist insurrection.

Immediately post-independence, the localised communist led peasant uprising was tackled with the twin tactics of managing public perception and crushing the rebellion. Once the CPI withdrew their agitation, the state government enacted several land reforms laws in an effort to provide protection to the sharecroppers, landless peasants as well as the adivasis. However, the failure of the state government to effectively implement the land reforms caused widespread discontentment among the cultivators leading to the 1967 Naxalbari and associated peasant uprisings. This time around also, the state government employed coercive methods to deal with the Naxalites. The police was strengthened and additional battalions of Indian army and the central armed police forces were deployed to conduct anti-Naxal operations. The CPI (M) and Congress also pitted their cadres against the Naxalites to finish them off completely.

It was only after the Communist rebellion was put down firmly, that the CPI (M) government implemented the land reforms effectively. These efforts succeeded in addressing the long held grievances of the peasants. The CPI (M) government also co-opted the rural populace by providing them stakes in the local self-governance as well as distributing economic largesse. While these measures helped in satisfying the aspirations of the rural people, neglect of the tribal people in the forested tracts by the government proved detrimental to the peace and tranquillity of the state. The grievances of the tribal people was exploited by the Maoists and once again they started a movement. In response, the state government dealt with the Maoist rebels with a heavy hand. At the same time, it effectively implemented developmental package in the tribal dominated areas to address the tribal discontentment.

Thus by employing coercive methods against the Maoist rebels as well as by catering to the needs of the peasants as well as the tribal people, and providing socio-economic and political benefits to all sections of the rural areas, West Bengal successfully tackled the Maoist problem in the state.

NOTES

1. The Movement was spread across 19 districts of undivided Bengal.
2. D.N. Dhanagare, 'Peasant protest and politics – The Tebhaga movement in Bengal (India), 1946–47', *The Journal of Peasant Studies*, Vol. 3 (3), 1976, p. 360.
3. Ibid.
4. Ibid, p. 364-365.

5. D. Bandyopadhyay, 'Tebhaga Movement in Bengal: A Retrospect', *Economic and Political Weekly*, Vol. 36 (41), 13019 October 2001, p. 3906.
6. Susnata Das, 'Marginal Communities in Peasant Movement: The Sharecroppers' Struggle for "Tebhaga" In North Bengal (1946-47)', *Proceedings of the Indian History Congress*, Vol. 74, 2013, p. 640.
7. n. 2, p. 369.
8. Nandini Basistha, 'Revisiting Tebhaga Movement in Bengal: Resistance against Domination and Alternative Identities', *Indian Journal of Public Administration*, Vol. 65(4), 2019, pp. 940-941.
9. n. 5, p. 3907. Also see, n. 6, p. 640. n. 7, p. 372.
10. Sekhar Bandyopadhyay, 'The Communists in post-colonial Bengal, 1948-52: The untold story of 'second' Tebhaga', *16th Biennial Conference of the Asian Studies Association of Australia*, Wollongong 26-29 June 2006, p. 4 at https://researcharchive.vuw.ac.nz/bitstream/handle/10063/646/article.pdf?sequence=2, accessed on 25 October 2022.
11. Ibid, p. 5.
12. *Documents of the Communist Movement in India, Vol. V*, Calcutta: National Book Agency Ltd., 1997, p. 643.
13. n. 10, p. 9.
14. Ibid, p. 12.
15. Jonathan Kennedy and Sunil Purushotham, 'Beyond Naxalbari: A Comparative Analysis of Maoist Insurgency and Counterinsurgency in Independent India', *Comparative Studies in Society and History*, Vol. 54 (4), October 2012, p. 845.
16. Asish Kumar Roy, *The Spring Thunder and After, A Survey of the Maoist and Ultra-Leftist Movements in India*, Calcutta: Minerva Associates, 1975, pp. 81-82.
17. Saibal Gupta, 'Naxalbari revisited', *The Times of India*, 25 April 2015 at https://timesofindia.indiatimes.com/city/kolkata/naxalbari-revisited/articleshow/47044695.cms, accessed on 5 January 2022.
18. Bernard D'Mello, *India after Naxalbari: Unfinished History*, New York: Monthly Review Press, 2018.
19. Kanu Sanyal, 'Report on the Peasant Movement in the "Terai Region", *Liberation*, November 1968, p. 39.
20. Ibid, p. 28-53.
21. n. 16, p. 203.
22. Biplab Dasgupta, 'Naxalite Armed Struggles and the Annihilation Campaign in Rural Areas', *Economic and Political Weekly*, Vol. 8 (4/6), Feb., 1973, p. 173.
23. Ibid, p. 174.
24. n. 16, p. 205.
25. Sumanta Banerjee, *India's Simmering Revolution*, London: Zed Books, 1984, p. 141.
26. n. 22, p. 184.
27. Ibid, p. 183.
28. Ranjit Kumar Gupta, *The Crimson Agenda, Maoist Protest and Terror*, Delhi: Wordsmiths, 2004, p. 105.
29. n. 25, p. 173.
30. Ibid, p. 183.
31. n. 28, p. 105.
32. n. 25, p. 185.
33. n. 28, p. 129.
34. n. 16, p. 224.

35. n. 25, p. 212.
36. Ibid, p. 222.
37. Ibid, p. 224.
38. Subhasish Ray and Mohan J. Dutta, 'Insecure peace: understanding citizen and local government relations in a Maoist-affected region in India', *Critical Asian Studies*, Vol. 50 (1), 2018, p. 41.
39. Ibid.
40. Abhirup Sarkar, 'Political Economy of West Bengal: A Puzzle and a Hypothesis', *Economic and Political Weekly*, Vol. 41 (4), 28 January-3 February 2006, pp. 341-342.
41. Malini Bhattacharjee, 'The Lalgarh Story', *Economic and Political Weekly*, Vol. 44 (33), 15-21 August, 2009, p. 18.
42. PTI, 'The second coming of Maoists’ in West Bengal in 2009', *The Hindu*, Kolkata, 1 January 2010 at https://www.thehindu.com/news/national/other-states/The-second-coming-of-Maoistsrsquo-in-West-Bengal-in-2009/article16835254.ece, accessed on 7 October 2022.
43. n. 38, p. 42.
44. Arnab Ganguly and Sukumar Mahato, 'Bengal CM survives Maoist attack', *The Times of India*, Salboni, 3 November 2008 at https://timesofindia.indiatimes.com/india/bengal-cm-survives-maoist-attack/articleshow/3665352.cms, accessed on 5 September 2022.
45. Suhrid Sankar Chattopadhyay, 'Lalgarh battle', *Frontline*, 17 July 2009 at https://frontline.thehindu.com/the-nation/article30187711.ece, accessed on 5 September 2022.
46. Ibid.
47. Ibid.
48. Sayoni Bose, 'Attachment to place and territoriality in Nandigram land struggle, India', *Human Geography*, Vol. 13 (2), 2020, pp. 142-143.
49. Ibid, p. 143.
50. Aloke Banerjee, 'Maoists admit role in Nandigram protests', *The Hindustan Time*, 15 May 2007 at https://www.hindustantimes.com/india/maoists-admit-role-in-nandigram-protests/story-8f6AWijvCt09VSWAEf3EVM.html, accessed on 14 September 2022.
51. Sanchita Das, 'Nandigram protests: 14 killed as violence spills over to Kolkata', *Live Mint*, 15 March 2007 at https://www.livemint.com/Politics/CAZYvJRNWnxOsvFMoYcFHI/Nandigram-protests-14-killed-as-violence-spills-over-to-Kol.html, accessed on 5 September 2022. Swagata Sen, '2007-Nandigram violence: A state of failure', *India Today*, 28 December 2009 at https://www.indiatoday.in/magazine/cover-story/story/20091228-2007-nandigram-violence-a-state-of-failure-741632-2009-12-23, accessed on 5 September 2022.
52. V.K. Shahikumar, 'Operation Nandigram: The Inside Story', *Indian Defence Review*, Vol 23.1 Jan-Mar 2008, at http://www.indiandefencereview.com/news/operation-nandigram-the-inside-story/0/, accessed on 21 September 2022.
53. *Annual Report 2007-08*, New Delhi, Ministry of Home Affairs, 2008, p. 142.
54. *Annual Report 2012-13*, New Delhi: Ministry of Home Affairs, 2013, p. 18.
55. n. 10, p. 7.
56. *The West Bengal Security Act, 1950, West Bengal Act XIX of 1950*, p. 1 at https://www.indiacode.nic.in/bitstream/123456789/14575/1/1950-19.pdf, accessed on 26 August 2022.
57. Ratan Ghosh and K. Nagaraj, 'Land Reforms in West Bengal', *Social Scientist*, Vol. 6 (6/7), Jan.-Feb., 1978, p. 52.
58. *The West Bengal Bargadars Act, 1950*, 15 March 1950, at https://www.indiacode.nic.in/bitstream/123456789/14369/1/act2.pdf, accessed on 26 August 2022.
59. Tim Hanstad and Jennifer Brown, *Land Reform Law and Implementation in West Bengal: Lessons and Recommendations*, Seattle: Rural Development Institute, 2001, p. 13.
60. n. 57, p. 52-53.

61. Ibid, p. 52. Also see, Prakash Singh, *The Naxalite Movement in India*, New Delhi: Rupa, 2016, p. 5.
62. n. 59, p. 13.
63. Ibid, p. 16.
64. n. 57, pp. 53-54. Nripen Bandopadhayay, '"Operation Barga" and Land Reforms Perspective in West Bengal: A Discursive Review', *Economic and Political Weekly*, Vol. 16 (25/26), 20-27 June 1981, p. 40.
65. n. 59, p. 15.
66. n. 57, pp. 65-66. Suhas Chattopadhyay, 'Operation Barga', *Social Scientist*, Vol. 8 (87), October 1979, p. 41.
67. Amitabha Chandra, 'The Naxalbari Movement', *The Indian Journal of Political Science*, Vol. 51 (1), Jan-Mar 1990, pp. 26-27.
68. n. 16, p. 87.
69. n. 67, p. 29.
70. n. 16, p. 205.
71. n. 25, p. 140.
72. n. 25, p. 141.
73. n. 28, p. 107.
74. n. 61, p. 50.
75. n. 25, p. 193.
76. n. 28, pp. 183-191.
77. Ibid, pp. 134-136.
78. n. 16, pp. 226-227.
79. n. 25, p. 212.
80. n. 16, pp. 233-234.
81. Sourjya Bhowmick, *Gangster State: The Rise and Fall of the CPI (M) in West Bengal*, Kolkata: Macmillan, 2021.
82. 'Keep your poll promises: Maoists to Mamata', *The New Indian Express*, 16 October 2011 at https://www.newindianexpress.com/nation/2011/oct/16/keep-your-poll-promises-maoists-to-mamata-300961.html, accessed on 23 September, 2022.
83. 'Mamata a threat to national security, used Maoists to win power: BJP', *The Hindustan Times*, 29 November 2018 at https://www.hindustantimes.com/india-news/mamata-a-threat-to-national-security-used-maoists-to-win-power-bjp/story-H6RtjPXuabLjTEGwr1Aa2K.html, accessed on 22 September 2022. Also see, Rahul Shivshankar, 'Mamata's Rally Exposes The Drift In Govt', *The Times of India*, 13 August 2010 at https://timesofindia.indiatimes.com/blogs/beyond-the-headline/mamata-s-rally-exposes-the/, accessed on 22 September 2022.
84. Gautam Navlakha, 'People's War as Strategy and Peace Talk as Tactics', *Frontier*, Vol. 44 (44), 13-19 May 2012 at https://www.frontierweekly.com/archive/vol-number/vol/vol-44-2011-12/vol-44-44/peopleswar-44-44.pdf, accessed on 7 October 2022.
85. Snigdhendu Bhattacharya, 'What Mamata Banerjee did right to wipe out Maoist violence in West Bengal', *The Hindustan Times*, 10 May 2017 at https://www.hindustantimes.com/india-news/what-mamata-banerjee-did-right-to-wipe-out-maoist-violence-in-west-bengal/story-tq1GX8PGGHBKVoxjGzvVKJ.html, accessed on 23 September 2022.
86. Ceasar Mandal, 'Comrades once, now nemesis', *The Times of India*, Jhargram, 29 November 2011 at https://timesofindia.indiatimes.com/city/kolkata/comrades-once-now-nemesis/articleshow/10912502.cms, accessed on 6 October 2022.
87. PTI, 'Mamata gives fresh call to Maoists to return to mainstream', *The Economic Times*, Kolkata, 25 August 2011 at https://economictimes.indiatimes.com/news/politics-and-nation/mamata-

gives-fresh-call-to-maoists-to-return-to-mainstream/articleshow/9732905.cms?from=mdr, accessed on 22 September 2022.

88. Ibid.
89. Sujato Bhadra, 'Peace-talk Process in Junglemahal', *Mainstream*, Vol. 50 (1), 24 December 2011 at https://www.mainstreamweekly.net/article3221.html, accessed on 6 October 2022.
90. Tamal Sengupta, 'Maoist peace talk in bengal ends', *The Economic Times*, Kolkata, 28 November 2011 at https://economictimes.indiatimes.com/news/politics-and-nation/maoist-peace-talk-in-bengal-ends/articleshow/10908724.cms?from=mdr, accessed on 6 October 2011.
91. n. 16, p. 89.
92. Charu Mazumdar, 'A Few Words about Guerilla Warfare', *Liberation*, Vol. III (4), February 1970.
93. n. 25, p. 141.
94. Ibid, p. 140.
95. n. 16, p. 206.
96. Report of the Bengal-Bihar Orissa Border, as quoted in n. 16, p. 206.
97. n. 25, pp. 186-187.
98. n. 28, p. 126.
99. Ashoke Kumar Mukhopadhyay, 'Through the Eyes of the Police: Naxalites in Calcutta in the 1970s', *Economic and Political Weekly*, Vol. 41 (29), 22-28 July, 2006, p. 3229.
100. Ibid, p. 3229.
101. n. 28, p. 131.
102. n. 25, p. 194.
103. n. 28, p. 132.
104. Ibid, pp. 137-140.
105. Ibid, p. 141.
106. n. 25, p. 195.
107. n. 28, p. 143.
108. Allegations which were refuted by the Police Commissioner of Kolkata at that time in his book. See n. 28, pp. 196-198.
109. n. 25, p. 197. Also see, n. 99, p. 3230.
110. n. 25, pp. 206-207.
111. Thomas F. Lynch III, *India's Naxalite Insurgency: History, Trajectory, and Implications for U.S.-India Security Cooperation on Domestic Counterinsurgency*, Washington: Institute for National Strategic Studies Strategic Perspectives, 2016, p. 28.
112. Sujan Dutta, 'Clamour to let army fight Maoists rises - Bengal, only state with military experience, adds voice to chorus', *The Telegraph*, Delhi, 26 September 2009 at https://www.telegraphindia.com/india/clamour-to-let-army-fight-maoists-rises-bengal-only-state-with-military-experience-adds-voice-to-chorus/cid/592261, accessed on 12 January, 2022.
113. n. 61, p. 77.
114. n. 25, p. 225.
115. Ibid.
116. ET Bureau, 'West Bengal govt 'bans' Maoists', *The Economic Times*, Kolkata, 24 June 2009 at https://economictimes.indiatimes.com/news/politics-and-nation/west-bengal-govt-bans-maoists/articleshow/4698305.cms, accessed on on 6 October 2022.
117. Raktima Bose, 'Special force to tackle Maoists', *The Hindu*, 20 March 2010 at https://www.thehindu.com/news/Special-force-to-tackle-Maoists/article16578458.ece, accessed on 6 October 2022.
118. n. 45.

119. Abhijit Dasgupta, 'Lalgarh ops launched, then stalled', *India Today*, 19 June 2009 at https://www.indiatoday.in/latest-headlines/story/lalgarh-ops-launched-then-stalled-50334-2009-06-18, accessed on 22 September 2022.
120. Shiv Sahay Singh and Ananya Dutta, 'Kishenji killed in encounter', *The Hindu*, 24 November 2011 at https://www.thehindu.com/news/national/Kishenji-killed-in-encounter/article13499991.ece, accessed on 7 October 2022. Soudhriti Bhabani, 'Naxal leader Kishenji killed in encounter: Reports', *India Today*, Kolkata, 25 November 2011at https://www.indiatoday.in/india/east/story/maoist-leader-kishenji-killed-in-encounter-146760-2011-11-23, accessed on 7 October 2022.
121. n. 10, p. 13.
122. n. 57, p. 56.
123. n. 16, pp. 87-88.
124. Ibid, pp. 94-95.
125. Charu Mazumdar, 'One Year of Naxalbari', *Liberation*, June 1968, p. 28.
126. n. 57, p. 57.
127. n. 59, p. 14. Also see, n. 57, p. 58.
128. 'A Peep into Future: A Case Study of the Next Phase of Land Reforms in West Bengal', Directorate of Land Records & Surveys, West Bengal, 1971, p. 39 as quoted in n. 57, p. 54-55.
129. n. 66, p. 42.
130. n. 59, p. 33.
131. n. 64, p. 40.
132. n. 64, p. 46.
133. n. 40, p. 342.
134. n. 38, p. 44.
135. Neha Banka, 'In their own language: a school in West Bengal's Birbhum for Santal children', *The Indian Express*, Birbhum, 31 March 2022 at https://indianexpress.com/article/cities/kolkata/in-their-own-language-a-school-in-west-bengals-birbhum-for-santal-children-7843955/, accessed on 7 October 2022.

5

PUNJAB

Punjab was ravaged by Sikh militancy throughout the 1980s and early 1990s. The spark for Sikh militancy in the state was lit on 13 April 1978 when a group of orthodox Sikhs led by Jarnail Singh Bhindranwale protested against an annual congregation of the *Nirankaris* (a sect considered to be heretical) in Amritsar. The protest soon degenerated into a clash between the two groups compelling the police to resort to firing to bring the situation under control. The firing by the police resulted in the death of eighteen followers of Bhindranwale and two followers of Sant Nirankari. Bhindranwale blamed the government and swore vengeance for the 'massacre'.[1] Thus, started Sikh militancy in Punjab. Another fallout of the incident was that it reinforced the existing chasm between the Hindus and Sikhs in the state. Even though, this episode was a case of intra-Sikh rivalry, the subsequent court verdict on this case which acquitted all the followers of Sant Nirankari on the ground of self-defence, was exploited by Bhindranwale and his followers to highlight an alleged anti-Sikh bias of the 'Hindu' State. The Sikh militancy or Khalistan movement was comprehensively defeated in 1993, but by that time it had consumed 21,469 lives.[2]

While Sikh militancy in Punjab has its roots in the politicisation of Sikh identity during the colonial times, the primary cause of militancy in the state was the outcome of a bitter political struggle between the Congress and the Akali Dal.[3] The British had formulated a policy in which apportionment of political privileges were based on the population preponderance of a particular religious groups. This led to an intense competition between the Sikhs and the Hindus, who declared Sikh as a sect of Hinduism. To counter the claims of the Hindus, the Sikh started asserting their religious identity and formed a number of political groups especially the Akali Dal, which propagated the Sikh identity and aspirations.[4] Thus, by the time of India's independence the Sikhs had established themselves as a separate religious group having their distinct ethnic identity.

The Politics of the Akali Dal

During the partitioning of the Indian subcontinent, the Sikhs had hoped that the British would create a separate state for them on the lines of Pakistan. However, the fact that the Sikhs did not constitute a majority in any area and did not reside in a contiguous territory that could be carved out for a separate state, negated their aspirations. So, in 1947 they reluctantly agreed to the partitioning of Punjab and remained with the Sikh-Hindu majority state of eastern Punjab.[5] This gesture, however, did not diminish their aspiration for a separate state within the Indian union. In 1948, the Akali Dal made the demand for a 'Punjabi Suba' arguing that they would rather have a separate state where they can safeguard their culture (Gurmukhi script), language (Punjabi) and religion (Sikhism).[6]

The Indian government smarting from the partition of India on religious lines, did not accede to the demands of the Akalis. However, the Union government did agree to several of their demands such as increased jobs in the public sector, equal number of seats for Hindus and Sikhs in the ministry of Punjab and dividing the state into Punjabi speaking and Hindi speaking segments where the respective language will be the medium of instruction till matriculation and the other would be taught as a compulsory language after fourth grade.[7] Throughout the 1950s and the 1960s, the Akali Dal campaigned for the creation of a Punjabi Suba (Punjabi speaking state). The State Reorganisation Committee however, found the demands of the Akali Dal for a separate state communal and therefore rejected their demand on the ground that it lacked the support of the general public. In response, the Akali Dal and other Sikh extremists, in order to garner Sikh support, tried to exploit the age old fears of the Sikhs that their identity and religion is under threat. These extremist elements of the Akali Dal even spread the propaganda that while the 'Hindu' government at the Centre had created several states based on language in 1956, but the Sikhs were denied their rightful demand.

In 1965, Fateh Singh of the newly created Akali Dal (Fateh) threatened the government that he would launch a 'fast undo death' until the demand for the creation of a Punjabi Suba is met. The Union government conceded to the demands of the Akalis and after the India-Pakistan war of 1965, the Punjab Suba was created on 1 November 1966. Creation of a separate Punjab state, however, did not end the tensions between the Congress and the Akali Dal. The Akali Dal claimed that the Sikhs were betrayed by the Centre because the control of Bhakra and Beas Dams were not given to the state, that certain Punjabi speaking areas were not added to the newly organised state, that Chandigarh, which was the capital of Punjab, was made an union territory thereby jeopardising the claim by Punjab over it, and that Punjab's share of river water was curtailed and was forced to share more water resources with Haryana and Rajasthan.[8]

It is important to note that following Independence, the Congress and the Akali Dal emerged as the two main political parties in Punjab. The irony is while the Congress Party crafted an enduring support base comprising the rural people, the lower castes (*Mazhabi* Sikhs) as well as a segment of Sikh population, the Akali Dal, despite representing the interests of the Sikhs, never enjoyed the full support of the entire Sikh community.[9] It had only the support of rich Jat Sikhs in the rural areas and a small segment of Sikhs in the urban areas. The demand for a separate Punjabi Suba by the Akali Dal was, therefore, essentially to appease the Sikh constituency and emerge as a governing party in the state. The Akali Dal did form two coalition governments in 1967 and in 1969, but because of intense infightings the government collapsed in 1969.[10] After the elections, the Congress-Indira (Congress-I) formed the government in 1972 with Giani Jail Singh as the Chief Minister.

On the Road to Sikh Militancy

The defeat of the Akali Dal at the hands of Congress Party pushed the Akalis towards adopting more extremist ideas to consolidate the Sikh support.[11] In its October 1973 annual congregation in Anandpur Sahib, the Akali Dal adopted a resolution, which defined the Sikhs as a *qaum* (nation) and called for the devolution of power from the Centre to the state and more autonomy to Punjab. The Akali Dal also placed itself as the 'very embodiment of the hopes and aspirations of the Sikh Nation and as such is fully entitled to its representation'.[12] The social, religious, economic and political policies in the Resolution were drafted with the objective to win over the Sikh 'nationalist'. The Congress on its part also tried to manipulate the Sikh community and attempted to divide them on the lines of caste and class to ensure that the Sikh votes remained divided. This tactics by the Congress propelled the Akalis to proclaim more extremist religious ideas to compete with the Sikh extremists.

In the ensuing tussle, the Congress Party extended political patronage to Jarnail Singh Bhindranwale, leader of a Sikh seminary (the *Damdami Taksal*), as an alternate to the Akali Dal. Bhindranwale attempted to narrow the definition of Sikhism to mean those who were baptised into *Khalsa* and who were *Amritdari* (baptismal nectar). He also espoused Sikh orthodoxy and austere living and argued that Sikhs were losing their identity because of internal decay and external threat.[13] He criticised the Akali Dal for embracing secular thoughts and ideas and claimed that Sikhs were suffering under the Hindu imperialist rulers of New Delhi.[14] The effective articulation of perceived grievances of the Sikh community by Bhindranwale and his charismatic personality received lots of support from Sikh extremists and attracted a large number of radicalised Jat Sikh youths under his fold.

Bhindranwale also gained lots of followers because of his relationship with Bhai Amrik Singh, the President of the All India Sikh Students Federation (AISSF). Bhindranwale was Amrik's Singh 'blood brother' and had succeeded Amrik Singh's father as the head of the *Taksal* after the latter's death in August 1977.[15] The *Akhand Kirthani Jatha* (Organisation for the Ceaseless Singing of Devotional Songs), the Babbar Khalsa, a political offshoot of *Akhand Kirthani Jatha*, and the *Dal* Khalsa, a militant Sikh organisation with avowed object of demanding the creation of an independent sovereign Sikh state, all created in 1978, together with the AISSF formed the core team of Bhindranwale. In addition, the Congress (I), some sections of Akali Dal and Pakistan (which offered him materiel support in his quest for a separate Khalistan) also provided Bhindranwale much needed support.[16]

Emboldened by the support he found, Bhindranwale adopted the strategy of terror to spread his clout. He publicly issued 'hit lists' of those who disagreed with his ideology and systematically killed the targeted persons one after another. He killed a number of *Nirankari* leaders including its head Baba Gurbachan Singh, who were allegedly responsible for the death of his followers in April 1978. He also targeted prominent Hindu leaders to intimidate the Hindus as well as to create a chasm between the Hindus and Sikhs. One such leader was Lala Jagat Narain, a respected newspaper owner and a Hindu leader, who was killed in 1981. The Congress Party, however, defended Bhindranwale in the Parliament by stating that he was not involved in the killings and even put pressure on the Punjab police to release Bhindranwale when he was arrested for these murders.[17] The unconditional release of Bhindranwale added to his persona of invincibility and the 'saviour of the Sikhs'.

Bhindranwale and his cohorts indoctrinated the Sikh youths in the ideology of separatism in militant terms under the façade of *gurmat* camps (camps held for expounding religious doctrines of Sikhs). They also used these camps to train the youths in the use of modern weaponry. The network of criminals and anti-socials were exploited for procuring arms and ammunition as well as for looting banks, jewellery shops and homes to replenish financial resources.[18] They also stockpiled weapons in the gurudwaras (Sikh Temples) and obtained external support from Pakistan and the Sikh diaspora.

Another tactic employed by Bhindranwale and his followers was to occupy the gurudwaras and exploit them for various purposes. First, by controlling the gurudwaras, the Sikh militants controlled the head priests and their sermons and suitably modified them for religious indoctrination and radicalising the youth for recruitment. Second, by occupying the gurudwaras, the militants projected themselves as religious and political leaders and often controlled their human and financial resources by threatening the gurudwaras' head. Third, the militants used the gurudwaras as operational centre because of their logistical and strategic benefits. Besides providing the place to dine and lodge, the gurudwaras were perfect sites as protected hideouts for them because the government was reluctant to send forces into gurudwaras lest it offended the Sikh sentiments.[19] Bhindranwale himself took up residence in the Akal Takht (Throne of the Timeless) and began to extol and instigate violence.[20]

As militancy was gaining currency in Punjab, the Sikh diaspora started supporting the cause of a separate Khalistan. Jagjit Singh Chouhan had in 1971 raised the demand for a separate Khalistan. In fact, the Khalistan movement had originated in the United Kingdom and between 1971 and 1978, a large number of organisations supported the movement. In 1980, Chouhan renewed his campaign in Punjab, hoisted the flag of Khalistan at

Anandpur Sahib in March and formed the National Council of Khalistan on 12 April 1980. Three months later he proclaimed the formation of Khalistan and issued Khalistani passports, stamps and currency notes from United Kingdom where he set up his 'government in exile'.[21]

Further, in February 1981 during a meeting of the Working Committee of the Akali Dal, the extremist faction led by Jagdev Singh Talwandi openly supported 'the Sikhs are a nation theory'. In March 1981, the Dal Khalsa came out in support of a separate Khalistan when they took out a procession of 60 activists wielding swords and a banner with a map of proposed Khalistan. In August 1981, the Dal Khalsa members also raised pro-Khalistan slogans from the visitor's gallery of the Punjab assembly. Significantly in September 1981, five members of the Dal Khalsa hijacked a Delhi-Srinagar Indian Airlines flight IC 423, with 117 on board, to Lahore as a protest against the arrest of Bhindranwale.[22] In fact throughout 1981, the Dal Khalsa indulged in looting, arson, mayhem and murder thereby creating an atmosphere of terror in the state. Finally, the Centre declared the Dal Khalsa and the National Council of Khalistan unlawful associations on 1 May 1982 under the UAPA. After the ban, the members of the Dal Khalsa quietly moved to other organisations such as the AISSF and Babbar Khalsa, and continued to indulged in arson, looting and indiscriminate killings.

Even as terrorism was escalating, the Akali Dal, which lost both the state and parliament elections in 1980, mounted political pressure on the state and the Union governments. In September 1981, the party presented a list of 45 demands to the Union government, which was revised to 15 demands a month later. Some of these demands were based on Anandpur Sahib Resolution and included issues such as declaration of Amritsar as a holy city, enactment of All India Gurdwara Act, increase in the share of river waters for Punjab, Chandigarh as Punjab's capital, greater autonomy to Punjab, etc.[23] In April-May 1982, the Longowal faction started the *nahar roko andolan* to block the building of the Sutlej-Yumana link canal. Meanwhile, Bhindranwale started a *morcha* against the arrest of Amrik Singh of the AISSF in July 1982.

This agitation was followed by the Talwandi faction's morcha for the creation of Desh (semi-autonomous Punjab) in August 1982. All these morchas combined and became a rallying point for the Sikhs to fight against the 'imperialist' Union government.[24] In fact, the Akali Dal, which had shifted its headquarters to the Golden Temple, intensified its agitation in August 1982 and termed it as *Dharma Yudh* (religious war). They even invited Bhindranwale to join their morchas. The merging of the Akali Dal and Bhindranwale morchas provided the Akali Dal the required appeal and foot soldiers to carry out violent agitations. The Akali Dal particularly chose national holidays to stage protests to lower the prestige of India and even threatened demonstrations during the Asian games in November-December 1982. By 1983, these violent demonstrations perpetrated by the Akali Dal became more frequent with calls for *rasta-roko* (road blockade), *rail roko* (stop rails) and *kam roko* (stop work).[25]

From 1983 onwards the security situation in Punjab became direr. While the political agitations became more violent, more and more youths were pulled into the extremist fold. A pattern of targeting and killing of innocent Hindus by the terrorists became more pronounced. In fact, the terrorists would hijack buses, segregate the Hindus and kill them in cold blood.[26] The terrorists also committed acts of sacrilege against Hindu temples and threw grenades at Hindu processions to create enmity between the Hindus and the Sikhs. The terrorists also targeted police men and officers and killed several of them during encounters. The murder of Deputy Inspector General A.S. Atwal on 25 April 1983 was particularly heinous.[27]

The Akali Dal never criticised these acts of terror and the state government's appeals to the *Shiromani Gurudwara Prabandhak Committee* (SGPC) to hand over the terrorists hiding in the gurudwaras drew no response.[28] However, this alliance between the Akali Dal and Bhindranwale also created tensions between the followers of Bhindranwale and Sant Harchand Singh Longowal. There were violent clashes between the two factions forcing Bhindranwale to move from the Guru Nanak Niwas to the Akal Takht with his armed entourage in December 1983. From his sanctuary Bhindranwale and his associates intensified their campaign of communal hatred and terror. Inside the Golden temple also, any dissent against Bhindranwale was met with intimidation and terror as several were tortured and killed.[29]

The deteriorating law and order situation forced the Union government to ask the Chief Minister Darbara Singh to resign and impose President's rule in October 1983.[30] The imposition of President's did not alter the grave security situation in the state. In fact, by the beginning of 1984, the situation in Punjab became more fraught because of Akali Dal's communal propaganda, violent mass agitations and increasing terrorist activities. The subversive activities of groups inside the Golden Temple assumed menacing proportions as the influence of external forces, with deep-rooted interest in the disintegration of India, became more evident. From 4 August 1982, when the Akali Dal intensified their agitation till 31 December 1983, there were over 425 violent incidents in which 112 persons were killed and more than 655 injured. However, from 1 January 1984 to 3 June 1984, there were over 775 violent incidents in which 298 persons were killed and more than 525 injured.[31]

Operation Blue Star and its Aftermath

Alarmed by the worsening security situation in Punjab, on 3 June 1984, the Indira Gandhi government ordered the Indian army to 'get rid' of all the terrorists ensconced in various gurudwaras of Punjab. Operation Blue Star was the codename given to the military operation to clear the Golden Temple of all the militants. Prior to moving into the Golden Temple in the night of 5 June 1984, the Indian army appealed for surrender to the terrorists. This appeal led to the surrender of Sant Harchand Singh Longowal and G.S. Tohra along with around 350 people in the midnight of 6 June 1984. The terrorists holed up in the temple premises, however, fired extensively to prevent the surrender, and ended up killing seventy persons.[32]

The army had moved with a strength of four infantry battalions, two specialist commando battalions, a squadron of Vijayanta tanks and one platoon of infantry combat vehicle.[33] Expectedly, the army faced determined resistance from the well-entrenched terrorists who fired at them with machine guns and rifle fires from fortified verandahs, minarets and rooftops. In fact, the Indian army took heavy casualties in the initial hours of the operation. It had to use heavy tanks to clear the fortifications and neutralise the terrorists, and even open fire on the Akal Takht from where terrorists were firing heavily. The entire operation lasted for two days and resulted in the killing of several militants including Jarnail Singh Bhindranwale and Amrik Singh.

Subsequent to the Operation Blue Star, Operation Woodrose was conducted as a follow up operation 'to capture Bhindranwale's surviving associates and to clear all Gurudwaras in the state of extremist elements.'[34] There was intelligence that the terrorists had taken sanctuary in a total of 42 gurudwaras in the state.[35] Based on this intelligence, the Indian army carried out coordinated operations against the terrorists in several districts of Punjab. Prior to the launching of these military operations, appeals were made to the terrorists to surrender. While in some place, the terrorists surrendered without much fight, in other places, the army had to move into the gurudwara premises to dislodge the terrorists. By the end of the month of June 1984, a total of 554 civilians/terrorists were killed including 493 in the Golden Temple. 4712 civilians/terrorists were apprehended, of which 1592 were from the Golden temple and 796 from other gurudwaras.[36] A large quantity of weapons, ammunition and explosives were recovered, including automatic weapons, mines and anti-tank weapons. A small factory for manufacturing hand grenades and sten guns was also found within the precincts of the Golden Temple.[37]

While the army operations were successful in evicting the terrorists, the extensive damage caused to the Golden Temple particularly the Akal Takht was perceived by the Sikh community as an attack on their religion. The complete media blackout regarding the military operation fuelled many rumours about the alleged atrocities committed by the Indian army. The Sikh community was highly agitated and simmering with anger. The 'mopping up' operation conducted by the Indian army following Operation Blue Star further compounded the problem. The mistrust of the local police and intelligence, hostile population and lack of credible intelligence forced the army to indiscriminately arrest a large number of people, most of whom could be described as innocent. The assassination of Indira Gandhi by her Sikh bodyguards in October 1984 as a revenge, and the consequent killings of Sikhs in Delhi were the proverbial last straw. Sikh youths joined militancy in large numbers and the demand for 'homeland for the Sikh' became more and more aggressive. Even Sikh officers and soldiers deserted the Indian military and joined the ranks of the militants.[38]

In their quest for a separate Khalistan, the militants found a willing ally in Pakistan. Pakistan, especially its Inter-Services Intelligence (ISI), set camps to train Sikh youths in handling weapons and explosives. Some of these camps were located as close as 75 metres from the international boundary. Sikh youths crossed over to Pakistan to receive training in various terrorist camps. The flow of Sikh militants to these training camps picked up in 1984 following Operation Blue Star, and increased substantially in the subsequent years.[39] Once their training was complete, these militants sneaked back into Punjab with sophisticated arms and explosives. Between 1986 and 1992, security forces in Punjab had apprehended 45,650 persons trying to cross the international border,[40] and had seized around 2500 AK series of assault rifles in the state.[41]

As was inevitable Sikh militancy raged in Punjab. Several terrorist groups such as the Khalistan Commando Force (KCF), the Khalistan Liberation Force (KLF), the Khalistan Liberation Organisation (KLO), the Bhindranwale Tiger Force of Khalistan (BTFK), etc. were formed. The terrorists belonging to these organisations unleashed a reign of terror in the state. The number of persons killed by the Sikh militants increased from 75 in 1983 to 359 in 1984, which further increased to 520 in 1986.[42] There were also high profile and sensational acts perpetrated by the militants such as the highjacking of the Indian Airlines plane from Chandigarh in 1984, the bombing of the Air India Flight 182 (*Kanishka*) in June 1985, which killed 329 passengers and crew, and the assassination of General A.A. Vaidya, who was the Indian army Chief of Staff during Operation Blue Star in August 1986.

Most significantly, the Golden Temple which was restored to the SGPC in January 1986, was once again taken control by the Sikh terrorists led by Damdami Taksal.[43] The terrorists were able to lodge themselves in the Golden Temple precinct because of the direct or indirect support of key Sikh leaders and institutions such as the SGPC, the AISSF and the *Jathedar* (leader) of the Akal Takht.[44] This time around also, the Union and the state governments looked the other way when the terrorists smuggled in large quantities of arms and ammunition inside the temple premises.

On 29 April 1986, a *Panthic Committee* to coordinate the activities of the terrorists was constituted, and a 'Declaration of Khalistan' was issued. The Barnala government made a feeble attempt to get rid of the terrorists from the Golden Temple and launched an operation often referred to as Black Thunder-I.[45] The operation, which was launched on 30 April 1986 with the help of the elite anti-terrorist force, the National Security Guard (NSG) was a non-starter as advance notice about the operation was already given out. As expected the operation did not result in the arrest of any terrorist of consequence, and the Sikh militants once again lodged themselves firmly inside the Temple complex and continued to kill civilians and police personnel. Between October 1985 to April 1988, 2866 lives (2207 civilians, 177 policemen, 482 terrorists) were lost.[46] Terrorism also spread far and wide in the state and gripped more districts than before. Thus, apart from the districts of Amritsar and Gurdaspur, Hoshiarpur, Jalandhar, Ludhiana and Faridkot were also badly affected. In May 1987, the Barnala government was dismissed by the Centre and President's rule was imposed in the state.

Operation Black Thunder and the End of Sikh Militancy

In 1988, the Union government was compelled, once again, to use force to clear the Golden Temple of Sikh terrorists. Learning from its earlier mistakes, the government desisted from employing the military and assigned the task to the NSG. The operation code named Black Thunder–II was launched on 11 May 1988. The operation was executed under the leadership of the Punjab police and assisted by the NSG and the CRPF.[47] Two battalions of the CRPF were deployed around the temple complex to control access. The NSG deployed 100 commandos to carry out the entire operation. Unlike the Indian army, the police and the NSG methodically gathered intelligence about the terrorists and their positions inside and systematically planned the entire operation before entering the Temple precinct.

The plan was 'to pin down the militants inside the complex by accurate sniper fire and then storm one part of the complex after another.'[48] So as a first step, snipers were positioned atop surrounding buildings to shoot at terrorists who came out of the rooms in the Temple complex. The first one to be killed by the snipers was the Panthic Committee spokesman, Jagir Singh, in the *parikrama* area. Shooting of Jagir Singh had a demoralising effect on rest of the militants. In the following three days, snipers killed 20 more militants.[49] Meanwhile, appeals were made by the police to the militants to surrender. For this purpose, the well-known Sikh saint Baba Uttam Singh was also brought in. On 15 May, 146 people, including 17 women and children surrendered, most of them were devotees trapped inside.[50]

As the next step, the NSG commandos took control of all the surrounding buildings and used heavy machine guns to break the fortifications and neutralise the militants. The administration had already cut off electric and water supply to the Temple complex and the CRPF and the police had laid a siege to break the will of the militants. Their patience paid off and on 18 May 1988, 46 terrorists, who had taken refuge inside the Harmandar Sahib three days earlier, surrendered. In all, 200 militants, including 50 hard core terrorists surrendered.[51] The surrender caused the militants to lose the aura of invincibility, which they had developed before the operation. Further, the fact that the entire operation was conducted in front of the media also helped a lot in shaping the narrative in favour of the government. The Sikhs appreciated the restraint shown by the government forces. At the same time they were dismayed by the desecration of the holy temple as well as the torture and murders committed by the militants.[52]

Operation Black Thunder-II had a profound impact on the militancy of Punjab. It exposed the militants, especially the leaders, by demonstrating that they did not have respect for the Sikh religious institutions. In fact, the Khalistan movement lost its veneer of religiosity it had acquired earlier and soon degenerated into criminal acts. A study had revealed that the Khalistan movement was populated with young, undereducated or illiterate youths with limited job prospects. Around 95 per cent of the youth joined the movement for 'fun' and only 5 per cent joined it in pursuit of Khalistan.[53] Armed with AK-47s, these youths rampaged through the rural areas indulging in loot, extortion, and even rape. As a result, the rural people were repulsed by the militants and stopped offering them food and shelter. Furthermore, the gurudwaras were also no longer available for the militants to hide.[54] Devoid of sanctuaries and safe houses, the militants were left in the open and soon either fell to the bullets of the police or their rivals or were arrested by the police.

Immediately following Operation Black Thunder-II, the terrorists had gone on an indiscriminate killing spree by killing 343 persons in May 1988 alone.[55] However, determined action by the police and lack of support from the masses constricted their areas of operation. By January 1989, the terrorists were confined to a thin strip of land along the international border and 70 per cent of their strikes limited to only three districts of Punjab – Amritsar, Gurdaspur and Ferozpur.[56] The number of Sikh militants killed in 1989 was 703 while the number of arrests reduced from 3,882 in 1988 to 2,466 in 1989 reflecting a shift in the strategy of the police.[57] Arrests and surrenders were not encouraged because the police felt that arrested militants would be invariably freed during a political compromise thus enabling them to go back to militancy once again.

While the police action against the militancy was highly successful as the level of violence was gradually coming down, the brutality and extrajudicial killings by the police and the detention of suspected militants without proper court hearing was creating a problem for the government at the Centre.[58] The defeat of the Congress (I) and the victory of the National Front at the Centre provided the much needed oxygen to the dying militancy in Punjab. Eager to arrive at a political solution, the National Front government, under V.P. Singh released a number of militants along with Simranjeet Singh Mann, who was the leader of Akali Dal (Mann), an extreme faction of the Akali Dal.[59] Even the DGP K.P.S. Gill was posted out of the state as a goodwill gesture towards the militants.

The détente period was exploited by the militants to increase violence in the state. In fact, the number of civilians killed in 1990 and 1991 were the most since the Khalistan movement begun. In 1990, 1,961 civilians were killed by the militants, which increased to 2,094 in 1991. The militants also increased their area of operation from the border districts to include urban areas in previously little-affected districts.[60] Distressed migration from the rural areas badly afflicted by militancy rose to 2524 families through 1990 and 1991. The number of terrorists killed also rose concomitantly from 1320 in 1990 to 2177 in 1991.[61] Despite the rise in the deaths of militants, some members of Khalistan movement felt emboldened enough to ask the United Nations to conduct a referendum on the secession. In fact, the leaders of Khalistan movement thought that victory was eminent and it was only the borders between India and Khalistan that had to be decided.[62]

The spurt in militancy was, however, short lived as the Congress party returned to power in the Centre in 1991. The Indian army was redeployed in the state and KPS Gill was once again posted as the DGP of Punjab. A combined effort at the union as well as the state level helped to effectively tackle the scourge of militancy in Punjab. In the face of a renewed and well-coordinated counterterrorism strategy, the militants groups could not offer a unified fight against the Indian state. Instead, they fragmented into multiple groups indulging in fratricidal killings and engaging in criminal acts. Even the political wing of the militant groups itself was divided into four groups – the First, the Second, and the Third Panthic Committee, and the Akali Dal (Babbar), all of which claimed to represent the Sikh community and their aspirations.[63]

The last nail in the proverbial coffin of the Khalistan movement was the successful holding of the elections in February 1992, which was boycotted by the militants and the Akali Dal (various factions). The Congress party came back to power in the state, which allowed the police to finish the task of eliminating terrorism from the state.[64] By the end of 1992, 537 terrorists had surrendered to the police, six of them hard core and in 1993, another 379, including 11 hard core terrorists, surrendered. The total number of civilian killed in 1993 also came down to only 48.[65] So in all respects, militancy came to an end in Punjab in 1993. Only a few intermittent terror episode continued for couple of years more, the major incident being the assassination of Chief Minister Beant Singh in 1995.[66]

The State Government's Response to Sikh Militancy

Initially, the Union government treated the militancy in Punjab as a law and order problem and expected the state police to tackle the problem. However, poor leadership, politicisation and sympathetic attitude of some personnel towards the extremist cause prevented the police from effectively tackling militancy.[67] Left with no option, the Union government had to intervene and placed Punjab under the President's rule after the security situation deteriorated. The Union government also undertook the overall responsibility of fighting the militants. The Indian state employed a mix of constitutional, political and security measures to address the problem of militancy in the state. The state police subsequently pulled up its socks and ably assisted the military and central armed police forces. In fact, it was a reinvigorated state police which eventually succeeded in ending the decade old militancy in the state.

Political Efforts

Successive governments at the Centre tried to accommodate the demands of the Akali Dal in order to come to a negotiated settlement. The first attempt after Sikh militancy broke out in the state was made in 1981. In response to the 15 points demands of the Akali Dal which was submitted in October 1981, Indira Gandhi immediately invited the leaders of the Akali Dal for talks and even met them twice in November 1981 and April 1982.[68] Further in October 1982, the government also released all arrested Akali Dal agitators as a gesture of goodwill and to facilitate talks. Several rounds of talks between the representatives of the Union government and the Akali Dal leaders took place. The talks essentially revolved around the broad topics which concerned the Sikhs as a religious community and those residing in other states besides Punjab and other issues.

The Union government tried to meet some of these demands such as imposing ban on the sale of tobacco, liquor and meat in the walled city of Amritsar including the Golden Temple, instead of conferring holy status to the city of Amritsar. The government also allowed the direct relay of *shabad kirtan* from the Golden Temple through the Jalandhar station of All India Radio for a duration of one and a half hours in the morning and half-an-hour in the evening. The government also allowed the Sikhs to carry *kirpans* (with specifications) in domestic flights from February 1983. Following the hijacking of an Indian Airlines plane, carrying kirpans was prohibited in flights.[69]

On the issue of river water sharing, an agreement was signed between the representatives of the Punjab, Haryana and Rajasthan governments and the Union government in December 1981. Under the agreement, the share of Punjab was raised to 4.22 million acre feet (MAF) and the share of Haryana was retained at 3.50 MAF. In addition, Punjab was allowed to utilise the surplus water of Rajasthan till the state was in a position to utilise its full share.[70] This settled issue was, however, raked up by the Akali Dal in 1983 demanding that the allocation of waters under the 1955 Agreement between pre-partition Punjab and Rajasthan should be reopened as Rajasthan was given more share. The Akali Dal also demanded that a share from Yamuna River should also be allocated to Punjab. This issue, however, remained inconclusive.

Regarding the transfer of Chandigarh to Punjab, the Indira government reiterated its 1970 position that Chandigarh will be transferred to Punjab provided Haryana gets its share of some Hindi speaking areas, which are now in Punjab. Akali Dal, however, insisted Chandigarh be transferred to Punjab and all other claims and counter claims including Abohar-Fazilka be referred to a Commission.[71] In response to the Akali Dal for restructuring Centre-State relations and granting autonomy to Punjab, the Indira Gandhi government constituted the Sarkaria Commission in June 1983 to look into the issue. The Akalis, however, wanted that the Anandpur Resolution be specifically mentioned, which was unacceptable to the government.

Further in January 1984, the Akali Dal submitted a fresh demand for the amendment of Article 25(2)(b) of the Constitution of India, which states that 'the reference to Hindus shall be construed as including a reference to persons professing the Sikh, Jaina or Buddhist religion, and the reference to Hindu religious institutions shall be construed accordingly.' In order to diffuse the situation, the Centre convened a tripartite meeting with the Akali Dal and the Opposition on 14 February 1984. After the first meeting, the Akali Dal decided not to participate in the talks any further.[72]

In the wake of Operation Blue Star, Indira Gandhi's assassination and the anti-Sikh riots in Delhi, the Rajiv Gandhi government restarted the stalled peace process with the Akali Dal. He invited Sant Harchand Singh Longowal, President of Akali Dal, for a dialogue to Delhi. His government also released around 1700 extremists along with several Akali Dal leaders who were arrested during and following Operation Blue Star to send positive signals.[73] Interestingly, the Rajiv Gandhi government also started a parallel dialogue with the AISSF, which was the prominent terrorist organisation at that time. However, the talks soon broke down with the AISSF as the government apparently favoured the Akalis.[74]

Finally, peace dialogues with the Akali Dal culminated into the signing of the Rajiv-Longowal Accord on 24 July 1985. The Accord took into account several demands of Sikhs including the transfer of Chandigarh to Punjab, setting up of separate Commissions to determine the transfer of villages to Haryana as well as other claims, referring the Anandpur Sahib Resolution on Centre-State relations to the Sarkaria Commission, and setting up of a Tribunal for River water sharing.[75] While the moderates welcomed the Accord, the extremists accused Longowal of 'selling the Sikh Community to the Hindu government.' In fact, only a few weeks after signing of the Accord, Longowal was killed by terrorists in August 1985. The Centre also announced state elections with the hope that the newly constituted government will be able to bring peace to the state. Despite threats from terrorist groups, state elections were held in September 1985 with 67 per cent voters' participation. The Akali Dal led by Surjit Singh Barnala, a moderate leader and an ally of Longowal, formed the government in Punjab.

Barnala, in an effort to bring normalcy in the state, made peace overtures to the terrorist groups and released around 2000 militants on the recommendations of the Bains Committee.[76] His government also looked the other way when on 26 January 1986, the Damdami Taksal and the AISSF ousted the SGPC and captured the Golden Temple and hoisted the Khalistan flag atop the temple.[77] From that day onwards, Punjab plunged into a renewed cycle of violence and lawlessness.

Rajiv Gandhi dismissed the Barnala government in May 1987 for its failure to establish law and order in the state and declared Emergency on the grounds of 'internal disturbance' in Punjab. During the Emergency, among other restrictions, the Right to Life as guaranteed by the Constitution of India was suspended in the state. His government also decided the futility of implementing the Rajiv-Longowal Accord under the circumstances, which many analysts argue, was not a wise decision and might have contributed in aggravating the already precarious situation.[78] These developments further marginalised the moderates, paving the way for the extremist faction of the Akali Dal led by Simranjit Singh Mann to dominate the political scene, which won six out of eight parliamentary seats in 1989.[79] After Rajiv Gandhi, the V.P. Singh government also tried to politically resolve the Punjab issue by holding talks with the Akali Dal led by Mann. The talks, however, failed as the Indian government could not concede to their demands. Another attempt at arriving at a negotiated settlement with the Akalis by the subsequent Chandrasekhar government in 1990 also failed.

The February 1992 state elections proved to be turning point for Punjab. Despite boycott calls from militant groups, people came out to vote for the elections. Even though the voter turnout was low (21.6 per cent), it reaffirmed peoples' faith in democracy. This faith was yet again displayed in the municipal polls in September 1992 when the voter turnout was 70 per cent and in the subsequent Panchayat polls in January 1993, when the voting percentage increased to 82 per cent.[80] The successful elections with high voter turnout highlighted the fact that people of Punjab were fed up with the reign of terror and that the militants had already lost their support base among the people.

Constitutional/Legal Measures

The outbreak of militancy in Punjab forced the Union government to bring Punjab under President's rule on 6 October 1983. The President's rule is imposed under Article 356 of the Indian Constitution. Under President's Rule, the state is ruled by the Governor, who is the representative of the President. After the proclamation of President's rule, the Punjab Disturbed Areas Ordinance, 1983 and the Chandigarh Disturbed Areas Ordinance, 1983 were promulgated on 7 October, 1983.[81] The Ordinances empowered the Governor of Punjab and the Administrator of Chandigarh to declare whole or part of the state and union territory as disturbed through a gazette notification. The Ordinances also allowed the central armed forces to be deployed in the state in aid of the civil administration. They provided special powers to the police such as firing upon or using maximum force (even causing death) against any person who seriously breaches public order in the disturbed area. The Ordinances also empowered the police to destroy arms dumps, fortifications and training camps from where an attack was made or perceived to be made. They provided immunity to policeman against any law suit brought in for discharging his duties under these Ordinances.[82] These Ordinances were later passed as Acts of Parliament on 8 December 1983.

Following the issuing of the Ordinances, the Punjab and the Chandigarh governments declared the whole state as well as the city of Chandigarh as a 'disturbed area' on 15 October 1983. The Union government deployed the CRPF and the BSF in the state to aid the state police. Later on, battalions of the ITBP were also deployed to guard the banks against attempted robbery.[83]

In conjunction to the Punjab and Chandigarh Disturbed Areas Ordinances, the Union government also promulgated the Armed Forces (Punjab and Chandigarh) Special Powers Ordinance on 15 October 1983 to enable the Indian army to operate in the state and the union territory.[84] The terms of the Ordinance broadly remained the same as that of the Armed Forces (Assam and Manipur) Special Powers Act of 1972 such as allowing the military to use maximum force (including lethal force), destroy ammunition dumps, training camps, etc., and arrest as well as enter any premises without warrant.

However, two sections were added, which provided additional powers to the armed forces. First, a sub-section (e) was added to Section 4 stipulating that any vehicle can be stopped, searched and seized forcibly if it is suspected of carrying proclaimed offenders or ammunition. Second, Section 5 was added specifying that a soldier has the power to break open any lock 'if the key thereof is withheld.'[85] This Ordinance enabled the Union government to deploy the Indian military in the state in June 1984 to bring the situation under control. The Ordinance was passed by the Parliament as the Armed Forces (Punjab and Chandigarh) Special Powers Act on 8 December 1983.

Furthermore, the Terrorist Affected Areas (Special Courts) Act, 1984 was enacted in July 1984 'to provide for the speedy trial of certain offences in terrorist affected areas and for matters connected therewith.'[86] Punjab and Chandigarh were declared 'terrorist-affected' areas in August 1984 and three judicial zones were created each with a Special Court. The Special Courts were established at Patiala, Jalandhar and Ferozepur. Subsequently, seven additional Special Courts were set up – two at Amritsar and one each at Hoshiarpur, Ludhiana, Patiala, Bhatinda and Chandigarh.[87] Under the Act, it is specified that the Special Courts could try scheduled offences, but other offences committed in the terrorist affected areas and pending before any court shall be transferred to the Special Court. The Schedule in the Act has been expanded to include offences ranging from offences against the State to criminal intimidation. The hearings of these courts were held *in camera* essentially to protect the witnesses against the terrorists.[88]

Another important legislation was the TADA. This Act was enacted 'to make special provisions for the prevention of, and for coping with, terrorist and disruptive activities and for matters connected therewith or incidental thereto.'[89] This anti-terrorism legislation came into effect in the year 1985 and remained in effect till 1995. It was the first anti-terrorism law introduced by the government for counter-terrorist activities against the backdrop of Punjab militancy. Special courts were set up under this act to deal with the cases of terrorism and disruptive activities. The act allowed judicial admissions of the confessions during investigation as evidence and relieved the police of the responsibility to produce the accused before the judicial magistrate within 24 hours. The accused could be detained for one year without trial under the Act.[90]

As the security situation in Punjab deteriorated further because of terrorist activities, the legislative assembly was dissolved and Emergency proclaimed in the state in 1988. The Union government also carried a series of amendments to the Constitution under the 59th Amendment Act in March 1988, which enabled the continuation of Presidential proclamation under Article 356(1) beyond one year to three years without the approval of the Parliament. Further, Article 352 and 358 were suitably amended to include 'internal disturbance' threatening India's integrity as one of the grounds to proclaim Emergency in the state. Furthermore, Article 359 was suitably amended to provide for automatic suspension of Article 21 that is, Right to Life, to restore order.[91] This offensive amendment was repealed by the 63rd Amendment on 6 January 1990.[92] In the intervening period, that is, for 21 months, the protection of life or personal liberty of the person was not guaranteed in Punjab.

Last but not least, Religious Institutions (Prevention of Misuse) Ordinance, 1988 was also passed as an Act on 1 September 1988, but was applied retrospectively from 26 May 1988.[93] This Act was enacted to prevent the misuse of religious institutions for political and other purposes. As mentioned, the Sikh militants as well as the Akali Dal (various factions) had been misusing the gurudwaras including the Golden Temple while the security forces were hesitant to enter the premises fearing adverse reactions from the Sikh community. The Act prohibited the use of religious institutions for promoting political activities, harbouring any accused or convicted person, storing arms and ammunition, building fortifications as well as conducting any activities which are in contravention to law, promoting societal disharmony and threatening the integrity of the country.[94] The Act also held the religious institution or the manager of the institution accountable for any offence under the Act. Most importantly, the Act clarified the legality of military operations inside the premises of the religious places, which enabled the security forces to exercise the writ of the law in the gurudwaras premises.[95]

Security Measures

While political efforts were made to find a political solution to Sikh militancy, it was a comprehensive counter terrorism response implemented by the security forces, especially the Punjab police, which ultimately defeated terrorism in Punjab. As mentioned above, entire Punjab was declared a 'disturbed area' in October 1983 and the CRPF, the BSF and the ITBP were deployed in aid of the state police. The police, which was at that time demoralised, ill-trained, ill equipped and politicised, did not possess the ability or the determination to challenge the militants. The police did not maintain any records of terrorist crimes and did not conduct any investigation. In fact, the police was extremely reluctant to undertake counter-terrorist assignments for fear of identification and reprisals.[96]

Unfortunately, the CAPFs also could not tackle the problem of militancy because first, they were not trained in counter terrorism operations. Second, the fact that they were an outside force meant that the CAPFs were unfamiliar with the terrain and people of the state. Inadequate knowledge about the terrain and inability to interact with the local people meant that the CAPFs could not generate their own intelligence and had to rely on the state police, which was not forthcoming. As a result, the anti-terrorist operations conducted by the CAPFs against the militants were marked by clumsiness, which further alienated the common people. They also operated in large conventional formations unlike the militants who were highly mobile and operated in small groups.[97] It was when the police and the CAPFs failed to bring the situation under control that the Indian army was brought in.

On 3 June 1984, the government deployed the Indian army in Punjab to aid the civil administration to maintain public order. The responsibilities assigned to the Army was: a) to tackle and control terrorist violence and to provide security to the common man, and b) to strengthen the international borders and to prevent infiltration of terrorists and smuggling of arms and ammunition. The CRPF, the BSF and the Punjab Armed Police (PAP) were placed under the command of the Indian army. The first task that the Indian army undertook after being deployed in Punjab was to flush out the militants from various gurudwaras including the Golden Temple. The disastrous consequences of military operations in Punjab revealed that like the CAPFs and the state police, the Indian army also did not have any experience in counter-terrorism at that point of time.

So despite deploying thirty-five battalions of Indian army and 350 companies of CAPFs during the peak of militancy, the central forces proved ineffective in defeating Sikh militancy in Punjab.[98] The main factors that prevented these forces to work together towards a coherent and unified counter-terrorism response were lack of 'actionable intelligence', forces acting in isolation and, more often than not, competing with each other, no sharing of intelligence/information, poor coordination among the central forces and the state police, and distrust and tensions between the Indian army, the CAPFs on one hand and the state police on the other. In fact, the Punjab police personnel had clashed openly with the CRPF at Amritsar in June 1986, and were close to exchanging fire.[99]

The counteroffensive by the Punjab Police: As stated earlier, Punjab police spearheaded the counter terrorist campaign in the state. The revival of the hitherto weak, demoralised and politicised force was initiated by two police officers: J.F. Ribeiro and K.P.S. Gill, who were appointed as successive DGPs in 1986 and 1988 (again in 1992) respectively. A number of measures were undertaken by these two to transform the state police into an effective counter-terrorism force. To begin with, the police was provided with more manpower, equipment, infrastructure and training. From 1989, massive recruitment drives were undertaken to fill the vacancies. Accordingly, the strength of the police rose from 32,855 in 1984 to 51,833 in 1989, which further increased to 65,658 in 1993.[100]

Further, to address the problem of lack of proficiency in counter terrorism operations, the Punjab police was trained by the Indian army and the NSG in operational tactics. Similarly, to counter the sophisticated weapons such as the AK-47s used by the Sikh militants, the weaponry of the police were upgraded from the World War II vantage .303 rifles and equally obsolete bolt-action 7.62s to Light Machine Guns (LMGs) and SLRs. General purpose guns were provided for police posts in the riverine areas. The upgradation of weaponry increased the capabilities of the police to repulse terrorist attacks and to confront the militants on a relatively equal footing.[101]

The police also received modern radio communication equipment and check posts were connected with wireless network. The force also received scores of vehicles including bullet proof vehicles. The police personnel were provided with bullet proof vests and were housed in specially constructed protective enclaves. These upgradations enabled the force to communicate quickly, patrol more frequently and widely, and respond timely and effectively in crisis situations.

A number of organisational improvements were also undertaken. First, police stations in severely affected districts were strengthened by increasing the number of police personnel as well as stationing senior level police inspectors such as the Deputy Superintendent of Police instead of a Sub-Inspector. Second, some of these district such as Amritsar and Gurdaspur were sub-divided into more police districts and new police stations were set up in these newly created police districts for more police presence.[102]

Third, a large number of police personnel tied to passive and static duties such as manning barricades, pickets and *nakas* were freed and reallocated to mobile-cum-naka contingent. Fourth, police personnel who were sympathetic to the terrorists' cause were discretely identified and assigned duties, which did not undermine anti-terrorist operations. The objective of reorganisation and upgradation of the police stations was to make each police station capable of reacting immediately and independently to any act of terrorist violence in its jurisdiction.[103] Furthermore, 15000 Home Guards were also recruited to assist the police.

Last but not least, SPOs were appointed in the villages and a Village Defence Scheme (VDS) was started. The SPOs, often ex-military or policemen, were paid a daily stipend, provided weapons, and were permitted to eliminate militants within their jurisdiction as well as adjacent villages. Under the VDS, volunteers were provided arms and trained in weapon handling, tactical plans were drawn for the defence of the villages, and the SPOs were made in charge of the village defence operations. According to Gill, 'the VDS was to play a significant role to the very end of the war against terrorism.'[104]

Revamping intelligence gathering: The next important reform that was carried out was establishing a system of intelligence gathering and analysis. Intelligence, which is the most important component for counter-terrorism campaign, was poorly gathered by the Punjab police. They did not keep records of militant activities as well as subsequent investigations, if any. Central intelligence agencies such as the IB, RA&W, MI, etc. did not have much presence in Punjab, which added to the dearth of intelligence.[105] The failure to gather basic information regarding militant activities prevented the police to understand the nature as well as the trends and patterns of militancy in the state. They also failed to identify the militant cadres and their active supporters.

To remedy this problem, an intelligence wing was instituted in 1984, which was manned by personnel borrowed from the CAPFs and the PAP. The manpower so acquired along with the civil police started maintaining databases on militant activities as well as conducting investigations. Over the next few years, the wing expanded and was able to organise and analyse the incoming intelligence, document their findings and disseminate to other security organisations. After Operation Black Thunder-II, intelligence gathering went deeper to understand the pattern of militancy at the grassroots level and identify villages who provided active support to militants through recruitment as well as logistical support.[106] The police was gradually but effectively able to identify the militants, their strength, their opponents, networks, safe houses, cross-border routes of infiltration and exfiltration, etc.

Such intelligence was verified as well as augmented through manual and electronic surveillance, informers, infiltrating militant organisations as well as Concealed Apprehension Techniques (CATs). CATs involved utilising the knowledge of a surrendered militant about his previous organisation as well as its members. These surrendered militants, who were paid handsomely and shielded against prosecution, worked closely with the police and often accompanied them to specific areas to identify their former colleagues. Termed as 'grossly illegal practices' by the police, CATs was, nonetheless, effective in the anti-terrorism strategy and had been successful in the elimination of several top militant leaders.[107]

Joint and coordinated operations: As stated above, various central forces deployed to fight militancy in Punjab were rendered ineffective because of poor coordination and intelligence sharing. These nagging issues were gradually resolved by taking corrective steps. First, to share intelligence among the forces involved, joint interrogation teams comprising the police and the CRPF were constituted and a system of intelligence sharing was set up. Second, a process of joint operations of the CRPF and the police were initiated so that over a period of time both the forces operated as one unit, thus improving coordination and cooperation. Third, officers from CAPFs as well as from outside Punjab police cadre were inducted to conduct and oversee operations at all levels.[108] As a result of these reforms, security forces could undertake joint operations successfully. The successful execution of Operation Black Thunder-II under the overall command of the Punjab police is one such example.

Another example of successful joint operation is Operation Rakshak I & II conducted in 1990-92. The objective of the operation was to stop militant violence in the border belt by preventing infiltration of militants and disrupting the movement of arms and weapons. In Rakshak I, which was launched in May 1990, the Indian army was deployed in strength along the ditch-cumbandh, which varied in distances from 300 metres to 5,000 metres from the international border. Even the company and battalion headquarters were located close to the border.[109] The army also actively engaged in search and seizure operations. The double line of defence comprising the BSF and the Indian army, the border fences and a curfew imposed in the villages falling within the border belt effectively stopped cross-border movement of militants.

In May 1991, the army was ordered to withdraw from the border districts. However, when Rakshak II was launched in November 1991, nine more divisions of the Indian army was deployed in the state. The Indian army, this time around did not conduct active anti-militancy operations and only assisted the police and the civil administration.[110] The success of Operation Rakshak I & II can be attributed to the enhanced coordination between the security forces facilitated by review committees set up at various levels. An apex Review Committee comprising the chief secretary and representatives from civil administration and army was set up at the state level. At district level, two committees consisting of deputy commissioners and representatives of both the army and the IB were set up for the co-ordination of the operation.[111]

Securing the international border: The crossing over of Sikh militants into Pakistan and returning with arms and explosives to perpetrate terror activities in the state and neighbouring areas compelled the Government of India to put in place measures to cut off their access routes into Pakistan from Punjab and back. These measures included erecting a barbed wire fence with wire obstacles along the vulnerable stretches of the border, floodlighting them, augmenting the strength of the BSF and procuring sophisticated electronic devices for border surveillance.[112] The project for fencing the international border was announced in April 1988 and by 1993, 433.92 km of border fences in Punjab was completed.[113] The fences played an important role as a physical obstruction and prevented easy egress and ingress of militants from Pakistan.

For strengthening the BSF, additional battalions of BSF were raised and deployed along the borders. For e.g. in 1986, a plan for raising 25 battalions of BSF for the India-Pakistan border was launched. Under the modernisation programme, the BSF was provided with night surveillance capabilities, such as Passive Night Vision Goggles (PNG), Night Weapon Sight (NWS), Hand

Held Search Lights (HHSL), Hand Held Deep Search Metal Detector (HHMD), Hand Held Thermal Imagery (HHTI), Long Range Reconnaissance Observation System (LORROS), Battle Field Surveillance Radars (BFSR), etc. for remote surveillance of the international borders.[114]

As mentioned above, the militants aided by Pakistan crossed the international border, and launch attacks, especially targeting border districts. As militant attacks increased, anxiety among the border population rose; people started moving out, investments in agriculture dwindled impacting farming output, and a sense of insecurity and depressed economic growth gradually enveloped the border areas.[115] In view of the distressing situation, the Union government realised that these areas required special government intervention for their overall development.

It concluded that a special scheme should be introduced to 'bring about over all development of these areas which encounter peculiar problems because of inaccessibility, remoteness, and a sense of insecurity in the people because of external aggression or cross-border terrorism and unlawful activities.'[116] Accordingly, the border area development programme was launched in 1986 in Punjab with the twin objectives of the 'balanced development of the sensitive border area in the western region through [the] adequate provision of infrastructure facility[ies] and [the] promotion of a sense of security amongst the local population.'[117]

The Present Situation: Resurgence of Sikh Militancy?

Efforts to revive Khalistan movement by the militant elements in the Sikh diaspora with the help of Pakistan's ISI have been continuous. In fact, it was in 2007 that the Indian intelligence agencies had warned that Pakistan's ISI is trying to revive Sikh militancy in the state. An incident of a bomb blast in a cinema hall in Ludhiana in the same year in which three suspected Babbar Khalsa militants were arrested was seen as evidence that Sikh militancy could be raising its head again.[118] This apprehension was further fuelled when the Sikh community organised a massive protest against the Dera Sacha Sauda chief Ram Rahim for sacrilege in May 2007.[119] Ram Rahim had imitated Guru Gobind Singh by wearing a pink robe during a congregation in Salabatpura on 13 May 2007, which infuriated the Sikh community.

Fortunately, for the next seven to eight years no incidence of violence or protests was registered in Punjab.

However, from 2015 onwards incidents of *beadabi* or sacrilege committed against the Guru Granth Sahib and the ensuing protests and killings have yet again reignited the discussion on the revival of Khalistan movement in Punjab. This is because in the 1980s the incidents of sacrilege were exploited to foment religious disharmony and fuel terrorism in the state.[120] In 2015 three incidences of sacrilege committed yet again by the followers of Dera Sacha Sauda were reported.[121] These incidents include the theft of a copy of the Guru Granth Sahib from a gurudwara in Burj Jawahar Singh Wala village in June and another when the pages of the holy book was torn and strewn in Bargari in October. The killing of three persons by the police in the ensuing protests in Faridkot and the failure of the state police to apprehend the culprits aggravated the simmering anger among the Sikh community in the state. Eventually, two of the suspected culprits were killed by unidentified gunmen in June 2019 and in November 2022.[122]

Many people believe that these sacrilege incidences were stage managed by Khalistani separatists 'to wake up a sleeping Sikh Qaum' and provoke them into believing that neither they nor their honour is safe in 'Hindu' India. Questions are raised as to why the persons who commit sacrileges are not closely questioned about their motives to bring out the 'truth'. Incidentally, politicians also exploit these sacrilege incidents to polarise the masses and win elections. In 2017, the Congress made this an election issue and promised that every sacrilege incidents in the past will be investigated. So, when the party came to power the Captain Amrinder Singh government constituted the Ranjit Singh Commission to investigate 'various incidents of sacrilege of the holy Guru Granth Sahib and other religious texts.'[123]

Furthermore, in August 2018, the Punjab Legislative Assembly passed the Indian Penal Code (IPC) (Punjab Amendment) Bill, 2018 and the Code of Criminal Procedure (CCP) Amendment Bill, 2018 to introduce amendments to the IPC and CCP (applicable only in the state of Punjab) that make committing sacrilege against certain religious texts punishable with life imprisonment.[124] Earlier the Punjab cabinet approved the insertion of Section 295AA to the IPC to provide that whoever causes injury, damage or sacrilege to Sri Guru Granth Sahib, Srimad Bhagwad Gita, Holy Quran and Holy

Bible with the intention to hurt the religious feelings of the people, shall be punished with imprisonment for life.[125] In 2016, the Shiromani Akali Dal (SAD)-Bharatiya Janata Party (BJP) government had passed a similar bill to punish desecration of Guru Granth Sahib with life imprisonment. That bill could not be implemented as the Union government raised objection to the fact that life imprisonment should not be limited to the desecration of holy book of only one religion but should be applicable for all religions.[126]

Despite the implementation of laws against sacrilege, incidents of desecration of the holy book and holy places have not abated, resulting in tensions and killings of people. For example, in 2018, torn pages of Guru Granth Sahib were found strewn in Amritsar. In December 2021, two incidences of sacrilege were reported. In the first case, a sword donated by Ranjit Singh was stolen from the Golden Temple and in the second case, the Nishan Sahib at a gurudwara in Kapurthala was desecrated. In the first case, the *sevadars* of the gurudwara apprehended the thief and lynched him to death.[127] In April 2023, yet again two incidents of sacrilege were reported in which three persons including a pastor were arrested for hitting two *granthis*, desecrating the Guru Granth Sahib in Morinda Gurudwara, and tearing the pages of the Gutka Sahib in Faridkot.[128]

Besides sacrilege incidences, killings of prominent persons belonging to different religions and sects were carried out to foment communal tensions in the state. To begin with, in April 2016, Durga Prasad Gupta, chief of the Shiv Sena's labour wing in Punjab as well as Mata Chand Kaur, wife of late chief of the Namdhari sect, were shot dead by assailants. In August 2016, a RSS leader, Brig Jagdish Gagneja (Retd), was shot and fatally wounded. Similarly, in 2017, Ludhiana witnessed a series of killings. In January of that year, a pastor, Sultan Masih and a leader of 'Hindu Takhat' were shot dead by assailants; in February, two followers of Dera Sacha Sauda were killed; and in October 2017 a RSS leader, Ravinder Gosain, was killed by two unidentified gunmen.[129] Fortunately, these incidents did not flare up into a major crisis in the state, much to the chagrin of the separatists residing on foreign soil.

The separatists got an opportunity to exploit the sentiments against the Union government during the farmers' protests in 2020-21. In September 2020, the Union government had enacted two new farm laws for agriculture, and modified the Essential Commodities Act 1951 for agri-food produce.[130]

These laws were projected as much needed reforms in India's agriculture sector, which would allow the farmers to sell their produce anywhere in India by deregulating the sale of farm produce from the APMC (Agricultural Produce & Livestock Market Committee) 'mandis' and removing the middlemen. The farmers, especially from Punjab and Haryana, however, feared that the laws would eventually dismantle the Minimum Support Price (MSP) system and push the 'arthiyas' or the commission agents who also help the farmers by providing loans, out of business.[131]

Consequently, the farmers held massive protests and demanded that the Union government either take back the laws or give them legal guarantee that the MSP system will be protected. As the protest rallies intensified, intelligence reports started emerging that Sikh separatist organisations such as the SFJ (Sikhs for Justice) was not only infiltrating the farmers' protest rallies but also trying to foment anti-India sentiments amongst them.[132] In fact, the SFJ had announced that it would provide all support for the planned 'Kisan Gantantra Parade' (tractor rally) on Republic Day and reward any person who would remove the Indian flag atop the Red Fort and hoist the Khalistani flag on that day.[133] Instigated by youth leaders as well as the SFJ, thousands of protesters stormed the Red Fort and hoisted the Nisan-e-Sahib on 26 January 2021, thereby making a political statement. As protests spread and became more violent, the Union government capitulated and repealed the three acts in November 2021.[134] The repeal was carried out to take away any opportunity for the extremist elements in the Sikh diaspora to incite the Sikhs in Punjab.

Interestingly, the farmers' agitation also threw up a few controversial personalities such as Deep Sidhu (alias Sandeep Singh). It is alleged that Deep Sidhu was a Khalistani sympathiser and wanted to widen the scope of the farmers' protest and 'challenge' the Union government. He was instrumental in instigating the farmers to resort to violence during the tractor rally as well as in the Red Fort. Later on he floated 'Waris Punjab De' (heirs of Punjab) on 30 September 2021, an organisation to act as 'a pressure group to protect and fight for rights of Punjab and raise social issues.'[135] He lent his support to the pro-Khalistan leader Simranjit Singh Mann and SAD (Amritsar) during the Lok Sabha bye-elections.

Following the death of Sidhu in February 2022, Amritpal Singh, a proclaimed Khalistani, who styled himself as Jarnail Singh Bhindranwale, allegedly anoint himself as the chief of Waris Punjab De and made Khalistan a priority issue for the organisation.[136] To gain popularity among the masses in the state, he also took up social and religious issues by urging the Sikh youths to shun drugs and become 'amritdhari' by strictly following the tenets of Sikhism. While Amritpal Singh had been actively propagating the idea of Khalistan, the Punjab government did not take any action against him. It was only after he and his supporters stormed the Ajnala police station to free one of his aides, Lovepreet Singh, in February 2023 that action was initiated against him. The state government invoked the National Security Act against Amritpal and registered at least half a dozen criminal cases in March 2023. Finally on 23 April 2023, Amritpal Singh along with nine of his aides were arrested by the Punjab police and transferred to the Dibrugarh jail.[137] His arrest brought to an end the drama of a possible revival of Khalistan movement in India.

The Sikh diasporas, especially in Canada, United States (US), United Kingdom (UK) and Australia, however continue with their propaganda for a separate Khalistan and indulge in violent activities which include arson and attack on Indian high commissions and consulates in the US and UK.

Summary

Punjab witnessed increased violence in the 1980s and early 1990s as the Sikh militants demanding a separate Khalistan carried out numerous terrorist attacks in the state. A combination of security, political, legal and economic tools were employed by the Union government to tackle the problem of militancy in the initial years. However, in the end it was the reinvigorated Punjab police, which was successful in dealing a death blow to militancy in the state. Here it is important to mention that non-interference by political parties, both at the union as well as the state level, in the efforts of the police greatly helped the force to strategise and conduct counterterrorism operations without constraints. In fact, it was the political will of the ruling political party not to tolerate terrorism of any kind that provided the police the much needed support to successfully complete its assigned task.

Had this political will been displayed when terrorism first raised its ugly head in the state in the late 1970s, Punjab would not have had to experience the scourge of Sikh militancy in the first place. But the aspiration of gaining political power in the state and to sustain it by any means led both the

Congress (I) and Akali Dal to not only tolerate Sikh extremism but also foment it. It was the one-upmanship between these two political parties that proved costly for the people of Punjab and the country in the long run. Two factors which also contributed substantially in finishing off Sikh militancy in the state were degeneration of the Khalistan movement into avarice and wanton killings, and the withdrawal of support to the movement by Pakistan as it became more involved in fomenting cross-border terrorism in J&K.

While Sikh militancy was effectively put down in the early 1990s, the state police, in subsequent years had to face severe criticism in the way counter-terrorism operations were conducted by it. A number of police officers and personnel were indicted for committing excesses and had to face court trials. In fact, sentiments against the alleged atrocities committed against the 'Sikh quam' by the Indian government continue to simmer. These sentiments are stronger in the Sikh diasporas located in Canada, the US, the UK and Germany, mostly among the Sikh èmigres who left India in the 1980s and the 1990s. It is this diaspora that has kept the flames of a separate Khalistan alive.[138] Their focus of attention changed from demanding separate Khalistan to highlighting the alleged atrocities committed by the Indian government on the Sikh community, particularly during Operation Blue Star and in November 1984.[139] In this respect, organisations such as the Khalistan Council, the World Sikh Organisation (WSO) and the SFJ are particularly active.

NOTES

1. Ved Marwah, 'India's counterinsurgency campaign in Punjab', in Sumit Ganguly and David P. Fidler (eds.), *India and Counterinsurgency, Lessons Learned*, London: Routledge, 2009, p. 92.
2. K.P.S Gill, 'Endgame in Punjab 1988-93', *Faultlines*, Vol.1, May 1999 at https://www.satp.org/Docs/Faultline/1_Endgame-in-Punjab—1988-93.pdf, accessed on 28 January 2022.
3. n. 1, p. 90.
4. Satnam Singh Deol, 'Sikh Ethnonationalism and Militancy: Manifestation and Prognosis', *Asian Ethnicity*, Vol. 20 (2), 2019, p. 189.
5. Rajshree Jetly, 'The Khalistan Movement in India: The Interplay of Politics and State Power', *International Review of Modern Sociology*, Vol. 34 (1), Spring 2008, p. 62.
6. n. 4, p. 273.
7. Ibid, pp. 66-67.
8. Ibid, p. 67.
9. n. 5, p. 63.
10. Jugdep S. Chima, 'The Punjab Crisis: Governmental Centralization and Akali-Center Relations', *Asian Survey*, Vol. 34 (10), October 1994, p. 852.
11. Hamish Telford, 'The Political Economy of Punjab: Creating Space for Sikh Militancy', *Asian Survey*, Vol. 32 (11), November 1992, p. 971.

12. Ibid.
13. Ibid, p. 975.
14. Ibid.
15. n. 10, p. 854.
16. Virginia Van Dyke, 'The Khalistan Movement in Punjab, India, and the Post-Militancy Era: Structural Change and New Political Compulsions', *Asian Survey*, Vol. 49 (6), November/ December 2009, p. 985.
17. Ibid, p. 986.
18. *White Paper on the Punjab Agitation*, New Delhi: Government of India, 1984, p. 2.
19. C. Christine Fair, 'Lessons from India's experience in Punjab, 1978-1993', in Sumit Ganguly and David P. Fidler (eds.), *India and Counterinsurgency, Lessons Learned*, London: Routledge, 2009, p. 112.
20. n. 18, p. 26.
21. n. 18, pp. 35-36.
22. Kamaldeep Singh Brar, 'Akal Takht to honour one of the five who hijacked Indian Airlines plane to Lahore', *The Indian Express*, Amritsar, 30 August 2020 at https://indianexpress.com/article/cities/chandigarh/akal-takht-to-honour-one-of-the-five-who-hijacked-indian-airlines-plane-to-lahore-6575484/, accessed on 31 January 2022.
23. n. 18, p. 5.
24. n. 11, p. 984.
25. n. 18, p. 27.
26. Ibid, p. 28.
27. Ibid, pp. 27-28.
28. Ibid, p. 26.
29. Ibid, p. 29.
30. Ibid, p. 28.
31. Ibid, p. 32.
32. n. 18, p. 49.
33. K.S. Brar, *Operation Blue Start: The True Story*, New Delhi: UBS Publishers' Distributors Pvt. Ltd, 1993, p. 61.
34. n. 2.
35. n. 18, p. 51.
36. Ibid, p. 169.
37. Ibid, pp. 170-171.
38. n. 1, p. 100.
39. n. 2.
40. Praveen Swami, 'Failed Threats and Flawed Fences: India's Military Responses to Pakistan's Proxy War', *India Review*, Vol. 3 (2), 2004, p. 157.
41. Chris Smith, 'Light Weapons and Ethnic Conflict in South Asia,' in Jeferry Boutwell , Michael T. Klare and Laura W. Reed (eds.), *Lethal Commerce: The Global Trade in Small Arms and Light Weapons*, Cambridge: American Academy of Arts and Science, 1995, p. 69.
42. n. 1, p. 100.
43. n. 2.
44. C. Christine Fair, 'The Golden Temple: A Tale of Two Sieges', in C. Christine Fair and Sumit Ganguly (eds.), *Treading on Hallowed Ground: Counterinsurgency Operations in Sacred Spaces*, Oxford: Oxford University Press, 2008, p. 44.
45. n. 2.
46. Ibid.

47. Ibid.
48. n. 1, p. 101.
49. Vipul Mudgal and Shekhar Gupta, 'Success of Operation Black Thunder in Amritsar clears Golden Temple complex of terrorists', *India Today*, 15 June 1988 at https://www.indiatoday.in/magazine/cover-story/story/19880615-success-of-operation-black-thunder-in-amritsar-clears-golden-temple-complex-of-terrorists-797338-1988-06-14, accessed on 4 February 2022.
50. Ibid.
51. n. 1, p. 101.
52. n. 19, p. 121.
53. Harish Puri, Paramjit Singh Judge, and Jagrup Singh Sekhon, *Terrorism in Punjab: Understanding Grass Roots Reality*, as quoted in Virginia Van Dyke, 'The Khalistan Movement in Punjab, India, and the Post-Militancy Era: Structural Change and New Political Compulsions', n. 16, p. 991.
54. n. 2.
55. Ibid.
56. Ibid.
57. Philip Hultquist, 'Countering Khalistan: Understanding India's Counter-Rebellion Strategies during the Punjab Crisis', *Journal of Punjab Studies*, Volume 22 (1), Spring 2015, p. 112.
58. For a detailed exposition on Police brutalities in Punjab see Kripal Dhillon, *Identity and Survival: Sikh Militancy 1978-1993*, New Delhi: Penguin, 2006, especially pp. 355-356.
59. n. 57, p. 113.
60. Ibid, p. 114.
61. n. 2.
62. n. 57, p. 114. Also see, n. 2.
63. n. 57, p. 114.
64. n. 58, pp. 342, 344-345.
65. n. 2.
66. n. 58, p. 346-347.
67. n. 1, p. 96.
68. n. 18, p. 6.
69. n. 18, pp. 9-10.
70. n. 18, p. 11.
71. Ibid, p. 15.
72. Ibid, pp. 101-102.
73. Prabhu Chawla, 'A chronicle of weeks leading to the historic Rajiv-Longowal accord', *India Today*, 31 August 1985 at https://www.indiatoday.in/magazine/indiascope/story/19850831-chronicle-of-weeks-leading-to-historic-rajiv-longowal-accord-801901-2014-01-02, accessed on 9 February 2022.
74. n. 2.
75. *Rajiv-Longowal Memorandum of Settlement (Accord), July 24, 1985* at http://www.sikhtimes.com/doc_072485a.html, accessed on 9 February 2022.
76. n. 2.
77. n. 11, p. 985.
78. n. 19, p. 118. Also see, Gurharpal Singh, 'Punjab since 1984: Disorder, Order, and Legitimacy', *Asian Survey*, Vol. 36 (4), April 1996, p. 412.
79. Ashutosh Kumar, 'Electoral Politics in Punjab: Study of Akali Dal', *Economic and Political Weekly*, Vol. 39, (14/15) 3-16 April 2004, p. 1517.
80. Ibid.

81. n. 18, pp. 28-29.
82. *The Punjab Disturbed Areas Act, 1983 Act No. 32 of 1983*, 8th December, 1983 at https://www.indiacode.nic.in/bitstream/123456789/1800/1/A1983-32.pdf, accessed on 8 February 2022.
83. n. 1, p. 96.
84. *White Paper on the Punjab Agitation*, New Delhi: Government of India, 1984, pp. 28-29.
85. 'Section 4 (e), & Section 5', *The Armed Forces (Punjab and Chandigarh) Special Powers Act, 1983 (34 of 1983)* at https://www.indiacode.nic.in/bitstream/123456789/1843/3/a1983-34.pdf, accessed on 8 February 2022.
86. *The Terrorist Affected Areas (Special Courts) Act, 1984 Act No. 61 of 1984* [31st August, 1984.] at https://www.indiacode.nic.in/bitstream/123456789/15425/1/the_terrorist_affected_areas_%28special_courts%29_act%2C_1984.pdf, accessed on 10 February, 2022.
87. 'Black Laws in Punjab: Report of an Enquiry', *Economic and Political Weekly*, Vol. 20 (19), 11 May 1985, p. 826.
88. n. 86.
89. *Terrorist and Disruptive Activities (Prevention) Act, 1987* at https://www.indiacode.nic.in/bitstream/123456789/15340/1/terrorist_and_disruptive.pdf, accessed on 14 February 2022.
90. Ibid.
91. *The Constitution (Fifty-ninth Amendment) Act, 1988* at https://www.india.gov.in/my-government/constitution-india/amendments/constitution-india-fifty-ninth-amendment-act-1988, accessed on 14 March 2023. Also see Vipul Mudgal and Inderjit Badhwar, 'President's Rule in Punjab neither wins over people nor deters killers', *India Today*, 30 April 1988, at https://www.indiatoday.in/magazine/special-report/story/19880430-president-rule-in-punjab-neither-wins-over-people-nor-deters-killers-798271-1988-04-29, accessed on 14 March 2033.
92. *The Constitution (Sixty-third Amendment) Act, 1989* at https://www.india.gov.in/my-government/constitution-india/amendments/constitution-india-sixty-third-amendment-act-1989, accessed on 10 February 2022.
93. *The Religious Institutions (Prevention of Misuse) Act, 1988 No. 41 of 1988* [1st September, 1988.] at https://www.indiacode.nic.in/bitstream/123456789/15336/1/religious_institutions_%28prevention_of_misuse%29_act%2C_1988.pdf, accessed on 8 February 2022.
94. Ibid.
95. n. 19, pp.113, 120.
96. n. 2.
97. n. 1, p. 98.
98. Ibid, p. 98.
99. n. 2.
100. n. 19, p. 114.
101. n 2.
102. n 1, p. 102.
103. n. 2.
104. Ibid.
105. n. 19, p. 116.
106. n. 2. Also see, n. 19, p. 116.
107. n. 19, pp. 116-117.
108. n. 2.
109. Kanwar Sandhu, 'In the second phase of Operation Rakshak, army tries to avoid mistakes of its earlier operations in Punjab', *India Today*, 15 March 1991 at https://www.indiatoday.in/

magazine/special-report/story/19910315-in-the-second-phase-of-operation-rakshak-army-tries-to-avoid-mistakes-of-its-earlier-operations-in-punjab-814145-1991-03-14, accessed on 14 February 2022.

110. n. 78, p. 414.
111. n. 109.
112. *Annual Report 1988–89*, New Delhi, Ministry of Home Affairs, 1989, pp.7–8.
113. 'First Report on Demands for Grants Nos. 42 & 44 of Ministry of Home Affairs for the Year 1993–94', Department Related Parliamentary Standing Committee on Home Affairs, *Rajya Sabha*, 28 April 1993, p. 25.
114. Anirudh Deshpande (ed.), *The First Line of Defence: Glorious 50 Years of the Border Security Force*, Delhi: Shipra Publications, 2015, pp. 241–244.
115. Prakash Singh, 'Impact of Terrorism on Investment Decisions of Farmers: Evidence from the Punjab Insurgency', *The Journal of Conflict Resolution*, Vol. 57, No. 1, Special Issue: Entrepreneurship and Conflict, February 2013, pp.143–168.
116. *Evaluation Report on Border Area Development Programme*, New Delhi: Planning Commission, 1999, p. 1, at http://planningcommission.nic.in/reports/peoreport/cmpdmpeo/volume1/177.pdf, accessed on 12 March 2018.
117. *8th Five Year Plan, Vol 2*, New Delhi: Planning Commission, 1992, at http://planningcommission.nic.in/plans/planrel/fiveyr/8th/vol2/8v2ch17.htm,accessed on 12 March 2018.
118. 'Six killed in Ludhiana cinema bomb blast', *Reuters*, Chandigarh, 15 October 2007 at https://www.reuters.com/article/idINIndia-29990620071014, accessed on 30 May 2023.
119. I.P. Singh, 'Punjab's 2015 Incidents Rooted In 2007 Blasphemy Case', *The Times of India*, 3 May 2023 at https://timesofindia.indiatimes.com/city/chandigarh/punjabs-2015-incidents-rooted-in-2007-blasphemy-case/articleshow/98378686.cms?from=mdr, accessed on 24 May 2023.
120. H.S. Panang, 'Religious intolerance main driver of insurgency in Punjab of 1980s. State's watching it again', *The Print*, 10 February 2022 at https://theprint.in/opinion/religious-intolerance-main-driver-of-insurgency-in-punjab-of-1980s-states-watching-it-again/825801/, accessed on 24 May 2023.
121. '2015 Bargari sacrilege cases: SIT blames Dera Sacha Sauda', *The Hindu*, Chandigarh, 3 July 2022 https://www.thehindu.com/news/national/other-states/2015-bargari-sacrilege-cases-sit-blames-dera-sacha-sauda/article65593528.ece, accessed on 24 May 2023.
122. Navjeevan Gopal, 'Explained: What are the sacrilege incidents that have Punjab on edge?', *The Indian Express*, Chandigarh, 27 June 2021 at https://indianexpress.com/article/explained/punjab-sacrilege-incidents-sit-probe-amarinder-singh-explained-7376954/, accessed on 24 May 2023. 'Bargari sacrilege: Key conspirator Sandeep Bareta arrested in Bengaluru', *The Indian Express,* Bengaluru, 24 May 2033 at https://indianexpress.com/article/cities/chandigarh/2015-bargari-sacrilege-case-sandeep-bareta-detained-8624247/, accessed on 24 May 2023. Aditya Menon, '2015 Bargari Sacrilege Accused Pradeep Gunned Down in Punjab's Faridkot', *The Quint*, 10 November 2023 at https://www.thequint.com/news/india/bargari-sacrilege-accused-pradeep-shot-dead-faridkot-punjab, accessed on 24 May 2023.
123. Government of Punjab, 'Justice Ranjit Singh Commission Report On Sacrilege Cases Will Be Tabled In Next Assembly Session, Says Capt Amarinder', *Directorate of Information and Public Relations*, Chandigarh, 25 July 2017 http://diprpunjab.gov.in/?q=content/justice-ranjit-singh-commission-report-sacrilege-cases-will-be-tabled-next-assembly-session#:~:text=Punjab%20Chief%20Minister%20Capt.,those%20found%20guilty%20by%20it., accessed on 30 May 2023.

124. PTI, 'Punjab Passes Bills Making Desecration of Religious Texts Punishable with Life Term', *The Wire*, Chandigarh, 28 August 2018 at https://thewire.in/law/punjab-bills-desecration-religious-texts-punishable-life, accessed on 30 May 2023.
125. Ibid.
126. Prabhash K. Dutta, 'What is sacrilege? Incidents and law in Punjab explained', *India Today*, 20 December 2021 at https://www.indiatoday.in/india/story/sacrilege-law-punjab-guru-granth-sahib-golden-temple-1889891-2021-12-20, accessed on 30 May 2023.
127. Sahil Sinha, 'From Bargari to Amritsar, sacrilege cases that rocked Punjab in recent years', *India Today*, 25 April 2023 at https://www.indiatoday.in/india/story/sacrilege-cases-punjab-gurdwara-kotwali-sahib-morinda-2364103-2023-04-24, accessed on 30 May 2023.
128. '2 sacrilege incidents in Morinda, Faridkot spark outrage; pastor among 3 held', *The Hindustan Times*, 25 April 2023 at https://www.hindustantimes.com/cities/chandigarh-news/punjab-police-arrest-3-over-sacrilege-incidents-including-pastor-and-sikh-priests-outrage-sparks-protests-and-condemnation-from-leaders-101682364439961.html#:~:text= Three %20people %2C%20including%20a%20pastor,a%20gurdwara%20in%20Morinda%20town., accessed on 30 May 2023.
129. 'Killing of RSS leader is eighth murderous attack since 2016', *The Tribune*, 17 October 2017 at https://www.tribuneindia.com/news/archive/punjab/killing-of-rss-leader-is-eighth-murderous-attack-since-2016-483569, accessed on 30 May 2023.
130. The two bills were: The Farmers' Produce Trade and Commerce (Promotion and Facilitation) Bill, 2020 and The Farmers (Empowerment and Protection) Agreement of Price Assurance and Farm Services Bill, 2020. 'Three bills aimed at transformation of agriculture and raising farmers' income introduced in Lok Sabha today; to replace ordinances promulgated on 5th June 2020', *Press Information Bureau*, 14 September 2020, at https://pib.gov.in/PressReleaseIframePage.aspx?PRID=1654007, accessed on 1 June 2023.
131. ' What is Farmers bill and and why farmers are protesting', *The Times of India*, 8 December 2020, accessed on 2 June 2023.
132. Express Web Desk, '"Khalistanis" have infiltrated farmers protest, will show IB inputs: Centre tells SC', *The Indian Express*, 12 January 2021 at https://indianexpress.com/article/india/khalistan-farmers-protest-supreme-court-7143649/, accessed on 2 June 2023.
133. Manjeet Sehgal, 'Khalistan terror group SFJ instigates farmers in Delhi to remove tricolour on Republic Day', *India Today*, 13 January 2021 at https://www.indiatoday.in/india/story/khalistan-terror-group-sfj-instigates-farmers-in-delhi-to-remove-tricolour-on-republic-day-1758674-2021-01-13, accessed on 2 June 2023.
134. Express Web Desk, 'PM Modi repeals farm bills: A timeline of events that followed since their enactment', *The Indian Express*, 20 November 2021 at https://indianexpress.com/article/india/pm-modi-repeals-farm-bills-a-timeline-of-events-that-followed-since-their-enactment-7630402/#:~:text=Here%27s%20a%20timeline%20of%20the,a%20%E2%80%9CDilli%20Chalo%E2%80%9D%20campaign., accessed on 2 June 2023.
135. Divya Goyal, 'What is Waris Punjab De, and who is Amritpal Singh?', *The Indian Express*, Ludhiana, 23 April 2023 at https://indianexpress.com/article/explained/waris-punjab-de-deep-sidhu-amritpal-singh-8464095/, accessed on 25 July 2023.
136. Kamaldeep Sigh Brar, 'How Amritpal launched Waris Punjab De online, made Khalistan his main plank, even planned school for NRI kids', *The Indian Express*, Amritsar, 23 April 2023 at https://indianexpress.com/article/cities/chandigarh/amritpal-waris-punjab-de-online-khalistan-akf-hola-mohalla-8511533/, accessed on 25 July 2023. Also see, 'What is Waris Punjab de, the group that went on the rampage in Amritsar?', *First Post*, 24 February 2023 at https://www.firstpost.com/explainers/what-is-waris-punjab-de-the-group-that-went-on-the-rampage-

in-amritsar-12204972.html, accessed on 25 July 2023.

137. The Hindu Bureau, '"Waris Punjab De" chief Amritpal Singh arrested from Punjab's Moga under NSA; shifted to Assam's Dibrugarh jail', *The Hindu*, Chandigarh, 23 April 2023 at https://www.thehindu.com/news/national/other-states/amritpal-singh-waris-punjab-de-punjab-arrested/article66769442.ece, accessed on 25 July 2023.
138. 'Sikh leader fears revival of Khalistan movement', *CTV News*, 21 April 2007 at https://www.ctvnews.ca/sikh-leader-fears-revival-of-khalistan-movement-1.238238?cache=yes%2F7.508111, accessed on 23 May 2023.
139. Dominika Sokol, 'The Sikh Diaspora in Cyberspace: The Representation of Khalistan on the World Wide Web and Its Legal Context', *Masaryk University Journal of Law and Technology*, Vol. 1 (2), 2007, p. 223-224. Shinder Purewal, 'Sikh Diaspora and the Movement for Khalistan', *The Indian Journal of Political Science*, Vol. 72 (4), Oct-Dec 2011, pp. 1138-1140.

6

CHHATTISGARH

Chhattisgarh, which was carved out of Madhya Pradesh and instated as the 26th state of the Indian Union on 1 November 2000, is the worst LWE affected state in the country. In 2021, the state recorded 255 violent incidents which claimed 101 lives,[1] which was 51 per cent of all LWE violent incidents and 70 per cent of resultant deaths.[2] In 2022, the number of violent incidents increased to 279 with a correspondent death of 56 people.[3] In Chhattisgarh, fourteen districts are Maoist-affected, including seven that are severely affected.[4] Bastar division, spread over 39,117 square kilometres with 15 lakh population, is considered a severely Maoist affected division. As per police estimates, about 4,500 Maoist cadres comprising both its political and military wings live in the jungles of Bastar.[5]

Chhattisgarh had its first brush with LWE in the early 1980s when cadres of the PW/PWG from the neighbouring Telangana and Andhra areas started entering into the Bastar region. The objective of the PWG cadres was to spread the Karimnagar/Adilabad Revolutionary movement to one of the most backward regions of India.[6] Later, as anti-PWG operations were intensified by the Andhra government, more and more PWG cadres, escaping the government crackdown, started spilling into Dandakaranya region of Chhattisgarh (then undivided Madhya Pradesh).

Significantly, the PWG had taken a conscious decision during that time to build bases in areas 'where the geographical conditions (mountains, hills, forests, and other favourable terrain) are more favourable for conducting the guerrilla warfare.'[7] Accordingly the leadership had identified the Dandakaranya area comprising the Bastar, Narayanpur, Bijapur, Dantewada and Kanker districts of Chhattisgarh as an ideal region to establish a base area and launch their guerrilla movement because the region has a hilly and heavily forested terrain and is predominantly inhabited by tribal people, especially the Gonds.[8]

Besides favourable geographical condition, the Dandakaranya region also had several socio-economic features, which favoured the Communists to start their activities. For example, the *Abujhmadh* in Dandakaranya was beyond the administrative reach of the state till only recently. The people of the region have a subsistence means of livelihood as they practice shifting agriculture, hunt and collect only forest produce. As a result, the people of the region live in extreme poverty and do not have access to basic amenities such as potable water, sanitation, health, education, transportation, means of livelihood, etc. To make matters worse, the economic policies of the Indian government focussing on setting up of big extractive industries as well as construction of big dams, alienated the tribals from their land. The tribals were also exploited by the money lenders, short changed by the contractors and maltreated by petty officials and policemen. Describing the dire plight of the tribals of Chhattisgarh, the Bhuria Commission had observed:

> The Government of India established a Dandkaranya Development Authority covering the tribal areas of Orissa and present Chhattisgarh State for the rehabilitation of East Pakistan (Bangladesh) refugees who were given land as well as other means of livelihood for their relief and rehabilitation. On the other hand, tribals did not receive due attention which also contributed as one of the causes of tribal discontent. The linking up of Raipur with Jagdalpur facilitated the entry of non-tribals into Bastar. Between 1992 and 1996, a nexus of officials and timber merchants conspired to strip Bastar of a significant amount of timber. The forest department started mono tree cultivation depriving tribals of their fuel, fodder and grass requirements. This, however, was stopped on account of protest by environmentalists. Exploitation of tribal women at the hands of non-tribals in developing urban centers led to great resentment among the tribals, although some steps were taken to meet the situation.[9]

As mentioned, such a socio-economic landscape provided the PWG, who had by 1980 discarded the 'annihilation line', found a conducive opportunity to harness the collective grievances of the tribal population, and to consolidate organisationally in the region. Initially, the PWG cadres operating in small armed squads consisting of five–six members each, took up particular cases in Bastar such as non-payment of minimum wages, teacher and doctor absenteeism, demands for bribes by policemen and forest guards, attack on their cultural identity through conversion, etc. As part of their strategy to endear themselves to the tribal people, the PWG cadres punished the corrupt officials, made the tendu leaves contractors increase the wages, disciplined teachers and doctors, fought for tribal rights on forest produce, and even held health and education programme. Such actions elicited awe and respect from the tribals and they gradually gravitated towards the Maoists.[10]

The Launch of Maoist Activities

From the mid-1980s onwards, the Maoists started consolidating their 'struggle' by organising the tribals and conducting sporadic violent incidents mostly aimed at the government.[11] For instance, during a severe drought in 1987-88, the Maoists organised the tribals and raided the houses of landlords and government godowns and looted food grains, clothes and vessels.[12] Beginning 1990, Maoists started violently opposing elections. During the 1991 Lok Sabha elections, they killed eight members of a polling party including six policemen by triggering a landmine blast. Similarly in November 1993, 10 CRPF personnel were killed when they were returning from election duties.[13]

By mid-1990s, the Maoists formed two mass organisations: the DAKMS and the *Krantikari Mahila Adivasi Sangathana* (KMAS). The DAKMS made several demands such as 'better wages and higher rates for the collection of minor forest produce, "pattas" regularising cultivation on forest land and the right of cattle to continue grazing in the forests and ending all harassment by forest officials and police and the arbitrary fines collected by them.'[14] These demands were aimed at providing the tribal people control over their land, water and forest resources. The KMAS, on its part, focused on issues affecting women and campaigned against social evils such as forced marriage and abductions, bigamy, domestic violence, consumption of liquor, etc. These two front organisations thus acted as a cover for the extension of Maoist guerrilla activities in the Dandakaranya region.

In 1994, the Maoists also formed the People's Committees, which was followed by the formation of Revolutionary People's Committees (RPCs) also known as the *Janatana Sarkar* (people's government) in the region. The main objective of such committees was to carry out administrative and judicial functions such as providing basic amenities, health, education, livelihood, developmental activities and dispensing justice. The aim was to organise the villagers through social, economic and cultural transformation in order to create a base area for the militia and the raiding guerrilla squads.

According to a Maoist document, each committee was formed for a population of 500 to 3500 persons and the committee members were the representatives of mass organisations and people who have been active in protecting and defending the guerrilla zone. It is stated that out of 4000-5000 villages in the area, nearly half of the villages had people's committees.[15] By 1997-98 most of the Dandakaranya region under the Maoists' influence had such RPCs[16] and by 2003, RPCs were formed in 500 villages of Dandakaranya and had influence over 2000 villages. Commenting on the establishment of RPCs, a senior Maoist leader had said,

> 'Now, we are forming RPCs which are geographically conducive for guerrilla warfare…RPC is the basic (form of) people's rule. When there is this basic people's rule in the villages then it becomes very difficult for any arm of the official machinery to function properly there. This is because when two forces are working at once, only one force can remain. This could be either ours or the enemy's.'[17]

The creation of a RPCs or Janatana Sarkar by overthrowing the authority of the government and establishing the political authority of the Maoists by coercion signified the first step towards creating a base area. According to Maoist literature, the base area thus created should have a self-sufficient economy to sustain the party and the people's war, which is essential to bring in the New Democratic Revolution. For this purposes, the Maoists who regarded the economic activities of the tribals as primitive, started carrying out developmental works to increase the productivity in their area of influence. In fact, Maoist literature boasts that they have been engaged in considerable developmental activities, especially in the fields of agricultural and livelihood improvement. According to their literature, 81 tanks were built in Dantewada district, four lakh fish seedlings distributed in the Konta squad area, 16,200 saplings distributed, diesel pump introduced in nine villages, cooperative paddy banks set up and agricultural cooperatives created in 220 villages, among other things.[18]

The Maoists had, however, implemented much of these developmental works such as building irrigation bunds and canals through forced labour from the tribals, which they euphemistically referred to as *shramdaan*. The Maoists also raided rich landlords and confiscated their grain and land. The confiscated grains and land, however, were not entirely redistributed to the tribals, but half of them were kept for sustaining themselves and their army.[19] For example, at the height of the conflict, the Maoists had reportedly confiscated approximately 1546 acres of land from landlords. While they distributed 743 acres of land to the landless, the rest were kept for the 'collective needs of the villages'. It is, however, not clarified what 'collective needs' meant and how much of the land and the produce is kept away for sustaining the people's army.[20]

At the same time, the Maoists had and continue to oppose developmental activities that are being launched by the government to improve the conditions of the tribals. In fact, the Maoists have violently prevented the implementation of developmental works including infrastructure such as railways, roads, power and telecom in their areas of influence to show to the tribal people that the governance structures at ground levels are ineffective.[21]

The Escalation of Maoist Activities

The formation of the PLGA in 2000 provided the much required teeth to the Maoist movement in the region. It was stated that the Maoists had organised several military camps in their strongholds to train the armed cadres. Besides using sophisticated weapons such as AK-47 rifles and SLR, the Maoists had also developed expertise in the fabrication and use of Improvised Explosive Devices (IEDs).[22] As a result, violent incidents and the resultant deaths started increasing in Chhattisgarh from 2000 onwards. In 2000, the state recorded 79 incidents with 48 deaths, which rose to 304 incidents with 55 deaths in 2002.

The Maoist movement in India got a major fillip in October 2004, when the PWG and the MCCI merged to form a political party called the CPI (Maoist) and the PLGA became its armed wing. The merger of the two units brought to the fore the proclivity of the Maoists towards mindless violence, which was demonstrated in increased attacks on policemen, landlords, so called collaborators, hapless villagers and tribals as well as on government buildings, infrastructure and jails. The number of violent incidents and resultant killings accordingly increased in the ensuing years. In 2004, Chhattisgarh recorded 352 violent incidents in which 83 persons were killed, which rose to 380 incidents and 165 deaths in 2005.[23] One of the reasons for the increase in the levels of violence in 2005 was the actions of an anti-Naxalite force called the Salwa Judum (purification hunt) against the Maoist cadres and the counter attacks by the Maoists. This trend of increased violence was observed till 2011 when the Supreme Court declared Salwa Judam as illegal.

The increased level of violence prompted the then Prime Minister Manmohan Singh in 2006 to declare the left wing extremism or Maoism as the 'single biggest internal security challenge.'[24] He suggested to the chief ministers of the Maoist hit states to consider undertaking joint operations and setting up of joint unified commands. He further suggested that police actions against the Maoist cadres should be followed by generous surrender and rehabilitation policies.[25] While a few chief ministers undertook some measures to counter the Maoist movement, majority of them either did not take any action or took half-hearted measures. Consequently, violence levels started increasing, especially in Chhattisgarh, which became the epicentre of Maoist violence in the country. By 2008, Maoist related violence escalated to 620 incidents and 242 deaths[26] and peaked in 2010 when 625 violent incidents and 343 deaths were recorded in the state.[27] In one of the incidents on 6 April 2010, 75 CRPF personnel were killed by the Maoists in the Tadmetla forest in Dantewada District.[28]

Maoist leadership termed the violence as a 'war of self-defence' or a counter violence in response to the 'brutal and violent repression campaign aimed at the suppression of the political movement of the people, and for exploitation of the minerals.'[29] The Maoist also rejected the appeal of the then union home minister P. Chidambaram to abjure violence and come for peace talks saying they would never lay down arms.[30] Ganapathy, in an interview in 2010, laid conditions for the Maoists to participate in peace talks. These conditions were: (1) All-out war had to be withdrawn; (2) the ban on the Party and Mass Organisations had to be lifted; and (3) Illegal detention and torture of comrades had to be stopped and they should be immediately released.[31] He further stated that if these demands were met, then the leaders who were released from the prisons will lead and represent the party in the talks. Since the Maoists did not stop violence, the Union government could not initiate peace talks with them.

Maoists' refusal to renounce violence and participate in peace talks forced the Union government, in cooperation with the state government, to redouble its efforts to counter the Maoist problem. Because of the renewed efforts, the Maoists started losing ground and as a result violence levels in Chhattisgarh started declining from 2011 onwards when 465 violent incidents and 204 deaths were reported, to 328 incidents and 112 killed in 2014. One of the reasons for the decline in the Maoist related incidents has also been attributed to the disbanding of Salwa Judum, which was responsible for increased attacks and counter attacks in the state. This declining trend in Maoist violence, however, did not mean that the Maoists were weakened. In fact, cadre base of the PLGA had increased from eight companies and 13 platoons in 2008 to 12 companies and more than 25 platoons by the end of 2013.[32]

The Jhiram Ghati attack of May 2013 in which 29 persons including senior Congress leaders were killed by the Maoists, is an example that Maoists were capable of launching successful and spectacular attacks, especially in their strongholds.[33] This fact is further corroborated by the statistics on number of violent incidents, which started rising again from 2015 onwards. In 2015, the state recorded 466 violent incidents in which 101 persons were killed.[34] The figures related to violent incidents in the state in 2018, 2019 and 2020 were 392, 263 and 315 respectively. The total number of causalities in these incidents were 341.[35]

As per National Crime Record Bureau (NCRB), a total of 533 cases against Maoists were registered in eight states in 2020 and Chhattisgarh accounted for 296 of these cases. The statistics further shows that of a total of 74 murders committed by the Maoists in 2020, 62 were reported in Chhattisgarh. Similarly out of total 41 registered cases of loot by Maoists, 39 were reported in the state. Chhattisgarh also topped the list with 139 cases of attempt to murder by the Maoists out of total 172 cases registered nationally.[36] Further, the year 2021 also saw a number of violent incidents. The most violent being the one which occurred on 3 April 2021 in Jonaguda village in Sukma district. In this incident 21 security personnel were killed and 31 others were injured. It was reported that the security forces came under attack when they were returning after a search for the top Maoist leader Madvi Hidma. It is also reported that the Maoist cadres and the Jan Militia used light machine guns and under barrel grenade launchers during the attack.[37]

Similarly, violence continued throughout 2022 and 2023. In one of the biggest attacks by the Maoists in two years, 10 personnel of the District Reserve Guards (DRG) including five former Maoists were killed in an IED blast triggered by the Maoists in the Aranpur area of Dantewada district on 27 April 2023. The attack happened during the TCOC (tactical counter-offensive campaign) period when the Maoists launch armed attacks in the months of March to June when the forests are devoid of any green cover and the targets are in plain sight of its well-trained cadres.[38]

The State Government's Response

The MHA's Annual Report of 2006-07 states that 'keeping in view that naxalism is not merely a law and order problem, the policy of the Government, is to address this menace simultaneously on political, security, development and public perception management fronts in a holistic manner.'[39] Despite implementing a comprehensive strategy towards tackling the Maoist problem, Chhattisgarh continues to experience largescale violence. In such a scenario, it is instructive to discuss the efforts of the Chhattisgarh government and highlight the shortcomings in the efforts of the successive state leaderships in tackling the Maoist movement.

Security Response

Even though the Union government does not treat LWE as a 'law and order' problem, the primary responsibility for tackling the Maoist insurgency rests with respective states. The Union government supplements the state governments by providing CAPFs to aid their efforts, reimbursing security related expenditure under the SRE scheme,[40] providing funds for modernisation of the police force under the MPF scheme, issuing guidelines to tackle the Maoist problems, so on and so forth.

The strategy adopted by Chhattisgarh for combating Maoist insurgency in the state is 'Clear Hold and Develop'. This strategy required the security forces to dominate an area to stabilise its security situation. Once security is ensured, developmental activities are undertaken to bring prosperity to the inhabitants of the area. The strategy essentially involves increasing the security personnel presence in the critical areas to saturate these areas so that they can carry out operations against the Maoist rebels. For implementing its security response, the state government depends upon the services of the CRPF, the state police and other civilian groups, which are formed from time to time to counter the Maoist insurgency.

The Central Reserve Police Force: Since Chhattisgarh did not have the required police force to tackle the Maoist problem as it was newly inaugurated in 2000, it requested the Union government for assistance. The Union government, in response, deployed the CRPF in the state in 2003 with the mandate to assist the state police during counter Maoist operations. However, the state police could not take up the leadership role as it did not possess the essential combat capabilities. Consequently, the CRPF had to unilaterally conduct counter insurgency operations. Since then, the CRPF has been at the forefront of counter LWE insurgency in Chhattisgarh.

In order to effectively deal with the escalating Maoist violence in the country, the Union government decided to raise counterinsurgency commando battalions called CoBRA in the CRPF. The CoBRA battalions are specialised force trained and equipped 'for commando and guerrilla/jungle warfare type of short and intelligence based quick operations.'[41] Between 2008 and 2011, ten CoBRA battalions were raised and a dedicated school for providing specialised training in jungle warfare and tactics for the CoBRA personnel was established. The CoBRA battalions have been effectively deployed against the Maoist rebels and have conducted several successful counter Naxal operations since then.

However, it is important to note here that while the CRPF is designated as the premier internal security force of the country and has been deployed in many theatres of conflict, the force initially lacked the skills to conduct guerrilla warfare. As a result, when deployed in insurgency prone areas, like in Chhattisgarh, the CRPF found it extremely difficult to face a determined and well trained Maoist rebels. This is evidenced by the fact that even five years after the deployment, 80 per cent of the CRPF personnel were engaged in passive defence duties such as protecting the Salwa Judum camps, government buildings and offices and VIPs.[42]

On its part, the state police had assigned only 300 of its personnel to fight the Maoist guerrillas. In a way the state police offloaded their responsibilities on the CRPF, who found themselves in an alien environment with no support from the police, lack of intelligence and non-familiarity with the local terrain and social fabric. On top of it, the CRPF itself suffered from many structural and operational deficiencies such as 'irrational and protracted deployments, inadequate training, almost no retraining, poor leadership, strategic and tactical stasis, fatigue and indiscipline, and an overwhelming posture of passive defence.'[43]

As a result, the CRPF suffered major setbacks during the counter insurgency operations and a lot of casualties. Some of the examples are, the April 2017 Sukma incident in which 26 CRPF jawans were killed,[44] the June 2010 incident when 26 CRPF jawans were killed,[45] and the worst of all – the April 2010 Dantewada incident in which 75 CRPF personnel were massacred by the Maoist.[46] That being said, over a period of time the CRPF started putting its house in order. The force concentrated on improving training of its personnel, gathering its own intelligence, achieving greater coordination with the police force, etc. in order to emerge as an effective counter insurgency force. However, it appears that inadequacies continue to plague the force and it still faces reverses. For example, in April 2021, 22 CRPF jawans were killed by the Maoist in Jagadalpur.[47]

Salwa Judum and *Koya* Commandos: Faced with the problem of a demoralised police force who were reluctant to take up anti-Maoist operations, the Chhattisgarh government tried to counter the Maoist problem by recruiting local ordinary villagers. The opportunity for such recruitment was provided on 2 June 2005, when villagers of Kutru village of Bijapur tehsil in Dantewada district protested against the Maoists diktats of ban on collection of tendu leaves and participating in elections. This protest movement was called the Salwa Judum. Arguing that Salwa Judum was a 'manifestation of the people's reaction to the atrocities perpetuated by the Naxalites,'[48] the state government backed the Salwa Judum activists. The Salwa Judum members organised themselves and started taking on the Maoist cadres gradually. By January 2007, villagers from 644 villages in Dantewada districts had joined the movement.[49]

Since, the Salwa Judum activists were also the easy targets of retaliatory attacks by the Maoists, they were housed in temporary relief camps located along arterial roads. These relief camps, based on the concept of 'strategic hamletting' isolated the insurgents from the people to some extent.[50] By 2007, 47, 238 people were living in 20 Salwa Judum 'relief camps', or base camps. Besides Salwa Judum, the state government also raised a vigilante force of SPOs under the Chhattisgarh Police Regulations. It appointed some of the Judum activists as SPOs on a monthly stipend of Rs 1500.[51] Many surrendered Maoists as well as persons who were victims of Maoists' violence were also recruited as SPOs. These SPOs were trained in handling weapons and provided with fire arms by the police and other CAPFs deployed in the state. The SPOs which numbered at 6,500 were named Koya Commandos, based on one of the tribes in the region.

Salwa Judum and the Koya Commandos, which were active mainly in Dantewada and Bastar districts, soon attracted a barrage of criticism, especially from human rights activists, of being high-handed and perpetrating atrocities. The 2008 Expert Committee Report had also observed that:

> Encouragement of vigilante groups such as Salwa Judum and herding of hapless tribals in make-shift camps with dismal living conditions, removed from their habitat and deprived of livelihood as a strategy to counter the influence of the radical left is not desirable. It delegitimizes politics, dehumanizes people, degenerates those engaged in their 'security', and above all represents abdication of the State itself.[52]

Disapproving the Salwa Judum, P. Chidambaram in December 2008, had also said that 'the Centre was not in favour of "non-state" actors taking the job of law enforcement in their hands.'[53]

Finally on 5 July 2011, the Supreme Court while delivering its verdict on writ petitions filed against the Salwa Judum in May and August 2007, declared arming of illiterate and semi-literate tribals to counter Maoists by the Chhattisgarh government as unconstitutional. It also directed the Chhattisgarh government to 'immediately cease and desist from using SPOs in any manner or form in any activities, directly or indirectly, aimed at controlling, countering, mitigating or otherwise eliminating Maoist/Naxalite activities in the State of Ch[h]attisgarh.'[54] It further directed the state government to 'take all appropriate measures to prevent the operation of any group, including but not limited to Salwa Judum and Koya Commandos, that in any manner or form seek to take law into private hands, act unconstitutionally or otherwise violate the human rights of any person.'[55]

Thus chastised by the Supreme Court, while the state government disbanded the Salwa Judum, the Chhattisgarh Assembly passed the Chhattisgarh Auxiliary Armed Police Force Act in September 2011. The Act authorises the state to 'establish a trained armed force of persons having knowledge of local area and topography and local language/dialect' since inaccessible tribal areas in Chhattisgarh are affected by Maoist violence.[56] In other words, the Act regularised existing SPOs and permitted them to be inducted into the auxiliary armed force of the state in utter disregard of the Supreme Court order.

The State Police: An efficient police force with effective combat and intelligence gathering capabilities has been successful in responding to internal security threats at the state level. The success of the Greyhounds of Andhra Pradesh and the Punjab police in fighting Maoists and Sikh terrorism respectively are some such examples. In states which continue to see high levels of LWE related violence, it has been observed that the state police are the weakest link. One of the main reasons for the failure of the police is the fact that the force, in general, is organised, equipped and trained for maintaining law and order, crime investigation and community policing, and not for combating insurgencies or terrorism. As a result, the police personnel deployed to conduct anti-naxal operations generally display lack of physical and mental courage, tactical know-how, shooting skills and discipline.[57]

In the case of Chhattisgarh, the state inherited a depleted police force as well as inadequate infrastructure. On top of it, the police personnel were reluctant to function in a state severely affected by LWE. Given the dire circumstances, the Chhattisgarh government, with the help of the Union government, gradually started strengthening its police force. The Eleventh Finance Commission in 2000 had recommended that Rs 984 lakhs would be required for Chhattisgarh to modernise its police force. Accordingly the Union government released Rs 664.88 lakhs over a period of four years.[58] In addition, under the MPF scheme, Chhattisgarh also received Rs 20.575 crore in 2001-02 and Rs 21.57 crore in 2001-2002 to modernise its police force.[59] These funds helped Chhattisgarh increase its police force from 22,592 personnel in November 2000, to 23,350 in 2005 and 46,425 personnel in 2009.[60] The number of sanctioned police stations also rose from 298 in November 2000 to 428 in June 2016.[61] At present, the Chhattisgarh police has a total 22 Armed Battalions including 9 IRBs.

Chhattisgarh also created the Special Task Force (STF) drawn from the state's armed constabulary as well as district police, as a specialised force for battling the Maoist insurgents. The STF undergo two months induction training and are organised into teams comprising 40-50 personnel when they are deployed on ground. The STF, which was raised in 2007, had approximately 2700-4000 personnel in April 2021.[62] The Task Force has its headquarters in Baghera in Durg district with four proposed hubs in Kanker, Sukma, Bijapur and Bastar districts, which will act as temporary camps and launching sites for anti-Maoist operations.

While the STF has shown success in operations against the Maoists in recent times, it faces various handicaps. First, although the force is organised in small teams, ideal for guerrilla warfare and is deployed in Maoist affected districts, decisions regarding its deployment pattern and various administrative tasks are taken by the headquarters instead of the district police superintendent. Experts argue that this centralisation of decision adversely affects the effectiveness of the STF because ground level situations are dynamic, which require quick responses and decisions.

The second handicap that the STF faces is lack of adequate training. Inadequate training is a matter concerning the entire police force, but it is acute for the STF as it is being developed as a special anti-Maoist force. Chhattisgarh started with poor police training infrastructure. The Police Training College and Schools located at Chandrakhuri, Mana, Rajnandgaon, Jagdalpur and Borgaon were established only after the state came into being. Even the CTJW School in Kanker established in 2004 was in its formative/conceptual stage for a few years before it could properly start training the police and CAPF personnel. The Chhattisgarh government also opened three CIAT schools in Mana, Rajnandgaon and Jagdalpur in July 2010, but their operationalisation took time.[63]

Interestingly, while Chhattisgarh was steadily increasing its police strength and establishing new police training schools, it did not allocate adequate funds for procuring infrastructure and manpower/trainers for these schools. For example, '[d]uring year 2004-05, the state police expended only Rs 77 lakh for training out of a total allocation of Rs 22 crores under the MPF scheme, accounting for 0.35 per cent of the total budget. Likewise, in 2006-07, only Rs 25 lakh was expended on training out of a total Rs 76 crore under the MPF scheme, which accounts for 0.0328 per cent of the total budget.'[64] That training is not accorded priority is evidenced by the fact that a substantial part of the budgetary allocation goes in pay and allowance, weapons, transportation, and communication, leaving very little funds for training purposes.

Lack of funds results in insufficient manpower and poor infrastructure in the training schools. Furthermore, the trainers who are assigned to these schools are a disgruntled lot. They feel that trainers' job is a punishment posting and are constantly looking for 'better' posting avenues. This is not only because of the mindset but also because of poor living and working conditions in the training schools. On top of it, the incentive for instructional assignments is a meagre Rs 15 per month in contrast to the 50 per cent of basic pay, which is paid as additional allowance to the STF personnel.[65] More often than not, the quality of the instructors is poor because they themselves have not undertaken specialised training courses. The trainers, on an average, display poor instructional ability, enthusiasm or motivation to train the recruits.

Insufficient infrastructure and resources as well as lack of trainers ensured that these training schools do not have the capacity to train substantial numbers of personnel, which is a must for raising an effective police force. Paradoxically, these training schools also recruit larger personnel than are officially sanctioned. As a result, the duration of the training is cut down, for example, from nine months to six months to accommodate the increased intake. In addition, police personnel are also regularly taken out of their training and assigned law and order duties during elections, VIP visits, etc.

Inadequate as well as poor training of the police personnel is reflected in their lack of physical and mental strength, poor commitment to the job and professional incompetence, especially in the areas of combat. [66] Presence of such tendencies often induce the police to take an easy approach instead of physically gruelling but viable options during combat. They also employ regular and stereotypical duties and administrative tasks devoid of elements of surprise and deception. More often than not, large numbers of personnel are involved in counter insurgency operations to hide operational incompetence. It is being argued that 'mass is being used to compensate for class.'[67] Such habits result in operational failures and frequently trap the police personnel in ambushes or IED blasts resulting in heavy causalities.

Another fallout of lack of proper training is the unwillingness of the Chhattisgarh police to take leadership role while confronting the well-trained Maoist cadres. Reinforcing this fact, a MHA official in 2021 had said, 'Central forces have the numbers and the training, but they have no local knowledge or intelligence.... Only local police can drive out Maoists. The reason we are not succeeding in Chhattisgarh is because the local police have not yet taken the leadership position, although things have improved over the years.'[68]

The District Reserve Group: Realising that the state police personnel continue to show reluctance in taking on the Maoists rebels in direct combat, the police leadership decided to raise a force which is populated by tribal youths familiar with the local terrain, ethos, culture and language. Accordingly, the DRG was raised over different periods of time starting 2008 in seven districts of Bastar division spread in an area of around 40,000 sq. kms. It was first set up in Kanker (north Bastar) and Narayanpur (comprising *Abhujmadh*) districts in 2008 and after a gap of five years, the force was raised in Bijapur and Bastar districts in 2013. Subsequently, the force was expanded in Sukma and Kondagaon districts in 2014, and in 2015 it was raised in Dantewada.[69]

The DRG is currently a 3500 personnel strong force. The recruitment to the DRG are at three levels – assistant constables, who are mostly SPOs of the disbanded Salwa Judum and former Maoists, constables who are recruited formally, and surrendered Maoists who are recruited as *gopniya sainiks* or informers.[70] The DRG personnel are provided with training in the state police academy and in the jungle warfare training facility in Kanker. Some of them are trained by the Greyhounds of Andhra Pradesh and also in the CIJWS in Vairengte. Being from the local areas and also having surrendered Maoists among their rank, the DRG track the Maoist cadres with the help of their own intelligence channels. The DRG is aware of the movement of the Maoists in the forests, their schedule, habits, operational pattern as well as location of their camps in different seasons. This information helps them in launching operations deep into the Maoist strongholds with success.

While the DRG has been successfully deployed to take on Maoist rebels, the force has been grappling with issues such as indiscipline, leadership issues and competition and poor coordination with other forces deployed in the state, all of which adversely affect their fighting capabilities. Many DRG personnel have been dismissed for unruly behaviour and for committing crimes. This indiscipline has also negatively affected their training as most of them do not take the rigorous drills seriously.

Another issue bedevilling the force is that while the hunter instincts of the tribal youths gave them the courage and grit to take on the well trained PLGA cadres, this aspect, however, proved to be a hurdle in making them a disciplined fighting force. It is being reported that during the time of combat or crisis, the hunter instincts kicks in and the youths react according to their instincts forgetting that they are a well trained specialised force. Such behaviour does prove deleterious during serious combats with the Maoists because during such battles only proper training helps in winning or getting out unscathed.[71] Furthermore, the leadership of the DRG is provided by non-tribal personnel, which more often than not creates friction between the officers and soldiers.

Surrender and Rehabilitation Policy: One of the measures implemented to tackle Maoist insurgency is the Surrender and Rehabilitation (S&R) Policy. The policy is aimed at weaning away misguided youths and hard-core rebels who have strayed into the path of Maoist movement. Chhattisgarh government announced its S&R policy in October 2004. Unfortunately, the policy was a nonstarter and hardly any armed rebels surrendered. For example, between 2005 and October 2010, only 115 armed cadres surrendered.[72] Faced with the failure to secure surrender of Maoist cadres, the Chhattisgarh government in 2015 modified the policy to make it more lucrative. It included 'housing for surrendered Naxals, compensation for ammunition apart from the weapons that they give up, as well as the possibility of all previous cases being removed from the record.'[73] This is over and above the benefits such as Rs 5 lakhs for a high ranking Maoist such as a state committee member, Rs 2.5 lakhs for a middle or lower ranking rebel; a monthly stipend of Rs 6,000 for a maximum period of 36 months; additional incentives for recovered weapons; so on and so forth. In fact, the state tried to ensure that rehabilitation starts immediately after a rebel surrenders as he or she is given Rs 10,000 as *protsahan rashi* (encouragement reward).

Despite a lucrative package, surrender figures in Chhattisgarh continues to be dismal. For instance, between 1 January 2018 and 25 September 2021, Police records revealed that 1462 Maoist rebels surrendered. Of these, 1,223 were in the three districts of Dantewada, Sukma and Narayanpur.[74] However, out of 1462, claims of only 113 were sent to the State Screening and Rehabilitation Committee (SRC), which found only 47 cases eligible for receiving the benefits.[75] This meant that only 3 per cent of the so called Maoist rebels who surrendered were genuine. This fact raises doubts about the veracity of the police claims that the security responses have been successful in cornering the Maoist rebels who are getting increasingly disillusioned by the Maoist ideology and therefore surrendering in large numbers. Human right activists, especially in Chhattisgarh, have been arguing that in reality the police coerce the poor and innocent villagers to surrender.

The police in its defence argue that many rebels who have bounties against them do not have their profiles in police records and as a result, it is difficult to verify their antecedents. Police also claim that most of the senior Maoist leaders prefer to surrender in their home states of Andhra Pradesh or Telangana where the S&R policy is more lucrative.[76] In view of the poor surrender records, the police in Chhattisgarh launched a new scheme called '*Lon Varratu*' (come back home in Gondi dialect), in Dantewada on 26 June 2020 to encourage 'misguided youths' to return home and start a new life with the help of the government.[77] Police claim that the campaign has been successful because within six months 226 rebels, including 61 hard core leaders had surrendered.[78]

Constitutional Provisions

The tribal areas of Chhattisgarh comes under the Fifth Schedule of the Constitution of India. Article 244(1) of the Constitution states that the provisions of the Fifth Schedule apply to the administration and control of the Scheduled Areas and Scheduled Tribes (STs) in any State other than the States of Assam, Meghalaya, Tripura and Mizoram.[79] The declaration of Scheduled Areas is based on the preponderance of tribal population, compactness and reasonable size of the areas, a viable administrative entity such as a district, block or taluk, and economic backwardness of the area as compared to the neighbouring areas.[80] Chhattisgarh has 14 districts as complete Scheduled Areas and six districts as partially Scheduled Areas. Out of 20,126 villages, 9,977 villages (49.5 per cent) are part of the Scheduled Areas in the state.[81]

The purpose of declaring any area as a Scheduled Area 'is to preserve the tribal autonomy, their culture and economic empowerment, to ensure social economic and political justice, and preservation of peace and good governance.'[82] For this purposes, the Fifth Schedule under Paragraph 4(1) provides for the establishment of a 20 member Tribal Advisory Council (TAC) with three fourth being the representatives of the STs in the state legislative assembly.[83] The duty of the TAC is to provide advice to the Governor on matters pertaining to the welfare and advancement of the STs of the state. The Fifth Schedule also vests enormous powers on the Governor. These are:

1. Preparing an Annual Report regarding the administration of the Scheduled Areas in the state by the Governor. (Part-A, Para-3)
2. Appointment of the Tribes Advisory Council; (Part-B, Para-4)
3. Regulating the application of Laws of the state and the Acts of Parliament to the Scheduled Areas; (Part-B, Para-5)
4. Making Regulations for the peace and good government of any or all Scheduled Areas in a state. (Part-B, Para-5) Under this the Governor is empowered to make Regulations regarding the – i) Prohibition and restriction of transfer of land from and between Scheduled Tribes, ii) allotment of land to tribals in Scheduled Areas; and iii) moneylending in Scheduled Areas to tribals.[84]

While constitutional safeguards have been provided for the development and wellbeing of the tribals, these safeguards have never been properly implemented. For example, the Annual Reports prepared by the Governors are crucial as they are the basis on which the Union government can formulate policies on tribal welfare and development as well as give directions to the state government for the administration of the Scheduled Area. Therefore, the Governor's Report should contain objective assessments of the quality of governance in the Scheduled Areas and the operationalisation of Acts, Regulations and Constitutional provisions for prevention of land alienation, regulation of money lending, protection of the interests of the tribals, abolition of bonded labour and prescription of special excise policy keeping in view the tribal customs.[85]

However, it has been observed that the reports prepared by the successive Chhattisgarh governors often read like a modified version of the Annual Reports of the Department of Tribal Affairs. In the earlier reports, there were no mention of issues such as the law and order situation, the Maoist problem, the political unrest, etc. in the Scheduled Areas and only matters related to development were covered.[86] It is only in the later reports that the law and order situation as well as the Maoist problem find mention in the Governor's reports.[87] Moreover, the mandatory inter-ministerial consultations on the Governor's reports were not conducted. In fact, there are allegations that the Governor does not exercise his/her extra-constitutional powers in administering the tribal areas lest it bring him/her in conflict with the state government. Allegations are also made that the Governor does not listen to the complaints of the tribals regarding forcible land grab.[88]

As regards the TAC, Chhattisgarh had set up a TAC soon after its inception as a state in 2000. The TAC comprises the Chief Minister as the Chairperson; the Minister of Scheduled Tribes and Schedule Caste Development Department as the Vice Chairperson); 15 Scheduled Tribes Members of Legislative Assembly as Members; three Members of Parliament (nominated as Members); and Secretary, Scheduled Tribes and Schedule Caste Development Department, Chhattisgarh government as Secretary. It is evident that the TAC comprises mainly state officials and a few nominated independent persons with little knowledge about tribal affairs.

Although the TAC was envisioned as body to provide informed suggestions and advices on the matters of concerns for tribal advancement, the manner in which it is constituted robs it of its effectiveness. The reasons being, firstly, the TAC can only discuss and recommend on matters referred to it by the Governor. The Chhattisgarh TAC rules states that apart from matters referred to it by the Governor, 'No issue shall be taken up for discussion and included in the proceedings and no proposals shall be passed in a meeting unless the issue has been mentioned in the notice for the meeting, however, the Chairperson can, using his discretion, permit such issues to be taken up for proceedings, that he thinks necessary and are in the direction of the motto of the Council at large but was excluded in the notice.'[89]

Second, the TAC does not have any powers to implement its own recommendations. Third, since the members of TAC are appointed by the state or the Governor and not through elections, the TAC is not answerable to the tribal population whom it represents and for whose betterment it is supposed to be working.[90] Furthermore, it is also observed that the meetings of the TAC is, more often than not, perfunctory and relevant issues such as land alienation of the tribal are seldom discussed.[91]

Besides Fifth Schedule, the Provisions of the Panchayats (Extension to the Scheduled Areas) Act (PESA) of 1996 has been implemented in Chhattisgarh.[92] PESA recognises the right of tribal communities to govern themselves according to their own systems of self-government and also acknowledges their traditional rights over natural resources. PESA also enjoins that a state legislation shall be in consonance with the customary, social and religious practices and traditional management practices of common resources. For achieving this objective, the Chhattisgarh Panchayat Raj Adhiniyam empowers *Gram Sabhas* (village assemblies) to approve plans for the socio-economic development, controlling all social sectors – including the processes and personnel who implement policies, exercising control over minor (non-timber) forest resources, minor water bodies and minor minerals, managing local markets, preventing land alienation, restoring alienated land, and regulating intoxicants among other things.[93] Unlike in other states, the Gram Sabhas in Chhattisgarh has the power to ensure accountability of the Gram Panchayats to them including the power to recall the *Sarpanch* or the *Panch* subject to certain conditions.

The Gram Panchayats are assigned with several civic, regulatory, welfare and maintenance functions, including financial functions to collect various types of taxes. Funds for 12 departments have been devolved to the Panchayats. Panchayats also appoint officials for nine departments. Chhattisgarh has Panchayats at the village, block and district levels. Out of total 11,664 Gram Panchayats in Chhattisgarh, 5,632 Gram Panchayats comprising 48.28 per cent are in Scheduled Areas. The fact that PESA has not been implemented effectively can be ascertained from the fact that Chhattisgarh has not formulated the rules of the Act yet. In fact, it is being argued that the Act has become toothless as its spirit has been violated by the state because the gram sabhas have no powers as their powers can be overridden. Moreover, many tribals living in the Fifth Scheduled areas do not figure in the voters' list and therefore cannot become member of gram sabhas.[94]

Governance

The raison d'être for the formation of Chhattisgarh was the social and economic underdevelopment of undivided Madhya Pradesh.[95] It was envisaged that the formation of a new state would bring about the desired levels of development, which would help fight left wing extremism plaguing the region. The Report of the Expert Group of the Planning Commission on 'Development Challenges in Extremist Affected Areas' had observed that:

> The areas in Central India where unrest is prevailing covers several States (like Andhra Pradesh, Orissa, Chhattisgarh, Madhya Pradesh, Jharkhand and part of Maharashtra) are minimally administered. State interventions both for development and for law and order had been fairly low. In fact there is a kind of vacuum of administration in these areas which is being exploited by the armed movement, giving some illusory protection and justice to the local population.[96]

The creation of Chhattisgarh to mitigate the problem of absence of administration, ironically, faced a peculiar problem. The officials who were posted in the newly created state were unwilling to reside in what was seen by them as remote and a banishment from the comfortable and well governed Bhopal.[97] The new cadre of the Indian Administrative Service (IAS) for the state lacked enough officials of appropriate seniority as well. This meant that officials with greater experience and knowledge about matters administration were not available to the new state.

Paradoxically, Chhattisgarh government's desire to bring in economic development in the state had in fact resulted in absence of administration because it pulled out whatever state machinery was functioning from the predominantly resource rich tribal areas to make way for the private investors. This policy of the government not only created a vacuum of governance but also took away the primary means of livelihood of the tribals, that is, land. Absence of governance at the grassroots meant that the people inhabiting these areas are deprived of basic amenities and provisions such as healthcare, education, sanitation, means of livelihood, so on and so forth. Not surprisingly, the 2011 Human Development Index (HDI) ranked Chhattisgarh the lowest amongst the state with a HDI of 0-0.358 indicating unequal access and high exclusion.[98]

In 2017 the Centre for Policy Research (CPR) conducted a comprehensive analysis of the implementation of four Union government sponsored social sector schemes: SSA for elementary education of children aged 6–14; the Midday Meal Scheme (MDM); Rashtriya Madhaymik Shiksha Abhiyaan (RMSA) for secondary education; and the Integrated Child Development Scheme (ICDS), in four districts of Chhattisgarh viz. Rajnandgaon, Surajpur, Janjgir Champa and Bastar. In its detailed Report, the CPR concluded that these four schemes suffer from 'limited human resources and weak internal management resulting in poor supervision; insufficient planning capacity and lack of prioritised resource allocation at the grassroots; and delayed fund flows and a complicated disbursement process.'[99]

According to the Report, the SSA and the RMSA suffer from teacher shortages, absenteeism and multi-grade teaching (a single teacher teaching several grades). These factors adversely affected the quality of education. The state government also found it difficult to recruit teachers for the secondary schools and those who were recruited never reported for work. Moreover, salaries of the decentralised teacher cadre – the *Shiksha Karmis*/Panchayat *Shikshaks* – were often delayed, thus robbing them of any motivation to teach.[100] According to the Annual Status of Education Report (Rural) 2021, Chhattisgarh has witnessed a decline in government school enrolment as the enrolment in the private schools are increasing steadily since 2010.[101]

The Multidimensional Poverty Index (MPI) of 2021 also indicates unbalanced development in districts such as Sukma, Dantewara, Bijapur, Bastar and Narayanpur as having around 45 to 50 percent of the population who are multidimensionally poor.[102] This means that these districts, which are also the hotbed of LWE, continue to suffer from acute deprivations in accessing education, nutritional status, and basic services like water, sanitation, energy, and asset ownership.[103]

That said, the Chhattisgarh government over the years have worked towards improving peoples' living standards. Several studies have also corroborated the fact that the state's performance in relatively improving literacy rates, access to health and sanitation, providing basic infrastructure such as roads, electricity, etc. has been noteworthy. In fact, the Report by the Public Affairs Centre (PAC), a Bengaluru-based non-profit think tank, puts Chhattisgarh as the fourth best governed state of India and third in the sustainability Index.[104]

However as indicated earlier, governance in the state is uneven. The LWE hit districts still continue to suffer from absence or lack of governance.

Summary

Chhattisgarh was chosen by the communist leadership precisely because of its hilly and heavily forested terrain to establish their 'base area'. Pervasive under-development and exploitation of the tribespeople by the outsiders provided them with issues around which they could mobilise people and instigate them to fight against the state. The limited presence (or total absence) of administration in the tribal areas meant that the inhabitants of these remote areas are deprived not only of basic amenities and infrastructure but also from grievance redressal and justice. All these factors alienated the people from the government as they gravitated towards the Maoists.

The state tried to suppress the Maoist threat through its coercive power, but the lack of capabilities and courage of its police force to fight the Maoists made it depend heavily on the CRPF. Unfortunately, the CRPF did not possess proper knowledge of the terrain and seldom got any intelligence about the rebels from the police. As a result, they found it difficult to combat the Maoist menace for a long time. The state government's efforts to wean the youths, especially the tribal youths from the Maoists' folds with generous surrender and rehabilitation schemes as well as positions in the police force, also failed.

Further, poor implementation of the constitutional safeguards under the Fifth Schedule and PESA provided to the tribals further alienated them as they have not yet been effective in bringing a meaningful transformation in the lives of the tribespeople. Last but not least, Chhattisgarh, for a long time, has performed poorly in the domain of governance. It is only in past few years that the state government has made some attempts to extend its administrative reach in the far flung areas. However, the developmental activities undertaken by the state government are uneven in their spread and reach, with the Maoist affected districts continuing to suffer from lack of basic amenities and infrastructure.

NOTES

1. 'Unstarred Question No. 1073: Naxal/Left Wing Extremism', *Lok Sabha*, 8 February 2022 at https://www.mha.gov.in/MHA1/Par2017/pdfs/par2022-pdfs/LS-08022022/1073.pdf, accessed on 16 March 2022.

2. The percentages are the figures till November 2021. 'Unstarred Question No.1968 Initiative To Control The Naxal Problem In Chhattisgarh', *Rajya Sabha*, 15 December 2021 at https://www.mha.gov.in/MHA1/Par2017/pdfs/par2021-pdfs/rs-15122021/1968.pdf, accessed on 1 April 2022.
3. Eradication of Left Wing Extremism', *Press Information Bureau*, New Delhi, 21 December 2022, at pib.gov.in/PressReleaseIframePage.aspx?PRID=1885482, accessed on 29 August 2023.
4. 'Review Categorization of Districts affected by Left Wing Extremism', *Ministry of Home Affairs*, 19 June 2021, at https://crpf.gov.in/writereaddata/images/pdf/815072021.pdf, accessed on 11 April 2022.
5. Ritesh Mishra, 'Maoist violence highest in Chhattisgarh in 2020, NCRB data reveals', *The Hindustan Times*, 15 September 2021, accessed on 1 April 2022.
6. Sudhakar, 'A Saga of Twenty-Five Years of Glorious Struggle, an Epic of People's Radical Transformation', *People's March*, January 2006, p. 3.
7. Maoist Documents - Strategy & Tactics of the Indian Revolution, Central Committee (P) CPI (Maoist) 2004, *SATP* at https://www.satp.org/satporgtp/countries/india/maoist/documents/papers/strategy.htm, accessed on 21 March 2022.
8. Ruchir Garg, 'Roots and Causes: The Case of Dandakaranya', in P.V. Ramana (ed.), *The Naxal Challenge, Causes, Linkages, and Policy Options*, Delhi: Dorling Kindersley (India) Pvt. Ltd., 2008, p. 31.
9. *Report of the Scheduled Areas and Scheduled Tribes Commission*, Vol. 1, New Delhi: Government of India, 2004, pp. 163-164.
10. n. 8, p. 36.
11. Archana Prasad, 'The Political Economy of 'Maoist Violence' in Chhattisgarh', *Social Scientist*, Vol. 38 (3/4), March-April 2010, p. 12.
12. n. 8, p. 37.
13. Prakash Singh, *The Naxal Movement in India*, New Delhi: Rupa, 2016, p. 127
14. Stephen Rego, 'Destructive Development and People's Struggles in Bastar', *Economic and Political Weekly*, Vol. 29 (7), 12 February 1994, p. 352.
15. n. 11, p. 17.
16. Ibid, pp. 16-17.
17. n. 8, p. 35.
18. Nandini Sundar, 'Bastar, Maoism and Salwa Judum', *Economic and Political Weekly*, Vol. 41 (29), 22-28 July 2006, p. 3190.
19. n. 11, pp. 18-19.
20. Ibid, p. 18.
21. *Annual Report 2009-2010*, New Delhi: Ministry of Home Affairs, 2010, p. 17.
22. *Annual Report 2003-2004*, New Delhi: Ministry of Home Affairs, 2004, pp. 41-42.
23. *Annual Report 2005-2006*, New Delhi: Ministry of Home Affairs, 2006, p. 24.
24. PTI, Naxalism biggest internal security challenge: PM', *Rediff.com*, 13 April 2006 at https://www.rediff.com/news/2006/apr/13naxal.htm, accessed on 31 March 2022.
25. Ibid.
26. *Annual Report 2008-2009*, New Delhi: Ministry of Home Affairs, 2009, p. 17.
27. *Annual Report 2013-2014*, New Delhi: Ministry of Home Affairs, 2014, p. 25.
28. HeadLines Today Bureau, '75 jawans killed in C'garh Naxal attack', *India Today*, 7 April 2010 at https://www.indiatoday.in/india/story/75-jawans-killed-in-naxal-ambush-in-chhattisgarh-71065-2010-04-05, accessed on 1 April 2022.
29. Jan Myrdal and Gautam Navlakha, 'In conversation with Ganapathy, General Secretary of

CPI(Maoist)', *Sanhati*, 12 February 2010 at https://sanhati.com/articles/2138/, accessed on 29 March 2022.

30. 'Maoists refuse to halt violence', *The New Indian Express*, New Delhi, 19 May 2010 at https://www.newindianexpress.com/nation/2010/may/19/maoists-refuse-to-halt-violence-155724.html, accessed on 30 March 2022.
31. n. 29.
32. India TV News Desk, 'Maoism in India: Know its history and King Pin "Ganapathy"', *India TV*, 26 June 2014 at https://www.indiatvnews.com/news/india/maoism-india-history-muppala-lakshmana-rao-alias-ganapathy-38451.html, accessed on 5 April 2022.
33. Neeraj Gupta, 'Jheeram Ghati Attack: When All Chhattisgarh Congress Members Died', *The Quint*, 10 November 2018 at https://www.thequint.com/videos/news-videos/jhiram-ghati-attack-chhattisgarh-congress-deaths, accessed on 1 April 2022.
34. *Annual Report 2018-19*, New Delhi: Ministry of Home Affairs, 2019, p. 10.
35. 'Unstarred Question No. 1187: Naxali Attacks', *Lok Sabha*, 27 July 2021 at https://www.mha.gov.in/MHA1/Par2017/pdfs/par2021-pdfs/LS-27072021/1187.pdf, accessed on 1 April 2022.
36. n. 5.
37. Rahul Tripathi, 'Chhattisgarh Naxal attack: 21 securitymen killed, 1 missing; Jawans ambushed by 400 Maoists', *The Economic Times*, 5 April 2021 at https://economictimes.indiatimes.com/news/defence/chhattisgarh-bodies-of-17-jawans-recovered-at-encounter-site/articleshow/81896131.cms, accessed on 1 April 2022.
38. PTI, 'Biggest attack by Maoists in Chhattisgarh in two years', *The Hindu*, New Delhi, 27 April 2023 at https://www.thehindu.com/news/national/foiling-ied-attacks-in-south-bastar-region-of-chhattisgarh-last-major-challenge-for-anti-naxal-ops-officials/article66782549.ece, accessed on 29 August, 2023.
39. *Annual Report 2006-07*, New Delhi: Ministry of Home Affairs, 2007, p. 25.
40. The SRE scheme was revised in 2004-05 in which funds reimbursed by the union government has been increased from 50 per cent to 100 per cent. Under the revised scheme, expenditure incurred by the affected states on various aspects are included. These are: compensation paid to the family of a civilian or a security personnel killed by Maoists; logistical support including hiring of helicopter, etc. for the CAPFs and state police; training for the state police force; payments to SPOs; community policing and Village Defence Committee (VDC)/Nagarik Suraksha Samiti (NSS); rehabilitation of surrendered Maoist cadre (applicable till 31 March 2013); strengthening of police stations, police outpost etc. not covered under (MPF Scheme); expenditure on publicity material to expose the Maoists unlawful activities, etc. For details, see, 'Revised Guidelines for Reimbursement of Security Related Expenditure to LWE Affected States under the SRE Scheme', *Ministry of Home Affairs* at https://www.mha.gov.in/sites/default/files/2022-09/NM-SRE-Scheme_160614_1%5B1%5D.pdf, accessed on 12 April 2022.
41. *Annual Report 2008-09*, New Delhi, Ministry of Home Affairs, 2009. P. 72.
42. Jason Miklian, 'The purification hunt: the Salwa Judum counterinsurgency in Chhattisgarh, India', *Dialectical Anthropology*, Vol. 33 (3/4), December 2009, p. 443.
43. K.P.S. Gill, 'Freedom From Fear-Sukma attack: Chhattisgarh police cannot hold back and fight Naxals in their stronghold through proxies', *SATP* at https://www.satp.org/satporgtp/kpsgill/governance/17KPS-Sukma_attack.htm, accessed on 12 April 2022.
44. Deeptiman Tiwary, Dipankar Ghose and Rahul Tripathi, 'Worst in Chhattisgarh in seven years: 25 CRPF men killed by Maoists in Sukma', *The Indian Express*, Raipur, 25 April 2017 at https://indianexpress.com/article/india/worst-in-chhattisgarh-in-seven-years-26-crpf-men-killed-by-maoists-in-sukma-4626755/, accessed on 12 May 2022.

45. Aman Sethi, '26 CRPF men killed in Chhattisgarh', *The Hindu*, Raipur, 29 June 2010 at https://www.thehindu.com/news/national/26-CRPF-men-killed-in-Chhattisgarh/article16272271.ece, accessed on 12 May 2022.
46. n. 28.
47. Asish Pandey and Kamaljit Sandhu, 'Chhattisgarh: 22 jawans killed, 31 injured in deadly encounter with Naxals on Sukma-Bijapur border', *India Today*, Raipur 4 April 2021 at https://www.indiatoday.in/india/story/chhattisgarh-encounter-naxal-maoists-tarrem-sukma-bijapur-cobra-crpf-jawans-missing-1786930-2021-04-04, accessed on 12 May 2022.
48. 'Unstarred Question No. 2521 Salwa Judum Movement', *Lok Sabha*, 16 December 2008 at https://eparlib.nic.in/bitstream/123456789/568419/1/67360.pdf, accessed on 1 April 2022.
49. 'Jan Jagaran Abhiyan (Salwa Judum): District South Bastar Dantewada' at https://cpjc.files.wordpress.com/2007/11/collectors-memo-2007.pdf, accessed on 1 April 2022.
50. Bela Bhatia, 'Judging the Judgment', *Economic and Political Weekly*, Vol. 46 (30), 23-29 July 2011, p. 15.
51. P.V. Ramana, 'A Critical Evaluation of the Union Government's Response to the Maoist Challenge', *Strategic Analysis*, Vol. 33 (5), 2009, p. 748.
52. 'Development Challenges in Extremist Affected Areas', *Report of an Expert Group to Planning Commission*, New Delhi, 2008, p. 77 at https://tribal.nic.in/downloads/Statistics/OtherReport/DevelopmentChallengesinExtremistAffectedAreas.pdf, accessed on 1 April 2022.
53. PTI, 'Govt disapproves of 'non-state' law enforcers like Salwa Judum', *The Economic Times*, New Delhi, 17 December 2008 at https://economictimes.indiatimes.com/news/politics-and-nation/govt-disapproves-of-non-state-law-enforcers-like-salwa-judum/articleshow/3850938.cms?from=mdr, accessed on 1 April 2022.
54. 'Writ Petition (Civil) No. 250 of 2007', Order, *Supreme Court Of India*, New Delhi, 5 July 2011, p. 76 at https://main.sci.gov.in/jonew/judis/38160.pdf, accessed on 4 April 2022.
55. Ibid.
56. Virginius Xaxa, et al., *Report of the High Level Committee on Socio-Economic, Health and Educational Status of Tribal Communities of India*, New Delhi: Ministry of Tribal Affairs, 2014, p. 355.
57. Om Shankar Jha, 'Combating Left Wing Extremism: Is Police Training Lacking? Case Study of Chhattisgarh', *IDSA Occasional Paper no. 3*, 2009, p. 7.
58. 'Unstarred Question No: 2918: Integrated Action Plan For Chhattisgarh', *Lok Sabha*, 22 March 2002 Questions: Lok Sabha (loksabhaph.nic.in), accessed on 12 April 2022.
59. Under the MPF Scheme, Chhattisgarh is placed under Category 'B', under which the union government assistance is 75 percent and state government's contribution is 25 per cent. 'Unstarred Question No. 6110: Modernisation of Police Force in Chhattisgarh', *Lok Sabha*, 7 May 2002 at https://sansad.in/ls/questions/questions-and-answers, accessed on 12 April 2022.
60. n. 57, p. 10.
61. 'Chhattisgarh Police', *Government of Chhattisgarh* at https://cgpolice.gov.in/about-us, accessed on 13 April 2022.
62. Rahul Noronha, 'Chhattisgarh's Maoist fighting force', *India Today*, Bhopal, 9 April 2021 at https://www.indiatoday.in/india-today-insight/story/chhattisgarh-s-maoist-fighting-force-1788801-2021-04-08, accessed on 13 April 2022.
63. 'Chhattisgarh opens three counter-insurgency schools', *Zee News*, Raipur, 16 July 2010 at https://zeenews.india.com/news/chhattisgarh/chhattisgarh-opens-three-counter-insurgency-schools_641412.html, accessed on 19 April, 2022.
64. n. 57, p. 15.
65. Ibid, p. 17.

66. Ibid, pp. 12-13.
67. H.S. Panag, 'How India's Maoist counter-insurgency is being undone by a flawed security strategy', *The Print*, 15 April 2021 at https://theprint.in/opinion/how-indias-maoist-counter-insurgency-is-being-undone-by-a-flawed-security-strategy/640124/, accessed on 19 April 2022.
68. Deeptiman Tiwary, 'Explained: Fighting Left Wing Extremism in Chhattisgarh, and elsewhere', *The Indian Express*, 7 April 2021 at https://indianexpress.com/article/explained/fighting-left-wing-extremism-in-chhattisgarh-elsewhere-maoist-attack-crpf-7260456/, accessed on 18 April 2022.
69. PTI, 'District Reserve Group adds impetus to anti-Naxal operations in Chhattisgarh', *The Economic Times*, Raipur, 13 July 2018 at https://economictimes.indiatimes.com/news/defence/district-reserve-group-adds-impetus-to-anti-naxal-operations-in-chhattisgarh/articleshow/50865986.cms, accessed on 13 April 2022.
70. n. 62.
71. Ibid.
72. P.V. Ramana, 'Taming India's Maoists: Surrender and Rehabilitation', *Strategic Analysis*, Vol. 37 (6), 2013, p. 720.
73. Dipankar Ghose, 'Chhattisgarh amends surrender policy for Maoists', *The Indian Express*, Raipur, 20 November 2015 at https://indianexpress.com/article/india/india-news-india/chhattisgarh-amends-surrender-policy-for-maoists/, accessed on 10 August 2022.
74. Ritesh Mishra, 'Dichotomy between Maoist surrender and rehab numbers', *The Hindustan Times*, Raipur, 20 October 2021 at https://www.hindustantimes.com/india-news/dichotomy-between-maoist-surrender-and-rehab-numbers-101634754443964.html, accessed on 10 August 2022.
75. Ibid.
76. Ibid.
77. Prithiviraj Singh, 'Get 500 Naxals of 1,600 in Dantewada to surrender – Chhattisgarh's new rehabilitation plan', *The Print*, Raipur, 16 July 2020 at https://theprint.in/india/get-500-naxals-of-1600-in-dantewada-to-surrender-chhattisgarhs-new-rehabilitation-plan/461534/, accessed on 11 August 2022.
78. Ejaz Kaiser, 'Lon Varratu: A "ghar wapsi" with a difference in Chhattisgarh's Dantewada', *The New Indian Express*, Chhattisgarh, 10 January 2021 at https://www.newindianexpress.com/good-news/2021/jan/10/lon-varratu-a-ghar-wapsiwith-a-difference-inchhattisgarhsdantewada-2247903.html#:~:text=Under%20the%20Lon%20Varratu%20campaign,local%20villagers%20and%20people%27s%20representatives, accessed on 30 August 2023.
79. 'Fifth Schedule, Article 244 (1)', *Constitution of India*, New Delhi: Government of India, 2022, p. 276 at https://cdnbbsr.s3waas.gov.in/s380537a945c7aaa788ccfcdf1b99b5d8f/uploads/2023/05/2023050195.pdf, accessed on 12 August 2022.
80. *Third Report of the Standing Committee on Inter-sectoral Issues Relating to Tribal Development on Standard of Administration and Governance in the Scheduled Areas*, New Delhi: Ministry of Tribal Affairs, 2009, p. 4.
81. R. Prasanna, 'Implementation of PESA in Chhattisgarh', *Ministry of Panchayat Raj* at https://cdnbbsr.s3waas.gov.in/s316026d60ff9b54410b3435b403afd226/uploads/2023/02/2023022126.pdf, accessed on 6 March 2022.
82. *Land and Governance Under the Fifth Schedule: An Overview of the Law*, New Delhi: Ministry of Tribal Affairs, nd, p. 2
83. 'Tribes Advisory Councils (TAC) have been constituted in all the ten states having Scheduled Areas', *Press Information Bureau*, 6 December 2021 at https://pib.gov.in/PressReleasePage.aspx?PRID=1778540, accessed on 16 August 2022.

84. 'Fifth Schedule, Part B', *The Constitution of India*, New Delhi: Government of India, 2022, pp. 277-278 at https://cdnbbsr.s3waas.gov.in/s380537a945c7aaa788ccfcdf1b99b5d8f/uploads/2023/05/2023050195.pdf, accessed on 16 August 2022.
85. n. 9, pp. 36-37.
86. Ibid, p. 38.
87. *Governor's Report on the Scheduled Areas of Chhattisgarh 2016-2017*, Government of Chhattisgarh at http://tribal.cg.gov.in/year-2016-17, accessed on 6 March 2022.
88. Jitendra, 'SC dismisses petition challenging functioning of Tribal advisory council in Chhattisgarh', *Down to Earth*, 24 November 2014 at https://www.downtoearth.org.in/news/sc-dismisses-petition-challenging-functioning-of-tribal-advisory-council-in-chhattisgarh-47529#:~:text=The%20Supreme%20Court%20last%20week,(TACs)%20in%20scheduled%20areas., accessed on 7 April 2022.
89. n. 56, p. 75.
90. Ibid, p. 74.
91. *The Tribes Advisory Councils: Time to be replaced by the Autonomous District Councils*, New Delhi: Asian Indigenous and Tribal Peoples Network, 2012, p. 7.
92. The Panchayati Raj Act of 1993 was automatically applicable to the Scheduled Areas. It was the PESA Act of 1996 which extended the Panchayati Raj Institution Act to be applicable in these areas. Accordingly, in 1997 the Madhya Pradesh state government added a new chapter to the existing Panchayati Raj legislation to make special provisions for panchayats in Scheduled Areas in Chhattisgarh. The Chhattisgarh Panchayat Raj Adhiniyam, 1993 forms the basis of the current panchayat system in place in Chhattisgarh at https://www.indiacode.nic.in/bitstream/123456789/12801/1/the_chhattisgarh_panchayat_raj_avam_ gram_ swaraj_ adhiniyam%2c_1993_no._1_of_1994_date_24.01.1994.pdf, accessed on 7 April 2022.
93. 'Section 4', *the Provisions of the Panchayats (Extension to the Scheduled Areas) Act, 1996* at https://www.indiacode.nic.in/bitstream/123456789/1973/1/A1996-40.pdf, accessed on 7 April 2022.
94. Suvarna Damle, *A study of contribution of the Tribal Parliamentarians in strengthening Panchayats (Extension to the Scheduled Areas) Act (PESA)*, Parliament, 2012, pp. 12-13 at http://164.100.213.102/rscmsnew/careers_documents/Suvarna_Damle.pdf, accessed on 7 April 2022. Kundan Pandey, 'Even after 25 years of its existence, the PESA Act fails to empower Adivasi communities', *Scroll.in*, 22 March 2021 at https://scroll.in/article/988729/25-years-on-many-indian-states-havent-implemented-the-law-that-empowers-adivasi-communities, accessed on 7 April 2022. Ambika Pandit, "Centre asks laggard states to expedite notification of PESA", *The Times of India*, New Delhi, 19 November 2021 at https://timesofindia.indiatimes.com/india/centre-asks-laggard-states-to-expedite-notification-of-pesa/articleshow/87787932.cms, accessed on 7 April 2022.
95. *Human Development Report - Chhattisgarh 2005*, Raipur: United National Development Programme, 2005, p. ix.
96. 'Development Challenges in Extremist Affected Areas', *Report of an Expert Group to Planning Commission*, New Delhi, 2008, p. 80 at https://tribal.nic.in/downloads/Statistics/OtherReport/DevelopmentChallengesinExtremistAffectedAreas.pdf, accessed on 8 April 2022.
97. Anindita Adhikari and Vasudha Chhotray, 'The Political Construction of Extractive Regimes in Two Newly Created Indian States: A Comparative Analysis of Jharkhand and Chhattisgarh', *Development and Change*, Vol. 51 (3), 2020, p. 17.
98. *Approach to 12th Five Year Plan 2012-17, Inclusion through Human Development*, Raipur; Government of Chhattisgarh, p. 1.
99. 'What ails Chhattisgarh's welfare schemes?', New Delhi: Centre For Policy Research, 22 August

2017 at https://cprindia.org/what-ails-chhattisgarhs-welfare-schemes/#:~:text= Insufficient %20 planning%20capacity%20and%20lack,and%20a%20complicated%20disbursement%20process., accessed on 18 May 2022.

100. Ibid.
101. *Annual Status of Education Report (Rural) 2021*, New Delhi: ASER Centre, 2021, p. 9.
102. *National Multidimensional Poverty Index Baseline Report Based on NFHS-4 (2015-16)*, New Delhi: Niti Aayog, 2021, pp. 76-77 at https://www.niti.gov.in/sites/default/files/2021-11/National_MPI_India-11242021.pdf, accessed on 18 May 2022.
103. n. 97, p. 1.
104. 'Chhattisgarh among top five best-governed states, at 3rd in sustainability index: Think tank report', *Times Now*, Raipur, 4 November 2021 at https://www.timesnownews.com/india/article/chhattisgarh-among-top-five-best-governed-states-at-3rd-in-sustainability-index-bengaluru-think-tank-report/829278, accessed on 19 May 2022.

7

MANIPUR

Manipur is the only state in the Northeast that has been witnessing prolonged insurgencies since decades. In fact, Manipur was the most violent state in 2019 accounting for about 57 per cent of the total incidents in the region.[1] In 2021, 112 insurgency related incidents were registered in the state in which nine civilians and five security force personnel lost their lives.[2] Violence in Manipur is perpetrated by myriad insurgent groups belonging to different ethnic groups such Meitei, Naga, Kuki, Zomi, Hmar and Muslim. Manipur's first albeit brief brush with insurgency was recorded in 1948-1950 when the Manipuri Communists under the leadership of Hijam Irabot started a struggle against feudalism. As a matter of fact, the communist struggle in the state was part of the larger anti-feudalism struggle, which the CPI had launched in India between 1948 and 1951. Some of the princely states and provinces which witnessed such struggles at that time beside Manipur were Hyderabad, Tripura and Bengal.

The Communist Rebellion

In October 1948, Hijam Irabot established the underground Communist Party of Manipur (CPM), which was not a full-fledged unit of CPI because it was recognised only as a District Organising Committee (DOC) of the Assam Branch of the CPI.[3] Be that as it may, Hijam Irabot launched the 'National Democratic Revolution' to establish a communist society free from exploitation and oppression. The main focus of his struggle was to change the political regime through social revolution. The objectives of the movement were:

installation of a popular responsible government, Panchayati Raj, revision of the land tenure system, cessation of forced labour, and so on and so forth.[4]

After Manipur state's merger with the Indian Union on 15 October 1949, Hijam Irabot strove to establish 'Independent Peasant Republic' and decided to undertake an armed revolution. To achieve its objective, the CPM raised the Manipur Red Guards Army in March 1950, which started training in the use of arms and guerrilla warfare.[5] The Red Guard Army had striking force of 32 trained red guards, supported by about 500 village guards.[6] Armed with the objective to overthrow the present Government in Manipur by violent means, the Red Guard started their terrorist activities including attacking the Manipur police, Manipur Rifles and the Assam Rifles. In fact, in a significant attack on 31 March 1951, the Red Guards attacked the Assam Rifles in Moirang Kampu and inflicted causalities on the paramilitary force.

Besides the armed wing, the CPM had also created a number of front organiations such as the Student's Federation, the Youth League, Mahila Samity, Peace Committee, etc. to spread the revolutionary fervour in the state. Hijam Irabot also travelled to Myanmar in September 1950 to enlist the help of the Communist Party of Burma.[7] The communist rebellion however could not sustain itself for long as the Indian state came down heavily on them. A large number of communist cadres were arrested and tried under the 'Manipur Conspiracy Trial' in 1951. The death of Hijam Irabot on 26 September 1951 and the decision of the CPI to end armed rebellion and participate in the electoral process effectively brought an end to the communist rebellion in the state.

While the Communist rebellion in Manipur, which is also termed as the first 'Meitei insurgency' had petered out, causes for new insurgencies were laying roots. One such cause was the 'humiliation' the people felt on the manner in which the Manipur state was incorporated in the Indian Union. Prior to Independence, Manipur was one of 565 odd princely states, which were indirectly ruled by the British. When the British paramountcy lapsed, Manipur signed the Instrument of Accession to the Indian Dominion and a Standstill Agreement on 11 August 1947.[8] Meanwhile, the state had enacted the Manipur State Constitution Act of 1947 on 26 July 1947,[9] which provided for a constitutional monarchy with an elected State Assembly.

The State Assembly was to be elected on an adult franchise with the Hill People occupying about 36 per cent of the seats in the Assembly. The Manipur Constitution also provided for a State Council of Ministers, consisting of six ministers elected by the State Assembly, and the Chief Minister, appointed by the Maharajah in consultation with the elected ministers of the Council.[10] Accordingly, elections for the formation of a government were held in June 1948. Since not a single party won a majority, the Praja Shanti Party formed a government in coalition with the Krishak Sangha and the Hill members.[11] On 21 September 1949, the Maharaja of Manipur signed the Agreement of Merger and Manipur state was merged with the Indian dominion on 15 October 1949. With the merger, Manipur was categorised as 'Part C' and made a Chief Commissioner's province. The State Assembly was dissolved and in its place an Advisory Council comprising five members was constituted.[12]

The people of Manipur, especially the political elites, who had enjoyed popular government before merger were discontent with the bureaucratic set up and started agitating for the restoration of a responsible elected government. In response, the Union government converted Manipur from Part C state to a Union Territory and provided for the constitution of a Territorial Council elected through universal suffrage under the Constitution (Seventh Amendment) Act of 1956.[13] The Territorial Council that came into existence in 1957 had its jurisdiction only in the rural areas outside Imphal.

The limited scope provided to the people of Manipur to fulfil their political aspirations fuelled further frustration and discontentment. The masses under the aegis of the Assembly Demand Coordinating Committee started agitations for installation of full democratic government and offered *Satyagarha*.[14] In fact, there were apprehensions that the political agitation for restoration of the State Assembly had gradually slipped into the hands of the radical leftist parties. Finally in June 1963, the Union government passed the Government of Union Territories Act, which converted the Territorial Councils into Territorial Legislative Assembly. The Act provided for a Legislative Assembly of 30 elected members and a Council of 3 Ministers with the Chief Minister.[15]

The Meitei Insurgency

The fact that Manipur remained a Union Territory while the Nagas, who had started an armed secessionist movement against the Indian state, got statehood in 1963 rankled the people of Manipur, especially the Meiteis. The dissatisfaction among the Meiteis was already aggravated by the fact that India, in 1953, accepted the transfer of Kubaw Valley, which according to them, formed a part of the Manipur kingdom and which was given to the Burmese by the British after the Treaty of Yandaboo in 1826. The ranks of the discontented political elites were joined by the educated youth who found their economic aspirations thwarted by the large number of non-locals who held government positions and dominated the economic activities. Lack of access to political and economic opportunities propelled the Meitei community to 'politicise their identity and mobilise support for a Meitei state-building project.'[16]

The movement was based on two main issues: 1) revival of Sanamahi, the Pre-Vaishnava religion, and 2) secessionism from India. The argument forwarded was that a 'Hindu' India had enslaved the Meiteis through Vaishnavism and are further exploiting them through economic dominance. Consequently, several youth organisations including the Pan Manipuri Youth League (PMYL) were formed to 'sensitise' the youths about their political, economic and socio-cultural situation and carrying forward the movement.

It was during this period that in November 1964 Arambam Samarendra Singh founded the United Liberation Front (UNLF) with the aim to 'secede from India through armed struggle' and establish a 'socialist society'. Soon differences among its cadres cropped up and in December 1968, and a more radical group led by Oinam Sudhirkumar broke away from the UNLF and established a government-in-exile called Revolutionary Government of Manipur (RGM).[17] The primary objective of the RGM was to 'liberate' Manipur through an armed struggle. The RGM had an elaborate administrative set-up including a home minister, a finance minister, a foreign minister and an army chief of staff with Sudhirkumar as the general secretary.[18] The RGM was based in Bangladesh (erstwhile East Pakistan) with its headquarters in Sylhet.

The cadres of UNLF and RGM carried out series of subversive activities especially looting of treasury in 1968-1969. They also reportedly established links with the Naga insurgents in 1970. In response, the security forces conducted counter insurgency operations against the RGM rebels and most of them were arrested while they were trying to crossover to erstwhile East

Pakistan.[19] The Bangladesh Liberation War of 1971 ensured that the rebels did not find safe haven in erstwhile East Pakistan. The final blow to the RGM was inflicted when Manipur was granted statehood in 1972 after the North-Eastern Areas (Reorganisation) Act was passed in 1971.[20] With the inauguration of Manipur as a state, the base of RGM was lost and a number of its cadres were arrested and incarcerated in Agartala jail. In 1972, the Meitei rebels with no cognisable offence were granted amnesty by Chief Minister Alimuddin. Three years later Chief Minister R.K. Dorendro Singh granted full amnesty to all of them and gave land and cash under the government rehabilitation policy.[21]

Once released from the jail, the rebels including Nameirakpam Bisheswar Singh along with 16 others, who were indoctrinated with Maoist thought while in jail, left for Lhasa on 14 June 1975, to seek Chinese assistance. The team returned to Manipur in 1976 after receiving extensive training in 'Marxism-Leninism and Mao Thoughts' as well as guerrilla warfare. Two years later, on 25 September 1978, Bisheswar formed the Revolutionary People's Front (RPF) and its armed wing the People's Liberation Army (PLA) modelled on the Zomiese PLA to achieve independence through armed struggle.[22] This was the first underground organisation which openly declared itself as Maoist. Nearly a year earlier on 9 October 1977, R.K. Tulachandra founded the People's Revolutionary Party of Kangleipak (PREPAK) with a primary demand to expel 'outsiders' from Manipur and establish an independent Manipur.[23] The UNLF had also reorganised itself under Rajkumar Meghen.

In 1978, these three insurgent organisations started urban guerrilla warfare in the Imphal Valley.[24] Another organisation, the Kangleipak Communist Party (KCP) which was formed on 13 April 1980, with the twin objectives of preservation of Meitei culture and demands for secession of Manipur from India, further contributed to the violence.[25] The number of persons killed in acts of violence went up from two in 1978 to 14 in 1979, 36 in 1980, and 51 in 1981.[26] The Meitei insurgency however, was partially tackled by the Indian security establishment when it was successful in either eliminating or incarcerating a number of top leaders and cadres. Besides counter insurgency operations, splits and surrenders further weakened these insurgent groups. At the same time, it is to be noted that the fighting capacities of these insurgent groups, especially the PLA remained intact.

As a result, while the Meitei insurgency did subside, but after a hiatus of few years it raised its head again. A fresh impetus to insurgency in Manipur was received when the UNLF and the PLA secured the assistance of the Kachin Independence Army (KIA) to arm and train their cadres in the late 1980s. However, after the KIA signed a truce with the Myanmar government in 1990, it withdrew its support to the Indian insurgent groups. It was at that point that the UNLF and the PLA shifted their bases from Myanmar to Bangladesh. In Bangladesh, these groups received material support from the Bangladesh government as well as the Pakistan's ISI.[27] In addition, the insurgent groups were able to procure arms and ammunition from the black markets of Cambodia and other Southeast Asian countries.

In the early 1990s, the three major Meitei insurgent groups namely the PLA, the PREPAK and the KCP also formed a united front of Meitei extremists called the Revolutionary Joint Committee (RJC) to coordinate their secessionist activities and to fight as a united front. The Meitei insurgents who had hitherto confined their activities only to the Imphal valley gradually started operating in the hills of Manipur also. In 1994, another insurgent group named the Kanglei Yawol Kanna Lup (KYKL) was formed after the merger of various factions of the UNLF, the PREPAK and the KCP. The objective of the KYKL is to 'rebuild' the Manipuri society by clearing it of all vices like immoral activities, drug trade and corruption.[28] In fact, a number of Meitei insurgent groups had redefined struggle against societal vices as one of their objectives. Furthermore, in March 1999, the UNLF, the PREPAK and the RPF who had been fighting separately for an 'independent Manipur', decided to form a common front called the Manipur People's Liberation Front (MPLF) to 'remove the slow progress of liberation struggle because of lack of unity among the revolutionary parties.'[29]

By the late 1990s, the Meitei insurgent groups had stepped up their activities. Easy access to financial resources through extortion and siphoning off developmental funds had enabled them to procure weapons and recruit a large number of cadres. Safe havens in Myanmar and Bangladesh allowed them to recoup, train, plan, and launch future offensives and hide in the neighbouring countries when pursued by the Indian security forces. The nexus between insurgent groups, politicians and bureaucrats ensured that the insurgent groups not only get lucrative contracts but are also shielded from arrests and judicial trials. As a result, violence levels had gradually increased since 2000s and peaked in 2009. For example, in 2003 there were 243 violent incidents in which 365 rebels were either killed or arrested.[30] In 2009, this figures rose to 659 incidents with 336 rebels killed and 1532 arrested.[31]

Since then violence levels have come down gradually, but have not stopped altogether. In fact, in 2019 Meitei insurgency accounted for about 60 per cent of insurgency related incidents in the state.[32] This is because unlike insurgent groups belonging to other ethnic groups in the state such as the Nagas and the Kukis who have suspended their activities and some are also engaged in peace talks with the Union and the state governments, the Meitei insurgent groups (except few splinter groups) have not suspended their activities or come forward for peace talks.

The reason for the Meitei groups' refusal to enter into a political dialogue with the Union government is the fear that the Union government could compromise the territorial integrity of Manipur in order to placate the Nagas in the ongoing Naga Peace Talks given that the Nagas have always demanded the incorporation of Naga inhabited areas of Manipur in Greater Nagalim. The Meitei resistance to the demands of the Nagas can be gauged by the fact that the decision of the Union government to extend the ceasefire with the NSCN (I-M) 'without territorial limits' in 2001 was understood by the Meiteis as an implicit recognition of the Naga demands by the government thereby drawing sharp reaction from them.[33]

The Naga and Kuki-Zomi Insurgencies

Besides Meitei insurgency, Manipur has also been witnessing violence perpetrated by the Naga and the Kuki insurgent groups. Manipur has two major tribes in the state namely the Nagas and the Kukis.[34] The Nagas inhabiting the northern Manipur hills identified themselves with the Nagas of the erstwhile Naga Hills District of Assam and espoused the secessionist demand raised by the Naga National Council (NNC) and Federal Government of Nagaland (FGN) in 1956, and later on by the National Social Council of Nagalim – Issac-Muivah (NSCN-IM) in 1980s. In fact, one of the founders of NSCN (IM), T. Muivah is a Tangkhul Naga who belongs to the Somdal (Shongran) village in Ukhrul district of Manipur. Consequently, the Manipur hills have been affected by Naga insurgency and have witnessed widespread insurgent activities.

Like the northern hills, the southern hills of Manipur also bore the brunt of Mizo insurgency during the 1960s onwards. Mizo insurgents have been demanding the unifications of Kuki-Zomi (who are akin to the Mizo tribe) inhabited areas of Manipur into Mizoram. In fact, during the Mizo insurgency, Churachandpur district was an important base for the Mizo National Front (MNF) insurgents.[35] While the insurgency in Mizoram ended with the signing of a peace accord between the MNF and the Union government in 1986, the Kuki-Zomi groups in Manipur continue to harbour discontentment and a desire to have a separate Kukiland. This desire to safeguard their interests was reinforced by the fact that the Kukis do not share cordial relationship with the preponderant Meitei community in the state. The Kukis are resentful towards the Meiteis because they feel that successive Meitei-dominated state governments kept their areas backward and did not provide them adequate political representation. The Kukis also lament the fact that the Manipur government did not make available a clearly defined territorial space for them.[36]

Added to this mix of fear and apprehension of the Kukis is their conflict with the Nagas. The Nagas and Kukis share an adversarial relationship since ancient times. The Meitei kings and British had settled the migratory Kukis in the Manipur hills to act as a buffer between the settled plain districts and the marauding Naga tribes. Throughout the colonial times also, the Nagas and Kuki were engaged in a running battle of attrition. Once Independence came and the administration started penetrating in these isolated hills, conflict over space and welfare schemes accentuated competition between the two ethnic groups. The Naga insurgency also provided an opportunity to the Nagas to seek 'revenge' against the Kukis. In fact, the Naga insurgents had devastated 60 Kuki villages in the Tamenglong and Ukhrul districts between 1956 and 1964.[37] In response, the Kukis had, in October 1958, formed a militant organisation called the Kuki National Volunteers (KNV) to reunite all Kukis residing in the Indian Union and its adjoining areas and defend themselves against the Naga militants. The organisation however soon became redundant.[38]

Since 1974, the Kuki community has been demanding the creation of a separate Sadar Hills autonomous district, made up of Kuki-dominated areas and carved out of Naga-dominated Senapati district.[39] The demand of the NSCN to include the hills inhabited by the Kukis into the Greater Nagalim in 1980s, further heightened the sense of unease among the Kukis. The Kukis were also convinced that the Union or the state government was not sensitive to their ordeal and will not protect them. So in 1988, the Kukis formed the Kuki National Organisation (KNO) and its armed wing, Kuki National Army (KNA) with an objective of uniting the Kuki inhabited lands of India and Myanmar into a single administrative unit called the 'Zalengam' (Land of freedom).[40] The simmering discontentment between the Nagas and the Kukis came to the fore in the early 1990s when Manipur witnessed one of the bloodiest clashes involving these two groups.

The clash between the Nagas and the Kukis, which started as a tussle to control smuggling network of the Moreh town in May 1992, soon went out of control. The refusal to pay 'house tax' to the Naga insurgents by the Kukis and the refusal to renew land agreement by the Nagas to the Kukis further contributed to the tensed situation.[41] What followed was a series of violent clashes between the militants belonging to the NSCN (I-M) and the KNA. In one of the bloodiest incidents on 13 September 1993, the Naga militants massacred around 115 Kuki civilians in what is known as the Joupi massacre.[42] Between 1992 and 1997, the NSCN (I-M) cadres allegedly killed scores of Kukis and destroyed about 350 villages.[43] Even though the NSCN (I-M) signed a ceasefire agreement with the Union government in 1997, clashes between the Naga and Kuki insurgents continue intermittently.

The Kukis, similarly clashed with the Paites (Zomi) in June 1997, who refused to be categorised as Kukis. This clash resulted in unspecified deaths and largescale internal displacement in Churachandpur.[44] Since then, several militant groups, each claiming to represent specific tribes have cropped up in the state. For example, the Zomi Revolutionary Army (ZRA), the Hmar People's Convention (HPC), the Hmar Revolutionary Front (HRF), the Indigenous People's Revolutionary Alliance (IRPA), etc. More often than not, multiple outfits claiming to represent the same tribe have also cropped up in the state. For example, there are 19 militant groups representing the Kuki tribes. Some of these are the Kuki Defence Force (KDF), the Kuki Independent Army (KIA), the Kuki International Force (KIF), the Kuki Liberation Front (KLF), the KNV, the Kuki Revolutionary Front (KRF), and the Kuki Security Force (KSF).

Besides, Pangals or Manipur Muslims also formed their own groups after Meitei-Pangal clash in May 1993.[45] The Meitei insurgents consider Pangal as *Mayang* meaning outsiders and therefore they resent the presence of Pangals in the valley. The Pangals have also formed their own armed groups. The People's United Liberation Front (PULF), North East Minority Front (NEMF), Islamic National Front (INF), Islamic Revolutionary Front (IRF) and United Islamic Liberation Army (UILA) are few such groups.

The Meitei-Kuki Conflict

The latest episode in ethnic conflict in the state was recorded in May-June 2023, when largescale conflict between Meitei and Kuki communities occurred. In the ensuing violence more than 180 persons were killed and property worth crores were destroyed. As mentioned earlier, the Meiteis and the Kukis shared an uneasy relation since long. However in recent years, because of some actions and decisions of the Meitei-dominated state government, the Kuki community felt a sense of discrimination and insecurity. To begin with, Chief Minister Biren Singh claimed that many illegal migrants from Myanmar who entered the state were settled by the Kuki community, mostly in the reserved and protected forests. Furthermore, the Biren Singh government also carried on with the land survey of reserve forests, protected areas, wetlands and wildlife to identify the 'encroachers', and served them eviction notices.

These drives against 'illegal encroachers' from Myanmar were interpreted by the Kukis as action against their own community because they identify the Chin refugees from Myanmar as members of their own tribe, that is, the Chin-Kuki tribe. Refuting the allegations of deliberate harassment against the Kuki community, the Manipur government claimed that of the total 291 encroachers removed from Manipur's forests between 1 January 2017 and 18 April 2023, 160 belonged to Meitei community, which shows that the Kuki community was not exclusively targeted.[46] But the Kuki community continued to remain aggrieved.

In addition, the Manipur government had also launched the 'War on Drugs' campaign in the state in 2017. The hills of Ukhrul, Senapati, Kangpokpi, Kamjong, Churachandpur and Tengnoupal districts were especially targeted as large-scale illegal cultivation of poppy was being carried out. The forcible destruction of illicit poppy cultivation and arrests of villagers were perceived by the Kuki community as depriving them of their livelihood because the 'affected cultivators' never received the compensation promised by the state government.[47] Consequently, these drives against encroachers and illicit poppy cultivators attracted large-scale protests, especially in the Kuki-dominated districts.

The state government viewed these protests as anti-government and claimed that the protesters were heavily influenced and instigated by the Kuki militant organisations especially the KNA and ZRA, who were not only providing shelter to illegal migrants from Myanmar, but also encouraging illegal poppy cultivation and drug trade. In fact, on 10 March 2023, the Biren Singh government decided to withdraw from the tripartite Suspension of Operations (SoO) agreement with the Kuki militant organisations.[48] This unilateral withdrawal from the agreement has not only upset the Kuki community but also put a question mark on the resolution of the Kuki militancy problem in the state.

The State Government's Response

Given the nature of insurgency and ethnic conflicts in Manipur, successive union and state governments have tried to bring the difficult situation under control through a series of measures. Some of these measures are discussed below.

Constitutional Measures

As discussed earlier, one of the factors that contributes to cycle of violence in Manipur is the tussle between the Meiteis residing in the plains and the tribes dwelling in the hills. Manipur has two distinct geographical features – the Imphal Valley and the Hills which surround the Valley. The Valley constitutes the five districts and the Hill constitutes 10 districts.[49] The Imphal Valley covers 10 per cent of the land area of Manipur and rest 90 per cent is covered by the Hills.

Ethnically, Manipur has three main groups – the Meiteis, the Nagas, and the Kukis. The Meiteis constitute 53 per cent of the total population and are primarily settled in the Valley districts of East and West Imphal, Thoubal, Kakching, Bishnupur and Jiribam. The Naga (17 per cent) and Kuki communities (26 per cent), which together constitute 41 per cent of the population are categorised into 34 Scheduled Tribes in the state. Both the groups of tribes inhabit the hills of Manipur. The Nagas are concentrated in the north consisting mainly of Senapati, Ukhrul, Tamenglong and Chandel districts. The Kuki tribes primarily populate the southern hills comprising Churachandpur, Kangpokpi, Chandel and Tengnoupal districts.[50]

This disproportionate spatial distribution between the Meitei community and the tribespeople is the crux of the problem. The Meitei community feels that even though they constitute 53 per cent of the population, they are confined to only 10 per cent of the land in the valley. Even in the valley, they argue that they are getting squeezed because tribespeople are buying land and settling there, while being non-tribal, they cannot buy land in the hills because of the protection provided to the tribespeople under Article 371(C) of the Constitution. The Meitei community further claims that in addition to the tribespeople, many 'outsiders' including illegal migrants from Bangladesh and Myanmar and people from rest of the country are settling in their land. They, therefore, argue that if the community has to 'preserve' and 'save the ancestral land, tradition, culture, and language', they need the ST status.[51]

The tribal communities, as evident, are opposed to the demand of the Meitei community for ST status on the grounds that Meiteis are a dominant community in the state with 40 of the 60 legislative seats occupied by them. They further argue that Meitei language is included in the Eighth Schedule of the Constitution and they are educationally, socially and economically better off than the tribespeople. Therefore, if ST status is bestowed upon the Meiteis, they will not only corner all the government jobs and other benefits, hitherto granted to the tribes by the Constitution, but also grab land belonging to the tribespeople as restrictions on purchasing land in the hills will not apply to them.

The Hill-Valley divide is most evident in the administration of these two geographical entities. During the colonial times, the British deliberately introduced the 'Hill-Valley divide' by separating the administration of the hills from the plains.[52] This divide was also accentuated by the religious divide between the two wherein the Meiteis embraced Vaishnavism patronized by the kings of Manipur and the hill people were converted to Christianity by the missionaries who were allowed to function in the Hill Areas.[53]

The British policy of keeping the tribes administratively separated from the Valley finally came to an end with lapse of British paramountcy and the enforcement of the Manipur State Constitution Act in 1947, which brought the Hills and Valley together as a common administrative unit. It is important to mention that the representatives of the Hill people tried to incorporate the rider that they will have the right to secede at the end of five years if the conditions under the Constitution are not found satisfactory.[54] This proviso was, however, not incorporated. Instead the Act states that 'it shall not apply in any matter where a specific reservation of powers is made to any Authority in the Hills under the provisions of the Manipur State Hill (Administration) Regulation, 1947.'[55]

In 1948, elections to the state Assembly were held and 18 out of 53 seats were allotted to the Hill people. Further, 17 per cent of the annual revenue was earmarked for the development of the Hill Areas.[56] The administration of the Hill Areas was laid down in the Manipur State Hill People (Administration) Regulation Act of 1947 where in the responsibility of the Hill Areas was entrusted to the Council of Ministers. The Council of Ministers had two elected Hillmen who were in charge of hill affairs, forests and agriculture. As for the administration of the Hill Areas, villages were grouped into Circles and Sub-Divisions. A Village Authority was formed where there were 20 or more tax paying houses and such an Authority was nominated by the village.

Likewise, Circle Authority was formed for each Circle who was responsible for maintenance of law and order, primary education, maintenance of bridle roads, land records, tax collections, improvement of agriculture, etc.[57] The administration of justice in the Hill Areas was conducted by the courts of Village and Circle Authorities. This system of administration in the Hill Areas of Manipur continued till 1956. In 1956, the Parliament of India passed the 'Manipur Village Authorities Act' for the administration of the Hill Areas which was implement in 1957. While the main provisions in the 1956 Act were more or less similar to that of the 1947 Act, but there were few changes also. For example, the Act determined the number of members in the Village Authority according to the number of tax paying houses in a village.

This Act provided for village councils to be democratically elected and provided reservation for women representatives. It also put certain limitations on the adjudicating power of the village chief by stipulating that the head of the state will appoint two or more members from the Village Authority to act as Village Court. The term of the members of the Village Authority was limited for a period of three years.[58] A total of 725 Village Authorities were constituted in seven subdivisions of the Hill Districts of Manipur.[59] It is important to note that while the Naga inhabited areas of Manipur had elected village chiefs, the Kuki inhabited villages did not. Kukis have a traditional system of hereditary village chieftains, who own all the land in the village. The Kuki community, therefore, opposed the elections arguing that the system of electing the village chief under the Village Authorities Act of 1956 was a means to 'do away with the rights of the chiefs over land.'[60] In fact, this fact also prompted the Kukis to demand for an autonomous homeland in 1960.

In 1963, when Manipur was declared as a Union Territory and provided with a Territorial Assembly with thirty members, the elected tribal members of the Assembly functioned as the Hill Standing Committee of the Assembly in charge of some of the affairs of the Hill Areas and some of them were also included in the Council of Minister.[61] In 1972, when Manipur was inaugurated as the 19th state of the Indian Union, the thirty member Territorial Assembly was increased to sixty member Legislative Assembly. Of these sixty members, nineteen were reserved for the STs and of the two Lok Sabha seats, one was reserved for the ST.[62]

A significant step towards the administration of the hill areas of the state was taken with the insertion of Article 371(C) in the Constitution of India. This Article provided for the enactment of the 'Manipur (Hill Areas) District Councils Act' in 1971, which was enforced in 1973 after Manipur attained statehood. Under the Act, the Hill Areas of Manipur was divided into five autonomous districts with six Autonomous District Councils (ADCs). The ADCs were: Senapti, Ukhrul, Tamenglong, Chandel and Churachandpur. The district of Senapati had two councils – Senapati and Sadar Hills, and the rest of the districts had four district councils.[63] The first elections to the Councils were held in 1973.

In addition to the ADCs, the Hill Areas Committee (HAC) was also constituted under the Manipur Legislative Assembly (Hill Areas Committee) Order of 1972. The members elected from the Hill Areas of Manipur comprise its members, who then elect a Chairman and a Vice Chairman. The HAC is the highest body 'at the legislative level to oversee the planning, implementation and monitoring of all development activities in the hill areas of the state.'[64]

Furthermore, as provided under Article 371(C) of the Constitution of India, the HAC also vets all laws affecting these hill districts.

The ADCs of Manipur are, however, fundamentally different from that of the ADCs in the other four north-eastern states, which were set up under the Sixth Schedule. First, the ADCs in Manipur were established by an Act of Parliament and not under the Sixth Schedule of the Constitution of India as Sixth Schedule was meant only for the Hill Districts of undivided Assam. Second, unlike the ADCs under the Sixth Schedule, the ADCs of Manipur are not entrusted with judicial and legislative powers. For example, the ADCs could make only byelaws on subjects of allotment, occupation or use of land for agricultural purposes and non-agricultural purposes, the use of unclassified forests, the use of canal or water courses and regulation of *jhuming* or other shifting agriculture. For appointment of and succession of Chief or headmen, inheritance of property, marriage and social reforms, the Councils could recommend to the Government of Manipur for legislation.[65]

Third, the ADCs are also given limited financial powers, which means that the ADCs are not allowed to raise revenue through other sources except imposing taxes on limited matters such as professionals, trades, callings, employment, etc.[66] Fourth, the 17 subjects that were supposedly under the 'control and administration' of the district councils were not so in reality because they were subjected to exceptions and conditions imposed by the Administrator.[67] As a consequence, the district councils were reduced to weak executive and administrative agencies.

The tribespeople of the Manipur Hill Areas could see that the ADCs in the Sixth Scheduled areas were much more powerful and autonomous compared to theirs, and, therefore, they started demanding the extension of Sixth Schedule in Manipur as well. A demand on this subject was first raised in 1974 by the HAC, following which the First Amendment to the Manipur (Hill Areas) District Councils Act of 1971 was carried on in which Section 23 was amended.[68] This amendment, however, did not satisfy the HAC. It continued to reaffirm its resolution for the extension of Sixth Schedule in the Hill Areas in 1978, 1983, and 1990.[69]

Meanwhile, a discussion on the demand for extension of Sixth Schedule for Manipur came up in Rajya Sabha in 1984 when the same was extended to Tripura. In May 1988, the Councillors and the Chairmen of the six ADCs also submitted a petition to the Union Home Minister on this issue. However between October 1988 and December 1990, the six ADCs were superseded and their administration was entrusted to the District officials of the districts concerned due to continuous resistance by the tribal groups.[70] It was during this time that the Sixth Schedule Demand Committee, Manipur (SSDCM) was formed, which along with the All Tribal Students Union, Manipur (ATSUM) carried forward the demand for extension of Sixth Schedule to Manipur.

In response to these demands, the Manipur state cabinet passed three resolutions in favour of extending the Sixth Schedule to the Hill Areas 'with certain local adjustments' on 13 May 1991, 17 August 1992 and 28 March 2001.[71] Despite committing to devolving greater autonomy to the ADCs, these resolutions could not be implemented because the state government failed to respond to the Union government's query as to what constituted 'local adjustments'.[72] One of the major factor which hinders the extension of Sixth Schedule in the Hill Areas is the strident opposition by the dominant Meitei community who fears that doing so would result in the disintegration of the state. Further, the inter-tribal tensions between the Kukis and the Nagas, and the Kukis and the Zomis in 1992 and 1997 respectively ensured that a consolidated tribal movement towards the extension of the Sixth Schedule in the Hill Areas could not be put up.[73]

Nevertheless, the demand for Sixth Schedule persisted throughout the 1990s. The tribal leaders voiced that the Autonomous District Council Act of 1971 has failed to safeguard the interests of the tribespeople of Manipur and therefore it should be repealed. An attempt at revoking the said Act was made in July 2000 when the Manipur Legislative Assembly enacted the Manipur Hill Areas Autonomous District Councils Act, 2000 (Manipur Act No.11 of 2000) which provided for repeal of the Manipur (Hill Areas) District Councils Act, 1971.[74] Since this Act was not enforced, the Legislative Assembly passed the Manipur (Hill Areas) District Councils (Second Amendment) Act of 2006, which repealed the Manipur Hill Areas Autonomous District Councils Act of 2000.[75]

Here it is important to mention that the National Commission to Review the Working of the Constitution in its Report of March 2002 had recommended the extension of the Sixth Schedule in the Hill Areas of

Manipur.[76] In September 2006, the Report of the Expert Committee observed that 'district level elected local bodies have been superseded or allowed to lapse, with interim measures continuing for decades.'[77] It further observed that there is fear that constituting elected councils would dilute the demand for Sixth Schedule status. Yet the Committee recommended that elections to district councils should be held soon, while the demand for Sixth Schedule could be examined independently.[78]

Subsequently in October 2008, the Manipur Legislative Assembly passed the Manipur (Hill Areas) District Councils (Third Amendment) Bill. The amendment reiterated the need to continue with the 1971 Act with 'necessary amendments'. It increased the total number of seats in the district council from eighteen to twenty four and provided that the elections to the district councils shall be conducted and supervised by the State Election Commission.[79] The Act also increased the number of subjects to be devolve to the ADCs from 17 to 26. The Act has been opposed on the ground that the new amendments do not provide any autonomy to the ADCs and it is the continuation of the same.

After a gap of 20 years, the Manipur government announced elections to the ADCs in April 2010. In protest, the All Naga Students' Association Manipur (ANSAM), the United Naga Council (UNC), the ATSUM, the NSCN (I-M) along with a clutch of Naga organisations imposed economic blockades between April and May 2010 by blocking the national highways that connect landlocked Manipur to rest of India. A counter-blockade was imposed by the All Manipur United Clubs Organisation and United Committee Manipur on 6 May 2010. The economic blockades were finally lifted in June 2010 after 69 days.[80]

Meanwhile, elections for the six district councils were conducted in two phases on 26 May 2010 and 2 June 2010 respectively.[81] However, voting turnout in the affected districts were uneven. For example, in the Naga dominated Senapati and Ukhrul districts, voting percentage were 33.4 and 0.86 respectively and almost all the candidates were returned uncontested. In contrast, in Chandel and Tamenglong, which are Kuki dominated districts, the voting percentage were 54.69 and 78.57 respectively.[82] The elected district councils functioned for the next five years till 2015.

The next elections for the ADCs were held in June 2015. Significantly, this time the Naga organisations did not boycott the elections because the Naga leaders realised that opposition to elections had deprived the Nagas in the hill areas not only from fulfilling their political aspirations but also from developmental funds. The UNC/ANSAM and the NSCN (I-M) also realised, albeit reluctantly, that barring people from exercising their democratic rights was preventing them from garnering popular support. Incidentally, the demand for the extension of Sixth Schedule in the Hill Areas does not find favours with the UNC and the NSCN (I-M) because they view it as a hindrance to their aim of realising the goal of integrating the Naga dominated areas of Manipur into the Greater Nagalim.[83]

It is argued that the winning pattern of the parties/candidates in the ADCs elections of 2015 indicated the preponderance of the ethnic issues and an alignment of respective desires of the Nagas and the Kukis. For example, the UNC and the NSCN (IM) tacitly supported the Naga People's Front (NPF), which also has the same objective of 'integrating all contiguous Naga inhabited areas' into the Greater Nagalim. That the NPF went on to win 43 seats in the District Councils with highest in Ukhrul (17) followed by Senapti (11), the strongholds of UNC and NSCN (I-M), underscores the fact that the Naga electorate also voted for the objective of an integrated homeland. Interestingly, the influence of these two organisations was limited in the other two Naga preponderant districts, that is, Tamenglong and Chandel, where the demography have also a mix of Kukis and Meities.[84]

Likewise, the impressive win of the Hill People's Alliance (HPA), an alliance of independent candidates in Churachandpur district indicated towards a strong desire for an autonomous Kukiland comprising Churachandpur, Chandel and the Sadar Hills. The HPA had an understanding with the United People's Front (UPF), an umbrella organisation of armed Kuki-Chin-Zomi groups, which seeks to establish an autonomous hill state for the Kukis.[85]

Be that as it may, the HAC continued with its demand for Sixth Schedule status for the Hill Areas. In continuation of their demand, the Hill Committee drafted the 'Manipur (Hill Areas) Autonomous District Councils Bill, 2021' and sent it to the state government in August 2021 for it to be tabled and enacted into legislation.[86] The new Bill proposes an increase in the number of council members from 24 to 31 with three members being nominated. It further proposes that the delimitation of the 28 constituencies be done in such a manner that three fourth of the seats are allocated according to the population and one fourth of the seats be reserved for socio-economically underdeveloped areas.[87] It proposes greater autonomy and financial powers for the ADCs. The Bill also proposes creation of Hill Areas Secretariat for managing, coordinating and monitoring the working of all the ADCs.[88]

The drafters of the new bill argue that the 1971 Act failed to achieve balanced development of the hill areas and therefore should be repealed. They further argue that the proposed Bill is drafted with the twin objectives of development of the hill areas and maintaining the territorial integrity of Manipur.

As expected the valley based civil organisations appealed to the state government not to table the bill as it contains maximum provisions for the creation of 'Naga Autonomous Territorial Council and Kuki Autonomous Territorial Council,' which are opposed by them.[89] In response, the tribal organisations have been holding protests and calling for bandhs and blockades to put pressure on the government to pass the bill. The state government on its part has been staving off tabling the bill by constituting a Committee to ascertain whether the state government has the mandate to pass such a legislation since the 1971 Bill was passed by the Parliament.[90]

These constitutional provisions were aimed at providing the tribespeople of the state an avenue to fulfil their political aspirations as well as preserve their socio-cultural practices. However, strident assertion of tribal identities, inter-community conflicts, insurgencies and inability of the ADCs to achieve objectives because of limited scope resulted in extreme polarisation of the society. It appears that till the contentious issue of extending Sixth Schedule to the Hill Areas of Manipur is not amicably resolved, the cycle of ethnic and political tensions will keep on recurring in the state.

The Legal Measures

The hills of Manipur have been witnessing insurgency related violence since the inception of Naga insurgency in 1956. The Nagas, who inhabited the hills of Assam and Manipur, had opposed the merger of their area with that of India at the time of Independence on the grounds that they were racially and socio-politically different from the Indians. The Nagas of the erstwhile Naga

Hill District of Assam had voted in favour of a referendum declaring independence in 1951, and raised the banner of revolt against the Indian Union. The Nagas of Manipur also identify themselves with the 'Naga cause' and supported the integration of contiguous Naga inhabited areas to create the Greater Nagalim. So, when the NNC formed the FGN on 22 March 1956 and intensified violence, it affected not only the Naga Hill District of Assam but also the Hill Areas of Manipur.

As the governments of the Assam and Manipur expressed their inability to tackle the insurgency, the Union government sent in the army to quell the rebellion and restore normalcy in the region. At the same time, the President of India promulgated the Armed Forces (Assam and Manipur) Special Powers Ordinance on 22 May 1958 to confer 'special powers' on the armed forces as well as to provide them with the legal framework to function in the 'disturbed areas' of Assam and Manipur.[91] A bill seeking to replace the ordinance was introduced in the monsoon session of the Parliament on 18 August 1958. The bill, however, faced opposition. Several members of Parliament argued that giving such sweeping powers to the armed forces would lead to the violation of the fundamental rights of the people. Laishram Achaw Singh, a Member of Parliament from Manipur, described the bill as a 'lawless law'.[92] The Bill was passed after a debate of seven hours and received the President's assent on 11 September 1958 and notified as the AFSPA, 1958.[93]

The preamble of the Act states that certain special powers are conferred upon the members of the armed forces in the disturbed areas of the state of Assam and the union territory of Manipur. Section 3 of the Act empowered the governor/administrator of the state/union territory to use the armed forces to aid the civilian power if he was of the opinion that the situation was disturbed enough to demand such an action. He could do so by declaring the entire state/union territory, or a part of it, as a disturbed area through a notification in the official gazette. This Section was amended in 1972 when the Union government was provided with concurrent powers to declare any state, or part of it, as disturbed given that the Union government under Article 355 of the Constitution of India is responsible for protecting every state against internal disturbance.[94]

As regards 'special powers', Section 4 of the Act confers upon any commissioned officer, warrant officer, non-commissioned officer or any other person of equivalent rank in the armed forces, the power to shoot, kill and arrest without warrant, any person he suspects; as well as enter and search without warrant or destroy any premises he believes are sheltering the rebels. The 'special powers' to open fire, even causing death, however, is not unfettered. It is qualified by two clauses. First, the power to open fire is given in a disturbed area where the assembly of five or more persons or the carrying of weapons is forbidden. Second, if a person is seen as violating such a law.[95]

Section 5 of the Act stipulates that any person who is arrested should be handed over to the nearest police station with least possible delay along with the report of his arrest. The 'least possible delay' being, within 24 hours of the person's arrest. Finally, Section 6 provides immunity to the armed forces personnel against arrest or prosecution for anything done or alleged to have been done in the discharge of official duties except after obtaining the consent of the Union government.[96]

In 1961, Ukhrul, Mao-Maram and Tamenglong sub-divisions were declared disturbed areas under Section 3 of the AFSPA, and the army took over the control of operations in these areas.[97] Envisaged to be enforced only for a period of one year, the AFSPA continued to be in force in the Naga-inhabited areas of Manipur. In 1964, an insurgent movement demanding the separation of Manipur from the Indian Union was launched by the UNLF. In 1969, as the insurgent activities of the RGM and the political activities of Meitei State Committee intensified, the Manipur government found it extremely difficult to contain the situation. As a result, President's Rule was imposed in Manipur on 16 October 1969.

This outbreak of insurgencies also necessitated enforcement of the AFSPA in Manipur, albeit, in a phased manner. In 1970, the State Home Department through a series of notifications declared parts of Manipur South (now Churachandpur) District, Manipur West (now Tamenglong) District, Manipur East (now Ukhrul) District, Manipur North (now Senapati) District, and Sadar Hills Sub-division of Manipur North District as 'disturbed areas' under the AFSPA. In October 1975, the entire Tengnoupal (now Chandel) District was declared disturbed. In May 1978, the whole area of Manipur South District, Jiribam Sub Division of Manipur Central District and Tengnoupal District were covered under the Act.

In 1980, the entire state of Manipur was declared 'disturbed area'.[98] Since then, the AFSPA has remained continuously enforced in the state. Most recently on 21 December 2021, the state government extended the 'disturbed area' provision of the AFSPA for one more year because of "the violent activities of extremist/insurgent groups" in the state.[99] The extension of the AFSPA continues even though there has been widespread protests against the Act and demands for revoking it because of several human rights violations by the security forces. The most prominent being in 2004 when Thanjam Manorama Devi was allegedly killed by the soldiers of Assam Rifles in cold blood.[100] Following the protests, the state government modified the notification under the AFSPA and excluded Imphal Municipal Area from 'disturbed area' status.[101] On 1 April 2022, the Union government withdrew the AFSPA from 15 police station areas in 6 districts of Manipur.[102] And a year later in April 2023, AFSPA was removed from four more police stations in view of 'significant improvement in law and order situation in the state.'[103]

In addition to the AFSPA, the West Bengal Security Act of 1950 was also extended to Manipur on 27 June 1961 with suitable modifications.[104] The Act 'make[s] special provision for the maintenance of public order by the prevention of illegal acquisition, possession or use of arms, the suppression of subversive movements endangering communal harmony or the safety or stability of the State and the suppression of goondas and for maintaining supplies and services essential to the life of the community.'[105]

The Act provided for declaration of any area as protected and denial of entry of persons in the said area without the authority for maintenance of law and order. The police was empowered to search and detain any person who entered such protected areas without permission. If found guilty the person is jailed for three years or fined or both. There are also provisions for jail terms for persons indulging in sabotage or carrying weapons or looting, etc. The Act also stipulated that the Chief Commissioner should constitute an Advisory Board and place before it the order to impose the Act within a month of issuance of the order for the Board to opine on the validity of the cause to impose the Act. The Act remained in force in Manipur till 25 January 1966.[106]

Besides, the Union government has also invoked the UAPA 'to provide for the more effective prevention of certain unlawful activities of individuals and associations, [and for dealing with terrorist activities,] and for matters connected therewith.'[107] Under this Act, a number of insurgent organisations are termed as terrorist organisations and are banned. These are: (i) the PLA and its political wing the RPF; (ii) the UNLF and its Armed wing the MPA, (iii) the PREPAK, (iv) the KCP, (v) the KYKL, (vi) Coordination Committee (Cor-Com), (vii) Alliance for Socialist Unity Kangleipak (ASUK), and (viii) the MPLF.

These legal measures facilitated the Union government to deploy the armed forces as well as the CAPFs in the state to fight insurgency. At the same time, these measures also provide the armed forces the required legal immunity to discharge their duties efficiently.

Security Measures

In the initially period, the Manipur police was the primary response instrument for fighting insurgency and restoring order in the state. For example, in 1948 when the Mao Nagas raised their demand for merger of Mao area with the Naga Hills and the Krishak Sangha under the leadership of Hijam Irabot started a secessionist movement, the Manipur police was called in to tackle the problems. At the time of Manipur's integration with the Indian union in 1949, Manipur had only five police stations and seven outposts with 46 officers and 330 constables in civil police and 115 personnel in Manipur Rifles.[108] However, as problems of insurgencies and ethnic clashes increased in the province, the strength of the state police proved inadequate and the government had to borrow additional companies of armed police from other states.

For example, when the Naga insurgency flared up in the later part of 1956 in the hill areas, in addition to the Manipur Rifles, which was deployed in Tamenglong, Mao and Ukhrul sub-divisions, the state government borrowed two companies of the Eastern Rifles from West Bengal and deployed them in Tamenglong sub-division.[109] Similarly, in 1960 when clashes between Kukis and Hmars broke out in Churachandpur, Jiribam and Tamenglong sub-divisions, the Manipur government deployed the companies of Bihar Military Police to bring the situation under control. Besides, the Assam Rifles was also deployed in the hill areas of Manipur to tackle the Naga insurgents in the state in 1956. Finally, the Indian army was deployed in 1961 to fight against the Naga rebels operating in the Manipur hills.

As a result of the sustained counterinsurgency operations against the Naga insurgents by the security forces, the law and order situation begun to improve from the later half of 1961. That rule of law was established in the affected areas of the state can be gauged from the fact that general elections were conducted successfully in 1962 despite a boycott call given by the Naga insurgents. In the subsequent years, the strength of the Manipur Rifles was periodically increased and as a result the force was successful in responding to the Naga insurgency. In addition, the Village Voluntary Force (VVF) was also raised by the Special Service Bureau (SSB) in 1966 'to protect the villages and deprive support for insurgents and also assist in counter-insurgency operations of the Indian Army and Central Paramilitary forces.'[110]

These measures contributed immensely in improving the security situation in the state. For example, during 1968-69 because of effective police action, Ukhrul sub-division was cleared of insurgent activities, and in Mao, civil administration was restored. During that time, a total of 301 Naga insurgents had surrendered, 439 were captured and 15 were killed in encounters with the police and the VVF. A large quantity of arms and ammunition were also recovered, which included 535 guns and rifles.[111] In 1970, the largescale deployment of the Indian army in the eastern part of the country because of the political turmoil in erstwhile East Pakistan enabled the government to carry out intensive counter insurgency operations against the Meitei rebels. As mentioned earlier, the Army along with the Assam Rifles were able to crush the RGM and its cadres.

In 1980 with the imposition of the AFSPA in entire state, the army, the Assam Rifles, the CRPF and the BSF were deployed to tackle the Meitei insurgency. The counter insurgency operations launched by the security forces were very effective not only in containing the violence but also in decimating the insurgent cadres and their leaders. For example, almost all the China trained leaders of the PLA were either captured or killed in just two encounters. The first encounter happened in 1981 which led to the arrest of N. Bisheshwar, and the second in April 1982 when his successor Kunjabehari Singh was killed.[112] In November 1985, the PREPAK leader R.K. Tulachandra was killed by the Manipur Rifles.[113]

Counter insurgency operations picked up again in the state after a resurgence in militancy in the end of 1980s. The valley based insurgent groups largely operated in the valley and the hills and jungles of the Chandel district where they had set up training camps. However by mid-1990s, because of the intense counter insurgency operations, some of the PLA rebels came over ground and even contested state elections.[114] However, insurgency in the state got a new fillip in 2001 when the Union government implemented the ceasefire agreement with the NSCN (I-M) 'without territorial limits'. This meant that the Manipur hills inhabited by the Nagas were also covered under the agreement, which was obviously unacceptable to the Meiteis and the valley based insurgent groups. As a result, large scale violence took place in the state in which the state assembly building was burnt down.[115]

In 2004, following agitations against the killing of Manorama Devi and for the withdrawal of the AFSPA, a Unified Command structure was constituted in Manipur. The Command was headed by the chief minister with representatives from the Indian army, the Assam Rifles, state police and Intelligence.[116] The idea was to launch joint operations of the Indian army and the Assam Rifles in coordination with the state police to provide better coordination and more transparency to such operations. In addition, a SOG was also constituted under the chairmanship of the chief secretary along with representatives from the Indian army, the Assam Rifles, the CRPF, the BSF, the state police and the Intelligence agencies to assess the security situation in the state, and plan and launch counter insurgency operations.

However, the Unified Command and the SOG remained in paper only. This can be ascertained from the fact that there were several counter insurgency operations which were carried by the Indian army but the state forces rarely participated. For example, in 2005, counter insurgency operations such as Stringer and Tornado were launched to 'flush out' militants from Loktak and Jiribam areas of the state. These operations resulted in the killing of 143 militants and arrest of 306 belonging to the UNLF, the PLA, and the PREPAK.[117] In the next few years also, similar operations were carried out. However, a look at the operations reveal that those were conducted primarily by the Indian army with the Assam Rifles and the Manipur Rifles occasionally participating in such operations.

These operations, however, could not make a dent in the fighting capacity of the valley based insurgent groups. Consequently, additional security forces were deployed in the state over the years. Thus, by November 2009, the number of security forces deployed in the state were as follows: Manipur Rifles and India Reserve Battalions: six battalions each (10, 396); civil police: 5056; CRPF and BSF: six battalions each (10,450), Army: ten battalions; Assam Rifles: 26 battalions; Home Guards: 2312.[118] All these security forces were mandated to maintain public order in the state. In addition to the security forces, Manipur has also raised VDF in 2008 as an informal layer of surveillance and defence against the insurgents. A Volunteer of the VDF is paid a sum of Rs 8500/- per month, provided with weapons and tasked with the duties of guarding vital installations, road opening duties during public unrest and sentry duties.[119]

Despite deploying large number of security personnel and constituting structures to create synergies among the various security forces engaged in counter-insurgency operations in the state, the security situation in the state continues to remain dire. One of the factors for this malaise is the lack of coordination and distrust among the security forces. It is argued that while the working relation between the Indian army, the paramilitary and the CAPFs is good, there is mutual distrust between the central security forces and the state police force. The central forces perceive the state police as a corrupt force which enriches itself by collecting money at check points or highways and colludes with insurgent groups.[120] The state police on their part distrust the central forces and are unwilling to cooperate claiming highhandedness of the central forces.

The dynamics of army deployment and the dynamics of ceasefire and SoO agreements also create constraints in effectively combating insurgency operations in the state. In recent times as tensions along the India-China border escalated, most units of Indian army were pulled out of the state and re-deployed. Even those that are presently deployed in the state are meant for quick mobilisation against external threats only. They are not mandated to carry counter insurgency operations. As a result, large gaps are created in the affected areas where there is no security presence to carry out counter insurgency operations.[121]

The withdrawal of the Indian army from the counter insurgency operations has put the entire responsibility of tackling the insurgents on the Assam Rifles. Unfortunately, the force finds it difficult to saturate the affected areas and dominate them because it is stretched to the maximum. In addition to counter insurgency duties, the Assam Rifles is also mandated to guard the India-Myanmar border. This dual role has affected the operational efficiency of the force[122] because challenges of smuggling of drugs, weapons and contraband

and cross-border movement of insurgents and people are increasing, and the Assam Rifles is compelled to deploy more battalions near the border leaving the hinterland loosely guarded for the insurgents to fill the vacuum.[123] The attack on a convoy of the Assam Rifles and the killing of the commanding officer along with his family and four jawans at Singhat subdivision in Churachandpur district in November 2021 is a case in point.[124]

The poor implementation of the ceasefire and SoO agreements also creates confusions and contributes towards violence in the state. A number of Kuki and break away Meitei insurgents groups have entered into ceasefire and SoO agreements with the Union and the state governments. However, the cadres belonging to various Kuki-Zomi rebel groups engage in fratricidal killings, turf wars, extortion, kidnappings, interfere in development programme, besides intimidating the masses.[125] Even though the security forces are aware that the crimes are perpetrated by the surrendered insurgent groups, they do not launch any counter insurgency operations because the insurgent groups are in SoO. And even when a rebel is apprehended, he claims that he belongs to one of the outfits under SoO agreement and the security forces do not have an option but to set him free.[126]

These cadres also influence elections to the state legislative assembly and the ADCs. In the recently held legislative Assembly polls, the Kukis had reportedly asked the people to vote for the BJP[127] after the Union government allegedly released around Rs16 crores for the Kuki militant groups under SoO agreement.[128] The ceasefire agreements with the NSCN-IM and NSCN (Khango) are not extended to the Manipur hills where both the Naga rebel outfits are active. As a result, the Naga rebels indulge in fratricidal and ethnic killings, extortion and kidnappings with impunity.

Organisational problems in the state police force in the form of poor morale, indiscipline and absence of dynamic and resolute leadership is another factor for the failure of successive state governments to combat insurgency. It is often alleged that the state police are a law unto themselves. For example in 2018, the state police department constituted a dedicated special commando unit to tackle law and order situation including insurgency. These commandoes comprising 20 officers and 256 men were selected from the state police pool and were given special training.[129] However, because of poor leadership this force reportedly soon deteriorated and even started functioning independently.

The police personnel not only indulged in extortion and kidnapping for petty monetary gains but also carried out several 'encounters' of rebels as well as innocent people.[130] Arbitrary arrests and detention by the police are also a routine feature in Manipur, which has alienated the general masses.

Another factor responsible for the lack of morale and discipline in the police force is political interference. This is evident from the following cases. In 2002, the personnel of Manipur Rifles refused to go on transfer postings arguing that it would dislocate their families.[131] Instead of taking disciplinary action against the personnel, the state government put on hold their transfers. Decrying the indiscipline in the state armed police, the opposition parties had accused the Ibobi Singh government of corruption in transfer and postings of these police personnel.

In fact such was the corruption in government postings and transfers that the N. Biren Singh's government approved a new Transfer and Posting Policy in December 2017 to address the malaise. The policy made it mandatory for every government servant to serve in the hills. It further states, 'Any Government servant who brings or attempts to bring any political or other external influence to bear upon any authority to further his/her interest in respect of matters pertaining to services under the Government, including transfers, shall be liable to be severely dealt with and action may be taken against him/her for violation of Rule 20 of the Civil Services Conduct Rules.'[132]

Political interference can also be observed in arrests of militants. It has been alleged that 'if an insurgent has a political connection, the police will not arrest him unless the matter is cleared by the political leadership.'[133] Such actions robbed the police force in Manipur of its professionalism and dedication to duty.

Political Measures

Insurgencies and ethnic tensions are best resolved through political dialogues and settlements. However, the political leadership in Manipur does not appear to be willing to engage with the insurgent groups to arrive at a political settlement. One example that can be cited to prove the argument is the claim by the then chief minister Ibobi Singh that he was not aware of the signing of the SoO agreement between the Kuki groups and the Indian army to cease hostilities and suspend operations in August 2005.[134] The Ibobi Singh government was reportedly opposed to the agreement and in one of the cabinet meetings on 21 September 2005, it 'decided not to respond to the Centre's directions to accept the army's suspension of operations (SOO) with the Kuki groups without further "clarifications."'[135] The state government also decided that 'any arrangement contemplated or finalised for SOO and subsequent negotiations will not be acceptable to the state government if these involve discussions/negotiation about issues relating to the territorial integrity of the state or adversely affects the interests of its people, at any stage or in any way.'[136]

This stand of the state government reflects the fact that the Meitei dominated political establishment is partisan and does not favour any concessions either to the Kuki or the Naga insurgent groups. It is reported that almost all the ministers including the chief minister belonging to the dominant Meitei community espouse the cause of the Meitei insurgents. Such a stand against any political settlement could also be because of the nexus between the political parties and the insurgent groups. These linkages have proved to be beneficial for both the parties as the political leaders take the help of the militant groups to influence the voters during elections and the insurgent groups exploit their proximity to the political leaderships to evade arrests and to siphon off development funds. In fact, the MHA citing an Indian army Report stated in Parliament on 25 April 2001 that five ministers of the Nipamacha Singh government had links with terrorists belonging to the NSCN-K, PLA, UNLF, KYKL and ZRA groups. This nexus was quite evident when in November 2000, two Kuki rebels were arrested from the then Transport Minister Haokholet Kipgen's official residence.[137] Even the Chief Minister Ibobi Singh had paid Rs. 50 Lakhs and Rs. 1 Crore to KYKL and RPF respectively, receipts of which were made available to the media.[138]

Be that as it may, successive state governments did try to reach out to the insurgent groups but did not succeed. In February 2001, Chief Minister Radhabinod Koijam offered a unilateral month-long cease-fire commencing 1 March 2001 to 17 outfits in the state. As a follow up to this gesture, on 19 March 2001, Governor Ved Marwah announced the setting up of a contact group to liaison with extremist organisations in the state. Unfortunately, these peace overtures of the state governments were rejected by the rebel outfits.[139]

A new beginning towards ushering in peace in the state was made on 22 August 2008, when 23 insurgent outfits (later increased to 25) belonging to the Kuki, Zo, Paite and Hmar groups organised themselves under two umbrella organisations, KNO and UPF, and signed a SoO with the Union and the Manipur governments.[140] According to the tripartite agreement, the groups agreed to abjure violence and not engage in any unlawful activities and agreed to be housed in 13 designated camps which are built away from major highways and the international boundary. For the enforcement of the ground rules and monitoring of the same a Joint Monitoring Group comprising representatives from the state government, the CRPF, Assam Rifles and the Indian army deployed in the state of Manipur was constituted.[141]

In another significant move to bring peace in Manipur, many breakaway rebels belonging to the KCP, the Manipur Army and the KYKL have come together and formed the United Revolutionary Front (URF) and entered into a ceasefire agreement with the Government of India in 2013. In 2017, in an effort to attract more and more rebels to surrender, the Union government increased the monthly stipend for the surrendered insurgent from Rs 4,000 to Rs 8,000, and the one-time financial grant was hiked to Rs 4 lakh from Rs 2.5 lakh.[142]

In addition to the ceasefire and SoO agreement, the KNO and the Naga National Political Group (NNPG) signed an accord on 10 January 2020, to end inter-tribal conflict by recognising the history and identity of each other.[143] These agreements have helped in reducing the number of violent incidents to some extent, but Manipur's security situation continues to be grim. One of the reasons is the failure of the union and the state governments to conclude a negotiated settlement with these surrendered groups. For example, tripartite talks between the Union government, the state government and the KNO/UPF to discuss the political demand of the KNO and the UPF was held on 15 June 2016, nearly eight years after signing of the agreements. This was followed by two more rounds on 19 October 2016 and on 9 August 2017.[144] Both the KNO and the UPF have submitted their political demands, but no headway could be made because of the disparity in the demands of these two outfits. While the KNO demands a separate Kuki State, the UPF has insisted on a state-within a state under Article 244A of the Indian Constitution.

While the state government does not seem to give in to the demands of the Kukis as it fears that the interests of the Meitei community will be compromised, ironically it blames the Union government and the security forces of insincerity as the reason for the failure to conclude a peace settlement. At the same time to show that it is sensitive to the demands of the Kuki groups, the Manipur government, on 9 December 2016, carved out the Kangpokpi district, which roughly conforms to the boundaries of the proposed Sadar Hills District. This decision, it claims will, fulfil the long held demand of the Kukis for a separate district for them.[145] The Kuki groups, however, lament that this decision is too little too late.[146]

That the Meitei dominated Legislative Assembly is biased towards the dominant community can be observed by how issues relating to land is handled in the state. Land is a major issue in Manipur and a source of conflict in the state. The land in the state is managed in two ways: a) by customary laws in the Hill Areas, and b) by the Manipur Land Revenue and Land Reforms (MLR&LR) Act of 1960 in the plain areas.[147] Although as a rule the Act is not to be implemented in the Hill Areas, over the course of time, the state has begun to implement the Act in the Hill Areas of the state as well.[148] Such actions by the state have allegedly resulted in land alienation among the tribespeople. The fact that the ADCs do not have the right to legislate on the subject of land has added to the apprehensions of the tribespeople.

To make matters worse, on 31 August 2015, the Manipur government passed three 'contentious' Bills'. These are: the Protection of the Manipur People Bill, the Manipur Shops and Establishments (Second Amendment) Bill and the Manipur Land Revenue and Land Reforms (Seventh Amendment) Bill.[149] The passage of the Bills in the Legislative Assembly resulted in widespread violence in the state, especially in the Hill Areas. The reason for the violence was the perception among the tribal people that the Bills, especially the Protection of the Manipur People Bill panders to the sentiments and pressures of the dominant community while undermining the interests of the hill people.

It is alleged that the Bill on Protection of the Manipur People addressed the anxiety and insecurity of the Meitei middle class who feel besieged by the migrant 'outsiders' and paved the way for the implementation of the Inner Line Permit system in the state to regulate the entry of 'outsiders' in the state.[150] The Bill, however, proved to be detrimental for the tribals because it defines 'Manipuri People' as 'Persons of Manipur whose names are in the National Register of Citizens of 1951, the Census Report of 1951 and the Village

Directory of 1951 and their descendants who have contributed collectively to social, cultural and economic life of Manipur.'[151] The tribespeople argue that since the village chiefs during the 1950s were illiterate they did not keep any records. The Census officials also hardly visited the Hill Areas during that time because of their remote location and poor connectivity. As a result there are no village or Census records of the residents of the Hill Areas. Given the lack of proper documentation in the Hill Areas, the tribespeople will find it difficult to prove that they are the 'natives' of Manipur.[152] The fact that these Bills were passed without consulting the HAC further reinforces the apprehensions of the tribespeople against the dominant Meitei community.

Governance

In 2021, Manipur was placed ninth in the overall ranking among the category of North-East and Hill States in the Good Governance Index (GGI).[153] The Index ranks states according to the status of governance. It revealed that Manipur had registered the highest decline of -11.2 per cent.[154] Manipur is also placed in the bottom of the table among its category of states as far as Human Development Index (HDI) is concerned. Manipur's score has also declined on quality of education, retention rate at Elementary Level and enrolment ratio among the ST and Scheduled Castes (SC).[155] Manipur is ranked the lowest in Commerce and Industry Sector and has registered higher debt to the Gross State Domestic Product (GSDP).

Manipur was also adjudged the worst governed state among the small states in India by a Bangalore based Public Affairs Centre in 2021. The assessment was based upon the performance in three categories – equity, growth and sustainability.[156] In other words, Manipur does not have adequate and quality governance and has poorly implemented the five centrally sponsored scheme, which have direct effect on the quality of life of the people, especially those residing in the rural areas. These schemes are: MGNREGS, NRHM, ICDS, SSA and the MMS. NITI Aayog's Sustainable Development Goal (SDG) India Index ranks Manipur at the lowest in decent work and economic growth.[157]

One of the reasons for Manipur to perform so badly on the governance index is the fact that the state is riddled with corruption. Corruption is a reality and an open secret in Manipur.[158] As is evident, corruption has resulted not only in failure of governance but also increasing the magnitude of scams in the state. One of the biggest scams was the siphoning off of allowances and dues amounting to crores of rupees from the Manipur Rifles personnel during 1996 to 1998 by top officials. The Public Distribution rice scam in 2013 and the scams over Loktak Lake and Mapithel Dam are other examples of widespread corruption in the state.[159] Such is the extent of corruption in the state that:

> Tankers carrying petrol, diesel and kerosene oil were diverted from the big authorized dealers and sold in the black market by all the major underground groups. These [insurgent] groups also diverted rice from the Public Distribution System (PDS) from all the dealers, with a part taken for supplying the underground camps. Rice, kerosene, petrol and diesel were also sold in the black market. Against the quota of five litres per family per month of kerosene oil, most people were getting only one or two litres in Imphal, while in the interior towns and villages, there was no penetration of the PDS supply at all.[160]

On top of it all, the state government's writ either does not run or is very tenuous is the insurgency affected areas. This aspect can be gauged from the fact that militant organisations continue to exact taxes from the residents of the state. Initially, the militant groups extorted money from the politicians, top bureaucrats and the businessmen, but later on all salaried persons were also asked to pay "taxes". In fact, by the 1990s the entire system of extortion had become institutionalised with the 'cashiers of different government departments were directed to deduct certain percentages according to the rank of the official and pay the amount to the underground organisation.'[161]

In fact, according to a media report, 'The "tax" imposed by the militants ranges from five percent (of the income) for a small farmer or petty trader to 12 or even 15 percent for a senior officer or an affluent businessman. And on top of this, 15 to 20 percent of the outlay on any project, even a small road repairing work, goes into the militants' pockets. Every item that's sold in Manipur is "taxed" by the militants.'[162] The militant groups also issue decrees dictating the masses to abide by them or face consequences. These decrees range from banning the sale and consumption of liquors and drugs, banning screening of movies, banning government doctors from working in private clinics, dictating people to wearing traditional local dress, etc. The militants have also succeeded in muzzling the voice of the civil society lest they raise their voice against the taxation and the decrees.

The fact that militants can operate in the state with such immunity is because of the political patronage. As mentioned earlier, several political parties in the state, including the national parties, have close connections with various insurgent groups. Manipur receives huge funds for fighting militancy, but most of the funds are siphoned off by politicians, bureaucrats, police officers and even high-ups in the army and para-military forces, besides the militant groups.[163] In fact, it is being argued that militancy in Manipur is allowed to flourish because once it ends, not only will the funds dry up but there will be clamour for development and transparency in governance, issues that do not suit the politicians, the bureaucrats and the security forces.[164]

Summary

Manipur has plunged into a cycle of violence since the communist rebellion of 1948-52. While the communist rebellion was called off, it did create grounds for future insurgencies to take roots. The perceived 'humiliation' felt by the collective Meitei community after the merger of the Kingdom and the granting of statehood to Nagaland triggered Meitei insurgency in the state. Besides the Meitei separatist movement, the Nagas and the Kukis who inhabit the Hill Areas of Manipur have also been up in arms against not only the Indian state but also against each other.

The union and the state governments have been trying to address the grievances of the people by implementing various constitutional, political and security measures. Towards this end, the granting of statehood as well as general amnesty to the Meitei rebels had, to some extent, assuaged the 'hurt sentiments' of the Meitei, but those were not enough. Similarly, to safeguard the interests of the Nagas and Kukis, the Union government bestowed ST status on them and reserved seats for them in the state assembly as well as in the Parliament. It also provided for setting up of ADCs and a Hill Area Council within the state assembly for vetting all laws affecting these hill districts.

However, the refusal of the major Meitei rebel groups to give up their separatist demands and enter into a political dialogue with the Union and/or state government is a major hindrance to peace in the state. Moreover, it appears that successive state governments, dominated by the Meitei community have not been keen on arriving at any political settlement with the Meitei rebels as most of them, espouse the rebels' cause. Furthermore, the politically dominant Meitei leaders do not want to give into the genuine demands of the Nagas or the Kukis, which they perceive would jeopardise the territorial unity of the state. In the absence of a common meeting ground among the three communities and in absence an efficient and inclusive governance, violence continues to persist making peace elusive in Manipur.

NOTES

1. *Annual Report 2019-2020*, New Delhi: Ministry of Home Affairs, 2020, p. 16.
2. *Annual Report 2021-2022*, New Delhi: Ministry of Home Affairs, 2022, p. 21.
3. Sanatomba Kangujam, 'Was Irabot in favour of complete independence', *E-Pao*, 2 October 2013 at http://e-pao.net/epSubPageExtractor.asp?src=manipur.History_of_Manipur. Article _ Hijam_ Irabot.Was_Irabot_in_favour_of_complete_independence, accessed on 17 February 2022.
4. Naorem Sanajaoba, 'The Genesis of Insurgency', in Naorem Sanajaoba (ed.) *Manipur Past and Present,* Volume I, Delhi: Mittal Publications, 1988, p. 246.
5. *Ngangam Mahendra Singh and Ors. vs Manipur State*, High Court of Gauhati, 19 November, 1951 at https://www.the-laws.com/Encyclopedia/Browse/Case?CaseId=601591120000&Case Id=601591120000, accessed on 17 February 2022.
6. n. 4.
7. E. Girani, 'Hijam Irawat And His Movements In Manipur: A Humanistic Revolutionary', *Journal of Emerging Technologies and Innovative Research*, High Court of Gauhati, Vol. 7 (4), April 2020, p. 1771.
8. *Manipur Merger Agreement, 1949* at https://www.satp.org/satporgtp/countries/india/states/manipur/documents/papers/manipur_merger_agreement_1949.htm, accessed on 17 February 2022.
9. *Manipur State Constitution Act, 1947* at https://www.ohchr.org/sites/default/files/lib-docs/HRBodies/UPR/Documents/Session1/IN/COHR_IND_UPR_ S1_2008anx_ Annex_IV_ Manipur_State_Constitution_Act%2C_1947.pdf, accessed on 18 February 2022.
10. S.K. Banerjee, 'Manipur State Constitution Act, 1947', *The Indian Journal of Political Science*, Vol. 19 (1), January-March 1958, pp. 35-36.
11. John Parratt and Saroj Arambam Parratt, 'Hijam Irabot and the Radical Socialist Democratic Movement in Manipur', *Internationales Asienforum*, Vol. 31 (3-4), 2000, p. 284.
12. Rajkumar Snahal, 'Post-Merger Political History of Manipur', in Naorem Sanajaoba (ed.) *Manipur Past and Present*, Volume I, Delhi: Mittal Publications, 1988, p. 176.
13. *The Manipur (Village Authorities in Hill Areas) Act, 1956, Act No. 80 of 1956, 22nd December, 1956* at https://www.indiacode.nic.in/bitstream/123456789/1666/1/195680.pdf, accessed on 18 February 2022.
14. n. 12, pp. 177-179.
15. Ibid, pp. 179-180.
16. M. Sajjad Hassan, 'Explaining Manipur's Breakdown and Manipur's Peace: The State and Identities in North East India', *Crisis States Programme Working Paper no. 79*, February 2006, p. 15 at http://eprints.lse.ac.uk/28150/1/wp79.pdf, accessed on 18 February 2022.

17. There is a debate if there was an organization called the RGM. According to Rajendra Kshetri, Sudhir Kumar had founded the Consolidation Committee (CONSOCOM) and CONSOCOM later came to be popularly known as RGM.
18. 'Manipur Backgrounder', *South Asia Terrorism Portal* at https://www.satp.org/satporgtp/countries/india/states/manipur/backgrounder/index.html, accessed on 18 February 2022.
19. E.N. Rammohan, 'Manipur: A Degenerated Insurgency', *USI Journal*, January-March 2002 at https://www.usiofindia.org/publication-journal/manipur-a-degenerated-insurgency.html#:~:text=Insurgency%20came%20to%20Manipur%20with,insurgency%20operations%20with%20the%20Army., accessed on 18 February 2022.
20. *The North-Eastern Areas (Reorganisation) Act, 1971* at https://www.indiacode.nic.in/bitstream/123456789/1534/1/197181.pdf, accessed on 18 February 2022.
21. Rajendra Kshetri, *The Emergence of Meetei Nationalism: A Study of Two Movements Among the Meeteis*, New Delhi: Mittal Publications, 2006, p. 95.
22. n. 18.
23. 'People's Revolutionary Party of Kangleipak (PREPAK)', *South Asia Terrorism Portal* at https://www.satp.org/satporgtp/countries/india/states/manipur/terrorist_outfits/prepak.htm, accessed on 18 February 2022.
24. R. Gopalakrishnan, *Insurgent North-Eastern Region of India*, Delhi: Vikas Publishing House Pvt Ltd, 1995, p. 81.
25. 'Kangleipak Communist Party (KCP)', *South Asia Terrorism Portal* at https://www.satp.org/terrorist-profile/india/kangleipak-communist-party-kcp, accessed on 21 February 2022.
26. n. 18.
27. Ibid.
28. 'Kanglei Yawol Kunna Lup', *South Asia Terrorism Portal* at https://www.satp.org/satporgtp/countries/india/states/manipur/terrorist_outfits/kykl.htm, accessed on 22 February 2022.
29. Phanjouban Taraport, *Bleeding Manipur*, New Delhi: Har Anand Publications Pvt Ltd., 2003, p. 181.
30. *Annual Report 2003-2004*, New Delhi: Ministry of Home Affairs, 2004, p. vii.
31. n. 1, p. 329.
32. Ibid, p. 18.
33. 'Centre to review Naga ceasefire extension', *The Times of India*, 9 July 2001 at https://timesofindia.indiatimes.com/india/centre-to-review-naga-ceasefire-extension/articleshow/1464658995.cms, accessed on 22 February 2022.
34. The recognized Naga groups are Anal, Chiru, Chothe, Kabui, Kacha Nagas, Koireng, Kairao, Lamkang, Mao, Maram, Maring, Monsang, Moyon, Sema, and Tangkhul (Thangal, Poumei, Liangmei, Tharao are yet to be listed as scheduled tribes separately). The Kuki-Chin-Zomi includes Zou, Vaiphei, Simte, Paite, Aimol, Gangte, Thadou, Shuhte, Ralte, and other are Kom, Hmar, etc.
35. n. 24, 1995, p. 91.
36. Sushil Kumar Sharma, 'Naga Peace Accord and the Kuki and Meitei Insurgencies in Manipur', *IDSA Policy Brief*, 5 January 2016 at https://idsa.in/policybrief/naga-peace-accord-and-the-kuki-and-meitei-insurgencies_sksharma_050116, accessed on 22 February 2022.
37. n. 24, p. 92.
38. Ch. Sekholal Kom, 'Militancy and Negotiations: A Study of Suspension of Operation in Manipur', *Journal of Peace Studies*, Vol. 18 (1&2), January-June, 2011, p. 77.
39. Ipsita Chakravarty, 'With Biren Singh saying pact with Kuki militant groups is a failure, will Manipur change tack?', *Scroll.in*, 23 May 2017 at https://scroll.in/article/838401/will-manipur-

change-tack-in-its-approach-to-militancies-that-have-riven-the-state-for-decades, accessed on 14 March 2022.

40. 'Kuki National Army', *South Asia Terrorism Portal* at https://www.satp.org/satporgtp/countries/india/states/manipur/terrorist_outfits/kna.htm, accessed on 22 February 2022.
41. Bhagat Oinam, 'Patterns of Ethnic Conflict in the North-East: A Study on Manipur', *Economic and Political Weekly*, Vol. 38 (21), 24-30 May 2003, p. 2032.
42. Arunabh Saikia, 'Naga-Kuki conflict: 25 years after clashes in Manipur, a reconciliation is still elusive', *Scroll.in*, 14 September 2018 at https://scroll.in/article/894324/25-years-after-naga-kuki-clashes-in-manipur-reconciliation-is-still-elusive#:~:text= An%20 elusive %20 reconcilia tion,protect%20us%2C%E2%80%9D%20said%20Gangte., accessed on 22 February 2022.
43. Karishma Hasnat, 'Manipur's Kuki rebels demand Bodoland-like territorial council, unhappy about delays in talks', *The Print*, 29 August 2020 at https://theprint.in/india/manipurs-kuki-rebels-demand-bodoland-like-territorial-council-unhappy-about-delays-in-talks/491204/, accessed on 23 February 2022.
44. U.A. Shimray, 'Ethnicity and Socio-Political Assertion: The Manipur Experience', *Economic and Political Weekly*, Vol. 36 (39), 29 September–5 October 2001, p. 3677. Also see, Bibhu Prasad Routray 'Unremitting Terror', *Outlook*, 3 February 2022 (updated) at https://www.outlook india.com/website/story/unremitting-terror/233017, accessed on 23 February 2022.
45. 'Muslim body demands compensation for 1993 riot victims', *E-Pao*, 11 January 2015 at http://e-pao.net/GP.asp?src=13..120115.jan15, accessed on 8 March 2022.
46. Bharti Jain, 'Manipur official: No tribal bias in evictions or in war on drugs', *The Times of India*, 17 May 2023 at https://timesofindia.indiatimes.com/india/manipur-official-no-tribal-bias-in-evictions-or-in-war-on-drugs/articleshow/100291179.cms?from=mdr, accessed on 8 March 2022.
47. For more on the consequences of the 'War on Drugs' campaign, see Lily Sangpui and Jenny Kapngaihlian, 'The Quest to End Illicit Poppy Cultivation in Manipur: Examining the War on Drugs Campaign', *Economic and Political Weekly*, Vol. 56, No. 32, 7 August 2021 at https://www.epw.in/engage/article/quest-end-illicit-poppy-cultivation-manipur, accessed on 17 May 2023.
48. Moushumi Das Gupta, 'Tripartite ceasefire pact to settle Kuki issues operational, says security adviser to Manipur CM', *The Print*, 14 May 2003 at https://theprint.in/india/tripartite-ceasefire-pact-to-settle-kuki-issues-operational-says-security-advisor-to-manipur-cm/1573514/#:~:text= Biren%20Singh%2Dled%20Manipur%20government,chief%20minister%2C%20told%20 ThePrint%20Thursday., accessed on 17 May 2023.
49. Valley districts are: East and West Imphal, Kakching, Bishnupur and Thoubal. Hill Districts are: Senapati, Kangpokpi, Ukhrul, Kamjong, Chandel, Tengnoupal, Churachandpur, Pherzawl, Noney, and Tamenglong. Jiribam district is an extension of the Cachar valley.
50. Richard Kamei, 'Tribal Land, Customary Law, and the Manipur Land Revenue and Land Reforms Act', *Economic and Political Weekly*, Vol. 53 (19), 12 May 2018, p. 52.
51. Tejas Harad, 'ST Status for Manipur's Meiteis: What is at Stake?', *The Quint*, 6 May 2023 at https://www.thequint.com/news/politics/manipur-violence-st-status-for-meiteis-valley-vs-hills, accessed on 17 May 2023.
52. H. Kham Khan Suan, 'Hills-Valley Divide as a Site of Conflict', in Sanjib Baruah (ed.), *Beyond Counter-Insurgency, Breaking the Impasse in Northeast India*, Oxford University Press, New Delhi, 2009, p. 273.
53. Rajendra Kshetri, *District Councils in Manipur, Formations & Functioning*, Akansha Publishing House, Delhi, 2006, p. 5.

54. U.A. Shimray, 'Naga Integration Movement: A Historical Perspective', *Nagaland Journal*, 22 April 2013 at https://nagalandjournal.wordpress.com/2013/04/22/naga-integration-movement-a-historical-perspective-by-u-a-shimray/, accessed on 28 February 2022.
55. n. 9.
56. 'Chapter VII-Hill People, Article 38', ibid.
57. *The Manipur State Hill Peoples (Administration) Regulation,* 1947, pp. 70-71, 74-75 at https://manipur.gov.in/wp-content/uploads/2017/06/act-1.pdf, accessed on 28 February 2022.
58. n. 13, pp. 3-4.
59. Bela Bhatia, 'Justice Denied to Tribals in the Hill Districts of Manipur', *The Economic And Political Weekly*, Vol. 45 (31), 31-July-31 August 2010, p. 41.
60. Ibid, p. 40. Also see, V. Ramachandran, 'Planning in the Sixth Schedule Areas and Those Areas Not Covered by Part ix and Part ix-a, 2006', *Report of the Expert Committee*, September 2006, p. 70 at http://nrcddp.org/file_upload/V.Ramachandran%20 Committee%20 report, %202007%20-%20Sixth%20Schedule%20Areas.pdf, accessed on 3 March 2022.
61. n. 53, p. 10.
62. Ibid.
63. Kham Khan Suan Hausing, 'From Opposition to Acquiescence: The 2015 District Council Elections in Manipur', *Economic and Political Weekly*, Vol. 50 (46/47), 21 November 2015, p. 79.
64. 'Comprehensive details about Manipur State and its Environmental & Social Sensitivities', *Government of Manipur* at https://manipur.gov.in/wp-content/uploads/2015/03/annexure-01-manipur-comprehensive.pdf, accessed on 3 March 2022.
65. n. 53, p. 23.
66. Ibid, p. 24.
67. n. 59, p. 41.
68. *The Manipur (Hill Areas) District Councils (Third Amendment) Act, 2008*, (Manipur Act No. 7 of 2003), *Manipur Gazette Extraordinary*, 27 October 2008 the_manipur_hills_ areas_ district_council_third_amendment_act,_2008.pdf (indiacode.nic.in), accessed on 2 March 2022.
69. n. 63, p. 80.
70. n. 60, p. 66.
71. n. 63, p. 80.
72. n. 59, p. 43.
73. n. 63, p. 80.
74. n. 68, p. 1.
75. Ibid.
76. 'Decentralisation And Devolution', *Report of the National Commission to Review the Working of the Constitution*, Vol. I, Department of Legal Affairs, Government of India, March 2002 at https://legalaffairs.gov.in/sites/default/files/chapter%209%20.pdf, accessed on 2 March 2022.
77. n. 60, p. 16.
78. Ibid, p. 72.
79. n. 74, p. 2.
80. 'Naga students call off Manipur blockade, finally', *The Economic Times*, 19 June 2010 at https://economictimes.indiatimes.com/news/politics-and-nation/naga-students-call-off-manipur-blockade-finally/articleshow/6067062.cms, accessed on 3 March 2022.
81. 'INC swept Manipur (Hill areas) District Councils elections', *E-Pao*, Imphal, 22 June 2010 at http://e-pao.net/epRelatedNews.asp?heading=18&src=230610, accessed on 3 March 2022.
82. n. 63, p. 81.

83. Ibid.
84. Ibid, p. 82.
85. Ibid, p. 83.
86. IFP Bureau, 'Manipur (Hill Areas) Autonomous District Councils Bill, 2021 introduced', *Imphal Free Press*, 20 August 2021 at https://www.ifp.co.in/manipur/manipur-hill-areas-autonomous-district-councils-bill-2021-introduced, accessed on 4 March 2022.
87. Ibid.
88. Ibid.
89. Jimmy Leivon 'Manipur: Civil bodies oppose Manipur (Hill Areas) Autonomous District Councils Bill 2021', *The Indian Express*, Imphal, 22 August 2021 at https://indianexpress.com/article/north-east-india/manipur/manipur-civil-bodies-oppose-manipur-autonomous-district-council-bill-2021-7465931/, accessed on 7 March 2022.
90. Rokibuz Zaman, 'Manipur divided over bill granting more autonomy to tribal councils', *Scroll.in*, 26 December 2021 at https://scroll.in/article/1013582/old-divides-have-surfaced-over-a-proposed-bill-in-manipur-as-elections-approach, accessed on 7 March 2022.
91. *The Armed Forces (Special Powers) Act, 1958*, Ministry of Home Affairs https://www.mha.gov.in/sites/default/files/armed_forces_special_powers_act1958.pdf, accessed on 7 March 2022.
92. Laishram Achaw Singh, as quoted in *The AFSPA: Lawless Law Enforcement According to the Law?* New Delhi: Asian Centre for Human Rights, 2005, p. 3.
93. n. 91.
94. Ibid.
95. S.B.Nakade, at al, *Report of the Committee to Review the Armed Forces (Special Powers) Act of 1958*, Ministry of Home Affairs, Government of India, 2005, p. 14 at https://andyreiter.com/wp-content/uploads/military-justice/in/Government%20Documents/India%20-%202005%20-%20Report%20of%20the%20Committee%20to%20Review%20AFSPA%20(Reddy%20Report).pdf, accessed on 7 March 2022.
96. n. 91.
97. 'History of Manipur Police', *Government of Manipur* at https://manipurpolice.gov.in/?page_id=4, accessed on 8 March 2022.
98. Irengbam Arun, 'A virus called AFSPA', *Kanglaonline*, 10 July 2016 at https://kanglaonline.in/2016/07/virus-called-afspa/, accessed on 7 March 2022.
99. K. Sarojkumar Sharma, 'AFSPA extended in Manipur for a year amid cry for repeal', *The Times of India*, 12 January 2022 at https://timesofindia.indiatimes.com/city/imphal/afspa-extended-in-manipur-for-a-year-amid-cry-for-repeal/articleshow/88843540.cms, accessed on 7 March 2022.
100. Simrim Sirur, '17 years since their naked protest against Army, 'Mothers of Manipur' say fight not over yet', *The Print*, Bishnupur, 22 July 2021 at https://theprint.in/india/17-years-since-their-naked-protest-against-army-mothers-of-manipur-say-fight-not-over-yet/700093/, accessed on 8 March 2022. Kranti Kumara, 'India: popular agitation against army atrocities engulfs the northeast state of Manipur', *World Socialist Web Site*, 15 September 2004 at https://www.wsws.org/en/articles/2004/09/mani-s15.html, accessed on 8 March 2022.
101. *Annual Report 2004-2005*, New Delhi: Government of India, 2005, p. 34.
102. *Annual Report 2020-2021*, New Delhi: Government of India, 2021, p. 15.
103. IFP Bureau, 'AFSPA withdrawn from more areas in Manipur', *Imphal Free Press*, 26 March 2023 at https://www.ifp.co.in/manipur/afspa-withdrawn-from-more-areas-in-manipur, accessed on 11 July 2023.
104. 'PART II – Section 3, Sub-section (1)', *The Gazette of India Extraordinary*, 27 June 1961, p. 1 at https://www.mha.gov.in/sites/default/files/A1967-37.pdf, accessed on 8 March 2022.

105. Ibid.
106. Ibid.
107. *The Unlawful Activities (Prevention) Act, 1967, Act No. 37 of 1967* [30th December, 1967] at https://www.mha.gov.in/sites/default/files/A1967-37.pdf, accessed on 9 March 2022.
108. n. 97.
109. Ibid.
110. The Sashastra Seema Bal was earlier known as the Special Service Bureau at https://ssb.gov.in/sHistory, accessed on 8 March 2022.
111. n. 97.
112. Subir Bhaumik, 'Insurgencies in India's Northeast: Conflict, Co-option & Change', *East West Center*, No. 10, July 2007, p. 17.
113. n. 29, p. 239.
114. E.N. Rammohan, 'Manipur: Blue Print for Counterinsurgency', *Faultline*, Vol. 12, May 2022 at https://www.satp.org/satporgtp/publication/faultlines/volume12/article1.htm, accessed on 10 March 2022.
115. G. Vinayak, 'Manipur speaker, 4 MLAs burnt in mob fury', *Rediff.com*, Imphal, 18 June 2001 at https://m.rediff.com/news/2001/jun/18mani.htm, accessed on 15 March 2022.
116. Khelen Thokchom, 'Joint forces in Manipur thrust', *The Telegraph*, Imphal, 6 June 2004 at https://www.telegraphindia.com/north-east/joint-forces-in-manipur-thrust/cid/711085, accessed on 9 March 2022.
117. Bibhu Prasad Routray, 'The State of Militancy', *South Asia Intelligence Review*, Vol. 4(26), 9 January 2006 at https://www.satp.org/south-asia-intelligence-review-Volume-4-No-26, accessed on 9 March 2022.
118. K.S. Subramanian, *State, Policy and Conflicts in Northeast India*, New Delhi: Routledge, 2016, p. 81.
119. Pradip Phanjoubam, 'The Assam Rifles lesson for Manipur', *The Telegraph*, 21 September 2021 at https://www.telegraphindia.com/opinion/the-assam-rifles-lesson-for-manipur/cid/1831502, accessed on 11 March 2022.
120. Lawrence E. Cline, 'The Insurgency Environment in Northeast India', *Small Wars & Insurgencies*, Vol. 17 (2), 2006, p. 143.
121. Author's interview with a senior Indian army official at New Delhi, March 2022.
122. Sanjiv Krishan Sood, 'Is Assam Rifles stretched with its dual role? Manipur ambush raises key questions', *The Print*, 17 November 2021 at https://theprint.in/opinion/is-assam-rifles-stretched-with-its-dual-role-manipur-ambush-raises-key-questions/767107/, accessed on 11 March 2022.
123. PTI, 'Assam Rifles to increase presence along Indo-Myanmar border', *Business Standard*, 27 December 2018 at https://www.business-standard.com/article/pti-stories/assam-rifles-to-increase-presence-along-indo-myanmar-border-118122700888_1.html, accessed on 11 March 2021.
124. Dinakar Peri, 'Assam Rifles Commanding Officer, family, four jawans killed in Manipur ambush', *The Hindu*, 13 November 2021 at https://www.thehindu.com/news/national/other-states/assam-rifles-co-others-killed-in-manipur-ambush/article37469920.ece, accessed on 11 March 2022.
125. William Gurumayum, 'The Kuki-Zomi Insurgency in Manipur Nearing Settlement', *Imphal Times*, 11 May 2018 at https://www.imphaltimes.com/articles/the-kuki-zomi-insurgency-in-manipur-nearing-settlement-2/, accessed on 11 March 2022.
126. Discussion with a senior Army officer with experience in counter insurgency operations in Manipur, March 2022. Also see, Aheibam Koireng Singh, 'Suspension Of Operation With

Chikimz Outfits In Manipur Part', *E-Pao*, 22 November 2016 at http://e-pao.net/epSubPageExtractor.asp?src=news_section.opinions.Opinion_on_Effects_of_Insurgency.Suspension_Of_Operation_With_Chikimz_Outfits_In_ Manipur_Part_I_By_Aheibam_Koireng, accessed on 14 March 2022.

127. Jimmy Leivon, 'Manipur polls: Kuki insurgent groups to support BJP candidates', *The Indian Express*, Imphal, 1 March 2022 at https://indianexpress.com/article/north-east-india/manipur/manipur-polls-kuki-insurgent-groups-support-bjp-7793375/, accessed on 11 March 2022.
128. Jimmy Leivon, 'Suspension of Operation funds: BJP says routine, Congress says bribe', *The Indian Express*, Imphal at https://indianexpress.com/elections/explained-suspension-operation-pact-kuki-militants-7801135/, 4 March 2022.
129. Robert Sapam,'Manipur police get special unit', *The Telegraph*, Imphal, 20 May 2018 at https://www.telegraphindia.com/north-east/manipur-police-get-special-unit/cid/1449408 #:~:text=The%20state%20police%20department%20has,counter%2Dinsurgency%2C%20in%20Manipur.&text=Imphal% 3A%20The%20state%20police% 20department,counter%2Dinsurgency%2C%20in%20Manipur., accessed on 10 March 2022.
130. n. 114.
131. PTI, '7th Manipur Rifles defies order', *The Tribune*, Imphal, 13 May 2002 at https://m.tribuneindia.com/2002/20020514/main5.htm, accessed on 10 March 2022.
132. The Sangai Express/DIPR, 'Cabinet approves new transfer policy', *E-Pao*, Imphal, 30 November 2017 at http://e-pao.net/GP.asp?src=9..011217.dec17, accessed on 10 March 2022.
133. E.N. Rammohan, 'Armed Forces Special Powers Act', *Dialogue*, Vol. 14 (4), April-June 2013, p. 119.
134. Aheibam Koireng Singh, 'Suspension Of Operation With Chikimz Outfits In Manipur Part I', *E-PAO*, 17 November 2016 at http://e-pao.net/epSubPageExtractor.asp?src=news_section.opinions. Opinion_on_Effects_of_Insurgency.Suspension_Of_Operation_With_Chikimz_Outfits_In_Manipur_Part_I_By_Aheibam_Koireng, accessed on 14 March 2022.
135. Saikat Dutta, 'Manipur CM Gave Rs 1.5 Crore To Separatists', *Outlook*, 12 December 2005 at https://www.outlookindia.com/magazine/story/manipur-cm-gave-rs-15-crore-to-separatists/229503, accessed on 14 March 2022.
136. Ibid.
137. Ajai Sahni, 'Survey of Conflicts & Resolution in India's Northeast', *Faultline*, Vol.12, May 2002 at https://www.satp.org/faultline-chapter-details/volume-12/survey-of-conflicts-resolution-in-indias-northeast, accessed on 11 March 2022.
138. n. 135.
139. n. 137, p. 71.
140. *Annual Report 2008-09*, New Delhi: Ministry of Home Affairs, 2009, p. 12.
141. n. 43.
142. n. 39.
143. 'KNO, NNPG sign Imphal AccordBoth agree to accept history and identity of each other', *The Sangai Express*, Churachandpur, 20 January 2020 at https://www.thesangaiexpress.com/Encyc/2020/1/20/Our-CorrespondentCCpur-Jan-19-A-major-Kuki-rebel-group-Kuki-National-Organsiation-KNO-has-signed-an-accord-with-the-Working-Committee-of-Naga-National-Political-Groups-NNPG-a-major-stakehold.amp.html, accessed on 22 February 2022.
144. 'Two Hundred Thirteenth Report: Security Situation in the North Eastern States of India', *Rajya Sabha*, 19 July 2018 https://sansad.in/getFile/rsnew/Committee_site/Committee_File/ReportFile/15/101/213_2019_5_16.pdf?source=rajyasabha, accessed on 14 March 2022.
145. Pradeep Singh Chhonkar, 'The Creation of New Districts in Manipur: Administrative Necessity versus Naga Territorial Aspirations', *IDSA Comment*, 23 December 2016 at https://www.idsa.in/

idsacomments/creation-of-new-districts-in-manipur_pschhonkar_231216, accessed on 14 March 2022.

146. n. 39.
147. *The Manipur Land Revenue and Land Reforms Act, 1960* at https://www.indiacode.nic.in/bitstream/123456789/1531/1/196033.pdf, accessed on 15 March 2022.
148. n. 50, p. 54.
149. The Sangai Express, 'All three Bills passed without any debate', *E-Pao*, Imphal, 31 August 2015 at http://e-pao.net/GP.asp?src=7..010915.sep15, accessed on 15 March 2022.
150. Kham Khan Suan Hausing, 'Manipur impasse: The hills are alive', *The Indian Express*, 22 September 2015 at https://indianexpress.com/article/opinion/columns/the-hills-are-alive-3/, accessed on 15 March 2022.
151. 'The Protection of Manipur People Bill, 2015', *Kangla Online*, 3 September 2015 at https://kanglaonline.in/2015/09/the-protection-of-manipur-people-bill-2015/, accessed on 15 March 2022.
152. Thangkhanlal Ngaihte, 'Manipur's blighted bills', *The Statesman,* 18 October 2015 at http://www.thestatesman.com/supplements/manipur-s-blighted-bills-97885.html, accessed on 15 March 2022.
153. *Good Governance Index 2020-2021*, New Delhi: Department of Administrative Reforms and Public Grievances, 2021, p. vi. Also see, Roopak Goswami, 'Good Governance Index: Manipur shows highest decline, Mizoram best', *East Mojo*, 28 December 2021 at https://www.eastmojo.com/assam/2021/12/28/good-governance-index-manipur-shows-highest-decline-mizoram-best/, accessed on 15 March 2022.
154. Ibid, p. 33.
155. Ibid, p. 65.
156. Vangamla Salle K.S., 'Manipur worst-governed small state in India; Sikkim, Mizoram best: report', *East Mojo*, Imphal, 5 November 2021 at https://www.eastmojo.com/northeast-news/2021/11/05/manipur-worst-governed-small-state-in-india-sikkim-mizoram-best-report/, accessed on 15 March 2022.
157. *Manipur Vision 2030 Leaving No-One Behind: Achieving Inclusive Growth and the Sustainable Development Goals*, Imphal: Government of Manipur, 2019, p. vii.
158. Angomcha Bimol Akoijam, 'Making Sense of Corruption in Manipur', *Kangla Online*, 4 September 2012 at https://kanglaonline.in/2012/09/making-sense-of-corruption-in-manipur/, accessed on 15 March 2022. Yenning, 'Corruption scam and issue of governance', *E-Pao*, Imphal, 23 February 2015 at http://e-pao.net/epSubPageExtractor.asp?src= news_section.opinions.Politics_and_Governance.Corruption_scam_and_issue_of_governance_By_Yenning, accessed on 15 March 2022.
159. Ibid.
160. n. 114.
161. Ibid.
162. Outlook Web Desk 'A Failed State?', *Outlook,* 3 February 2022 (updated) at https://www.outlookindia.com/website/story/a-failed-state/235387, accessed on 15 March 2022. Also see, n. 158.
163. Ibid.
164. Ibid.

8

CONCLUSION

India has been facing myriad internal security threats since independence. While a number of these threats have persisted since then, the country has been successful in tackling some of them. One of the first challenges that Independent India faced was communist inspired and communist led insurrections. The Communists, in order to seize political power from the democratically elected government, tapped into the grievances of the poor peasants and tribespeople, incited them and organised them to 'fight for their rights'. In the initial years, these communist rebellions were localised and challenged the local governments, but later on some of these rebellions fused together to become a pan-Indian phenomenon. In some cases, these communist rebellions sowed the seeds for future ethnic insurgencies in the country as well.

Given the wide spectrum of these threats, tackling them necessitates a whole of Government approach. Both the union and the state governments require to effect policy changes and interventions at the pan-India as well as at the state level, to address the issues of political disempowerment, economic deprivation, cultural discrimination, neglect, disenchantment, etc. which, more often than not, provide fodder for insurgency and secessionism. At the same time, maintaining public order and rule of law by strengthening state police forces and judicial systems assures common people of getting fair justice. In the initial decades, the Union government tried to confront insurgencies and militancy proactively by dismissing the state governments and deploying the armed forces to fight the insurgents and militants. It was successful in its efforts in cases such as in West Bengal (initial phase), and Mizoram.

However, in the later years, the Union government transitioned into the role of providing guidance as well as financial, logistical, legal and diplomatic support to the affected state governments. Issuing guidelines about tackling Maoist insurgency, providing financial and logistical assistance to the affected states, and refraining from imposing President's rule and deploying Indian army are examples of the supportive role played by the Union government. This transition has likely been brought about by a growing realisation in New Delhi that most of the internal security threats originate at the local or state level. More often than not, it is the disgruntled political elites who exploit the genuine or perceived grievances of the people to grab power by fomenting disaffection and unrest. Therefore, if issues of political, cultural and economic neglect are taken care of at the local levels, much of the conflicts could be resolved before they could transform into bigger problems and engulf wider areas. There is also a realisation that the solution to these internal security problems lie in political accommodation, positive social engineering, economic development and better governance at the lower levels, and not by imposing fragile peace through security forces.

In fact, discussions in the previous chapters have highlighted that states that have provided political inclusion, economic development and cultural expression to the politically and economically marginalised and cultural minorities have been successful, to a large extent, in assuaging the politico-economic and cultural aspirations of the aggrieved populace and therefore were able to wean the rebels away from the path of insurgencies and militancy. For example, landlessness among the peasantry and tribal people and exploitation by the landlords were genuine grievances which were exploited by the Communists to rally people and initiate violent movements to overthrow the democratically elected governments. States such as West Bengal, Andhra Pradesh, Tripura, etc. had to bear the brunt of communist rebellion not only prior to independence but also in the late1960s and early 1970s because successive state governments failed to distribute land equitably to the people despite enactment of Land Reforms Acts.

It was only when the land reforms were successfully implemented and tenancy rights given to the peasants that the main cause for communist insurgency was addressed in West Bengal, Tripura and to a large extent in Andhra Pradesh. Here, it is important to note that if reforms and governance remain non-inclusive then causes for disaffection are reignited leading to conflicts. This happened in Andhra Pradesh in 1980s and West Bengal in 2000s when left wing extremism raised its head again in the tribal dominated areas of the states. In both the states, land reforms were implemented in the plains areas where many intermediate and lower caste/class people, who hitherto formed the cadre base of the communists, benefitted not only economically but they were also accommodated politically. Political empowerment and economic growth motivated these beneficiaries to support the state governments and withdraw from the communist cause.

The tribal people, on the other hand, who also took active part in the communist rebellions remained deprived of land reforms, political empowerment and economic development. Their sense of neglect was exploited by the Communists who formed bases in the hilly and forested areas and attacked the state governments. Besides the Maoists, political elites of the states also contributed in fuelling the sense of deprivation among the tribal to gain political power. They also hobnobbed with the Maoists, especially during elections to win seats for their parties with the help of the rebels. But by providing political empowerment, ushering in development in the tribal belts as well as by providing them financial benefits, the state governments were eventually able to assuage their hurt feelings and win them over.

A good example of political accommodation of the tribals by the state political elites is Tripura. The state government addressed the issue of political alienation by providing the tribal people with self-governance by establishing the Tripura autonomous territorial council. The autonomous council covers two thirds of the area of the state. The government also ensured that the tribal people, especially the *Jamatias*, became economically self-sufficient by introducing forest and agro-based economic activities as a means of earning livelihoods. Similarly, the West Bengal and Andhra Pradesh governments launched special developmental packages as well as provided effective governance to satisfy the developmental as well as basic requirements of the tribal people. These efforts helped the state governments in weaning away the youths from the Maoists folds.

While effectively catering to the local socio-economic and political aspirations of the people at the ground level was instrumental in addressing root causes of alienation and disempowerment and thereby eliminating separatist tendencies among the common people, coercive actions by the state police forces also proved to be an effective method to counter determined insurgents and militants. This fact holds true for almost all the states who have successfully defeated insurgencies. However, Andhra Pradesh and Punjab are the two states where a motivated and effective police force broke the back of insurgency and militancy, almost singlehandedly. Andhra Pradesh defeated the Communist (Naxal/Maoist) insurgency predominantly through force centric counterinsurgency strategy. A coercive counterinsurgency strategy of raising special elite police force called the Greyhound backed by an effective and sophisticated intelligence to take the Maoist rebels head-on was responsible in eliminating Maoist insurgency in the state. This strategy resulted in either killing or arrest of a number of top Maoist leaders, forcing rest of the leadership to flee the state and take shelter in neighbouring states.

Similarly in Punjab, dynamic leadership helped in infusing a sense of motivation, courage and professionalism in a hitherto corrupt and partisan police force. Non-interference by the political leaders and a no-tolerance towards terrorism policy allowed the police to independently strategise and accomplish its task of eliminating militancy from the state. The police was ably supported by other security forces of the Union government such as the Indian army, the CRPF, the NSG and the BSF. In fact, effective police action was also responsible in ending Urban Naxalism in West Bengal during the early 1970s. Like the Punjab police, the West Bengal police had also become partisan and demoralised, which allowed the Naxalites to unleash a reign of terror in Kolkata and other urban centres of the state. The imposition of President's rule and subsequent change of government in the state ensured political non-interference in the workings of the police force.

While the abovementioned states have been successful in their efforts to eliminate causes of conflicts and build peace, there are other states, which continue to grapple with the problem of insurgencies because strategies employed by them to alleviate grievances and bring prosperity and security to their people are half-hearted. Of these, Chhattisgarh and Manipur, which continue to witness high levels of violence, indicate that the state governments' efforts to combat insurgencies have not yielded the desired results. A study of the two states reveals that factors such as location and terrain of the states, inter-ethnic conflicts, lack of political will and political accommodation, ineffective governance, lack of coordination among security forces, etc. play spoilsports and hinder the process of conflict resolution and peace building.

In the case of Chhattisgarh, the heavily forested and hilly terrain of Dandakaranya and its location at the tri-junction of Chhattisgarh, Odisha and Telangana (previously undivided Andhra Pradesh) provide an ideal base area for the Maoists. The remote and inaccessible location prevent the police forces to enter into the area thus allowing the Maoists to operate unmolested. In addition, the tri-junction ensures that the rebels could easily slip into the neighbouring state as the Chhattisgarh police does not have jurisdiction beyond the state borders. The problem is further compounded by the fact that coordination between the police forces of the three states is either non-existent or poor causing conducting counter-insurgency operations near impossible. A similar situation can be seen for Manipur as well. Being proximate to the international border with a politically unstable and complicit neighbour have ensured that insurgents could easily cross the border and take shelter in the neighbouring country. The forested and hilly tracts of the state also make counter insurgency operations difficult.

The terrain and location no doubt add to the difficulties of the police in these states, but the fact that the police in these two states are also weak and partisan does not help matter. In Chhattisgarh, the police is ill trained and ill equipped, which does not allow it to have the courage to fight the Maoists. The state relies heavily on union forces to take on the Maoists. In fact, such is the state of the police that the CRPF has become the prominent force to fight the determined Maoist rebels in the state. In Manipur, the police is divided on ethnic lines and its personnel are biased towards their own community. Political interference is also rampant. The ongoing Meitei-Kuki conflict have brought this fact to the fore and questioned the effectiveness of the police to ensure order and peace in the state.

Absence or lack of political accommodation and empowerment in Chhattisgarh and Manipur have also prevented political solutions and prolonged insurgencies in these states. In Chhattisgarh, poor performance of the tribal advisory committee and ineffective implementation of PESA have robbed the tribals of a chance for self-governance and control over their resources. Tribal people have been vulnerable to land grab by mining and other private companies as well as exploitations by revenue and forest officials. On top of it for a long time, the Chhattisgarh government have not been able to provide basic and effective administration to the Maoist affected districts. In fact, tribal population of Chhattisgarh are most politically deprived and socio-economically marginalised section in the state. Given such a scenario, it is obvious that the tribal people feel neglected by the government and gravitate towards the Maoists who have been able to provide them with some semblance of administration and justice.

In Manipur, the Meitei community dominated state government have been biased against the tribal people residing in the hill areas of the state. In fact, successive state governments have deliberately neglected the development of the Hill Areas. They have also been reluctant to give more autonomy to the tribal people of the state to manage their own affairs. This lack of political accommodation and economic development have alienated the tribal people against the Meiteis and exacerbated the security situation. The recent conflict between the Meitei and Kuki communities is an example of the extreme chasm that has developed between communities in the state. Furthermore, the refusal of the major Meitei rebel groups to give up their separatist demands and enter into a political dialogue with the government and the state government's apparent lack of interest to arrive at any political settlement with the rebels continue to make the state one of the most violent in the Northeast region.

Given that most conflicts start at the local levels and if not addressed promptly, they grow into a national concern, it can be concluded that in those states where the state political leadership have shown a resolve to combat insurgency and political violence, peace has prevailed and sustained. In these states, the leadership have tried to defeat the ideology of insurgents and win over the people with a judicious mix of coercion, political accommodation, justice and development. The effective implementation of measures such as granting land titles, allowing local self-governance, reservations for the deprived sections in politics as well as in government jobs, carrying out economic development, providing basic amenities, etc. were instrumental in bringing political, social and economic empowerment to the marginalised sections of the society, thus robbing the insurgent groups the cause to mobilise the people against the governments. At the same time, strengthening the law enforcement and intelligence agencies and forging better coordination among various security forces ensured that the insurgents and the militants could be contained effectively.

States where political will to fight insurgency is lacking or absent have to endure persistent conflict and violence. The failure of the political leadership to bring together disparate ethnic groups together and find a political solution is the primary factor for the persistence of insurgency. These states also fare badly with regard to governance and economic development. Consequently, the residents do not enjoy a better quality of life and mostly remain dissatisfied, providing ample opportunities for the insurgents to exploit people's grievances and strengthen their rank and file. The need of the hour, therefore, is for the leadership in the conflict afflicted states to display the will to effectively and urgently address the causes of conflict and build sustainable peace.

Here it is also important to highlight that given the multiplicity of faith, ethnicities, and other features in the country, the union and the state governments have to be ever vigilant lest issues of deprivation and disempowerment are not exploited by disgruntled political elites to mobilise people and agitate to capture power, thus jeopardising the internal security of the country. In fact, such instances are already been witnessed in the states such as Tripura and Punjab where insurgency and militancy have been successfully contained.

In Tripura, political parties such as the Indigenous People's Front of Tripura (IPFT) and the Tipra Motha, advocating a separate tribal state or a 'Greater Tipraland' have become quite prominent in recent times. The rise of these parties indicate that the tribal people remain dissatisfied and demand greater political powers. In fact, the Tipra Motha has intensified its agitation for a separate state. Further, the issue of Tipraland has caused tensions between the IPFT and its ally the BJP in the state. If these separatist demands are not nipped at the bud, Tripura might see resurgence of violence once again.

Similarly in Punjab, the SAD has been periodically pandering to the sentiments of the Sikh extremists. The SAD government in 2012 allowed a memorial of Bhindranwale to come up in the Golden Temple. More recently in 2022, the party President referred to Bhindranwale as a saint and eulogised his 'sacrifices' for the Sikh quam. Given that organisations such as the SFJ do not miss an opportunity to foment religious intolerance and separatists sentiments in the state, it is incumbent on the political parties to promote peace and harmony in the society and not contrive false grievances.

Maintaining internal security in an ongoing process that requires vigilance, commitment and political will both at the union as well as the state levels. It is however the states that can address issues of political disaffection and governance at the ground level and prevent flaring up of local conflicts into larger internal security threats. The need of the hour therefore, is for the state political leaders to refrain from fomenting ethnic, religious, casteist and sub-regional sentiments among the masses to garner political brownie points over others as these could have serious security repercussions. State governments should strive to provide inclusive and effective governance as well as employment opportunities so that all segments of the society are equally benefitted. State governments should strengthen the Police force and implement Police Reforms in letter and spirit to make the force professional and efficient. This will go a long way in curbing criminal and anti-national activities at the ground level. Last but not least, state governments should cooperate and work in tandem with the Union government to ensure national security.

BIBLIOGRAPHY

Acts, Agreements, Treaties and Memoranda of Understanding

Manipur Merger Agreement, 1949.

Manipur State Constitution Act, 1947.

Provisions of the Panchayats (Extension to the Scheduled Areas) Act, 1996.

Rajiv-Longowal Memorandum of Settlement (Accord), July 24, 1985.

Terrorist and Disruptive Activities (Prevention) Act, 1987.

The Andhra Pradesh Reorganisation Act, 2014 (Act No. 6 of 2014).

The Armed Forces (Punjab and Chandigarh) Special Powers Act, 1983 (34 of 1983).

The Armed Forces (Special Powers) Act, 1958.

The Bengal Suppression of Terrorist Outrages Act of 1936.

The Chhattisgarh Auxiliary Armed Police Force Act , 2011.

The Constitution (Fifty-ninth Amendment) Act, 1988.

The Criminal Law Amendment Act of 1908.

The Manipur (Hill Areas) District Councils (Third Amendment) Act, 2008 (Manipur Act No. 7 of 2003), *Manipur Gazette Extraordinary*, 27 October 2008.

The Manipur (Village Authorities In Hill Areas) Act, 1956, Act No. 80 of 1956, 22nd December, 1956.

The Manipur Land Revenue and Land Reforms Act, 1960.

The Manipur State Hill Peoples (Administration) Regulation, 1947.

The North-Eastern Areas (Reorganisation) Act, 1971.

The Police Forces (Restriction of Rights) Act, 1966.

The Punjab Disturbed Areas Act, 1983 Act No. 32 of 1983, 8th December, 1983.

The Religious Institutions (Prevention of Misuse) Act, 1988 No. 41 of 1988 [1st September, 1988.]

The Tamil Nadu Suppression of Disturbances Act, 1948 (Act 3 of 1948).

The Telangana Tenancy and Agricultural Lands Act, 1950 (Act No. XXI of 1950).

The Terrorist Affected Areas (Special Courts) Act, 1984 Act No. 61 of 1984 [*31st August*, 1984.]

The Tripura Land Revenue and Land Reforms Act, 1960.

The Tripura Tribal Areas Autonomous District Council Act, 1979.

The Unlawful Activities (Prevention) Act, 1967 Act No. 37 of 1967 [30th December, 1967].

The West Bengal Bargadars Act, 1950, 15 March 1950.

The West Bengal Prevention of Violent Activities Act, 1970.

The West Bengal Security Act, 1950, West Bengal Act Xix of 1950.

'A Peep into Future: A Case Study of the Next Phase of Land Reforms in West Bengal', *Directorate of Land Records & Surveys*, West Bengal, 1971.

'Decentralisation and Devolution', *Report of The National Commission To Review the Working of the Constitution*, Vol. I, Department of Legal Affairs, Government of India, March 2002.

'Development Challenges in Extremist Affected Areas', *Report of an Expert Group to Planning Commission*, New Delhi, 2008.

'Dr. Ram Manohar Lohia vs State of Bihar and others on 7 September, 1965', *Supreme Court of India*, New Delhi.

'First Report on Demands for Grants Nos. 42 & 44 of Ministry of Home Affairs for the Year 1993–94', Department Related Parliamentary Standing Committee on Home Affairs, *Rajya Sabha*, 28 April 1993.

'Ngangam Mahendra Singh and Ors. vs Manipur State', *High Court of Gauhati*, 19 November, 1951.

'Review Categorization of Districts affected by Left Wing Extremism', *Ministry of Home Affairs*, 19 June 2021.

'Romesh Thappar vs The State of Madras on 26 May, 1950', *Supreme Court of India*, New Delhi.

'Two Hundred Thirteenth Report: Security Situation in the North Eastern States of India', *Rajya Sabha*, 19 July 2018.

'Unstarred Question No. 1073: Naxal/Left Wing Extremism', *Lok Sabha*, 8 February 2022.

'Unstarred Question No. 1187: Naxali Attacks', *Lok Sabha*, 27 July 2021.

'Unstarred Question No. 1968 Initiative to Control the Naxal Problem in Chhattisgarh', *Rajya Sabha*, 15 December 2021.

'Unstarred Question No. 6110: Modernisation of Police Force in Chhattisgarh", *Lok Sabha*, 7 May 2002.

'Unstarred Question No: 2521 Salwa Judum Movement', *Lok Sabha*, 16 December 2008.

'Unstarred Question No: 2918: Integrated Action Plan for Chhattisgarh', *Lok Sabha*, 22 March 2002.

'Writ Petition (Civil) No. 250 of 2007', Order, *Supreme Court of India*, New Delhi, 5 July 2011.

8th Five Year Plan, Vol. 2, New Delhi: Planning Commission, 1992.

Annual Report 1988-1989, New Delhi, Ministry of Home Affairs, 1989.

Annual Report 2003-2004, New Delhi: Ministry of Home Affairs, 2004.

Annual Report 2003-2004, New Delhi: Ministry of Home Affairs, 2004.

Annual Report 2004-2005, New Delhi: Ministry of Home Affairs, 2005.

Annual Report 2004-2005, New Delhi: Government of India, 2005.

Annual Report 2005-2006, New Delhi: Ministry of Home Affairs, 2006.

Annual Report 2006-2007, New Delhi: Ministry of Home Affairs, 2007.

Annual Report 2007-2008, New Delhi: Ministry of Home Affairs, 2008.

Annual Report 2008-2009, New Delhi: Ministry of Home Affairs, 2009.

Annual Report 2009-2010, New Delhi: Ministry of Home Affairs, 2010.

Annual Report 2012-2013, New Delhi: Ministry of Home Affairs, 2013.

Annual Report 2013-2014, New Delhi: Ministry of Home Affairs, 2014.

Annual Report 2014-2015, New Delhi: Ministry of Home Affairs, 2015.

Annual Report 2018-2019, New Delhi: Ministry of Home Affairs, 2019.

Annual Report 2019-2020, New Delhi: Ministry of Home Affairs, 2020.

Annual Report 2020-2021, New Delhi: Government of India.

Annual Report 2021-2022, New Delhi: Ministry of Home Affairs, 2022.

Constitution of India, New Delhi: Government of India, 2022.

Evaluation Report on Border Area Development Programme, New Delhi: Planning Commission, 1999.

Good Governance Index 2020-21, New Delhi: Department of Administrative Reforms and Public Grievances, 2021.

Government Reports, Parliament Questions, Speeches, Court Orders

Governor's Report on the Scheduled Areas of Chhattisgarh 2016-2017, Government of Chhattisgarh, 2017.

Human Development Report - Chhattisgarh 2005, Raipur: United National Development Programme, 2005.

Implementation of Land Reforms: A Review by the Land Reforms Implementation Committee of the National Development Council, New Delhi, Planning Commission, 1966.

Malimath, V.S., *Committee on Reforms of Criminal Justice System, Vol. 1*, New Delhi; Ministry of Home Affairs, 2003.

Manipur Vision 2030 Leaving No-One Behind: Achieving Inclusive Growth and the Sustainable Development Goals, Imphal: Government of Manipur, 2019.

Nakade, S.B., at al, *Report of the Committee to Review the Armed Forces (Special Powers) Act of 1958*, Ministry of Home Affairs, Government of India, 2005.

National Multidimensional Poverty Index Baseline Report Based on NFHS-4 (2015-16), New Delhi: Niti Aayog, 2021.

Padmanabhaiah, K., *Committee on Restructuring Police*, New Delhi; Ministry of Home Affairs, 2000.

Punchhi, Madan Mohan, *Commission on Centre-State Relations Report Volume V*, New Delhi, Government of India, March 2010.

Ramachandran, V., 'Planning in the Sixth Schedule Areas and Those Areas Not Covered by Part ix and Part ix-a, 2006', *Report of the Expert Committee*, September 2006.

Report of the Scheduled Areas and Scheduled Tribes Commission, Vol. 1, New Delhi: Government of India, 2004.

Second Administrative Reforms Commission, New Delhi: Government of India, June 2007.

Third Report of the Standing Committee on Inter-sectoral Issues Relating to Tribal Development on Standard of Administration and Governance in the Scheduled Areas, New Delhi: Ministry of Tribal Affairs, 2009.

Tripura-Human Development Report 2007, New Delhi: Government of Tripura, 2007.

White Paper on the Punjab Agitation, New Delhi: Government of India, 1984.

Xaxa, Virginius, et al., *Report of the High Level Committee on Socio-Economic, Health and Educational Status of Tribal Communities of India*, New Delhi: Ministry of Tribal Affairs, 2014.

Books

Ahuja, Amit and Kapur, Devesh (eds.), *Internal Security in India: Violence, Order and the State*, New York: Oxford University Press, 2023.

Annual Status of Education Report (Rural) 2021, New Delhi: ASER Centre, 2021.

Banerjee, Sumanta, *India's Simmering Revolution*, London: Zed Books, 1984.

Bhaumik, Subir, *Insurgent Crossfire, Northeast India*, New Delhi: Lancer Publishers, 1996.

Bhowmick, Sourjya, *Gangster State: The Rise and Fall of the CPI (M) in West Bengal*, Kolkata: Macmillan, 2021.

Brar, K.S., *Operation Blue Start: The True Story*, New Delhi: UBS Publishers' Distributors Pvt. Ltd, 1993.

Calman, Leslie J., *Protest in Democratic India, Authority's Response to Challenge*, London: Westview Press, 1985.

Deshpande, Anirudh (ed.), *The First Line of Defence: Glorious 50 Years of the Border Security Force*, Delhi: Shipra Publications, 2015.

Dhillon, Kripal, *Identity and Survival: Sikh Militancy 1978-1993*, New Delhi: Penguin, 2006.

D'Mello, Bernard, *India after Naxalbari: Unfinished History*, New York: Monthly Review Press, 2018.

Documents of the Communist Movement in India, Vol. V, Calcutta: National Book Agency Ltd., 1997.

Global Peace Index 2023: Measuring Peace in a Complex World, Sydney: Institute for Economic and Peace, 2023

Gopalakrishnan, R., *Insurgent North-Eastern Region of India*, Delhi: Vikas Publishing House Pvt Ltd, 1995.

Gupta, Ranjit Kumar, *The Crimson Agenda, Maoist Protest and Terror*, Delhi: Wordsmiths, 2004.

Hanstad, Tim and Brown, Jennifer, *Land Reform Law and Implementation in West Bengal: Lessons and Recommendations*, Seattle: Rural Development Institute, 2001.

Kshetri, Rajendra, *The Emergence of Meetei Nationalism: A Study of Two Movements Among the Meeteis*, New Delhi: Mittal Publications, 2006.

Kumar, Kuldeep, *Police and Counter Insurgency, The untold story of Tripura's COIN Campaign*, New Delhi: Sage, 2016.

Land and Governance Under the Fifth Schedule: An Overview of the Law, New Delhi: Ministry of Tribal Affairs, nd.

Lynch III, Thomas F., *India's Naxalite Insurgency: History, Trajectory, and Implications for U.S.-India Security Cooperation on Domestic Counterinsurgency*, Washington: Institute for National Strategic Studies Strategic Perspectives, 2016.

Majumdar, Manabi, et al *Tripura Human Development Report II*, Kolkata: Pratichi Institute, 2018.

Nayak, Giridhari, *Neo-Naxal Challenge, Issues & Options*, New Delhi: Pentagon Press, 2011.

Oetken, Jennifer L., 'Counterinsurgency against Naxalites in India', in Sumit Ganguly, David P. Fidler (eds.), *India and Counterinsurgency: Lessons Learned*, Oxon: Routledge, 2009.

Roy, Asish Kumar, *The Spring Thunder and After, A Survey of the Maoist and Ultra-Leftist Movements in India*, Calcutta: Minerva Associates, 1975.

Saundaryya, P., *Telangana People's Struggle and its Lessons*, Calcutta: Communist Party of India, 1972.

Schendel, Willem Van, *The Bengal Borderland, Beyond State and Nation in South Asia*, London: Anthem Press, 2005.

Sharma, P.D., *Police and Political Order in India*, Delhi: Research Publications, 1984.

Singh, Prakash *The Naxalite Movement in India*, New Delhi: Rupa, 2016.

Subramanian, K.S., *State, Policy and Conflicts in Northeast India*, New Delhi: Routledge, 2016.

Taraport, Phanjouban, *Bleeding Manipur*, New Delhi: Har Anand Publications Pvt Ltd., 2003.

The AFSPA: Lawless Law Enforcement According to the Law? New Delhi: Asian Centre for Human Rights, 2005.

The Tribes Advisory Councils: Time to be replaced by the Autonomous District Councils, New Delhi: Asian Indigenous and Tribal Peoples Network, 2012.

Watts, Stephen, et al, *Countering Others' Insurgencies: Understanding U.S. Small-Footprint Interventions in Local Context*, Santa Monica: RAND, 2014.

Journals Articles

Adhikari, Anindita and Chhotray, Vasudha, 'The Political Construction of Extractive Regimes in Two Newly Created Indian States: A Comparative Analysis of Jharkhand and Chhattisgarh', *Development and Change*, 2020, pp. 843-873.

Balagopal, K., 'Maoist Movement in Andhra Pradesh', *Economic and Political Weekly*, Vol. 41(29), 22-28 July 2006, pp. 3183-3187.

Balagopal, K., 'People's War and the Government: Did the Police Have the Last Laugh?', *Economic and Political Weekly* , Vol. 38 (6), 8-14 February 2003, pp. 513-519.

Bandyopadhyay, D., 'Tebhaga Movement in Bengal: A Retrospect', *Economic and Political Weekly*, Vol. 36 (41), 13019 October 2001, p. 3901-3907.

Bandyopadhyay, Sekhar, 'The Communists in post-colonial Bengal, 1948-52: The untold story of 'second' Tebhaga', *16th Biennial Conference of the Asian Studies Association of Australia*, Wollongong 26 - 29 June 2006, pp. 1-17.

Banerjee, S.K., 'Manipur State Constitution Act, 1947', *The Indian Journal of Political Science*, Vol. 19 (1), January-March 1958, pp. 35-38.

Basistha, Nandini, 'Revisiting Tebhaga Movement in Bengal: Resistance against Domination and Alternative Identities', *Indian Journal of Public Administration*, Vol. 65(4), 2019, pp. 936-942.

Bhatia, Bela, 'Judging the Judgment', *Economic and Political Weekly*, Vol. 46 (30), 23-29 July 2011, pp. 14-16.

Bhatia, Bela, 'Justice Denied to Tribals in the Hill Districts of Manipur', *The Economic and Political Weekly*, Vol. 45 (31), 31 July-31 August 2010, pp. 38-46.

Bhattacharjee, Malini, 'The Lalgarh Story', *Economic and Political Weekly*, Vol. 44 (33), 15-21 August, 2009, pp. 17-19.

Bose, Sayoni, 'Attachment to place and territoriality in Nandigram land struggle, India', *Human Geography*, Vol. 13 (2), 2020, pp. 139-153.

Burton, Sir Michael, 'The Malayan Emergency: A Subaltern's view', *Asian Affairs*, Vol. 42 (2), 2011, pp. 251-260.

Catton, Philip E., 'Counter-Insurgency and Nation Building: The Strategic Hamlet Programme in South Vietnam, 1961-1963', *The International History Review*, Vol. 21 (4), December 1999, pp. 918-940.

Chakravarti, Mahadev, 'Insurgency in Tripura: Some Trends', *Economic and Political Weekly*, Vol. 36 (25), 23- 29 June 23-29, 2001.

Chandra, Amitabha, 'The Naxalbari Movement', *The Indian Journal of Political Science*, Vol. 51 (1), Jan-Mar 1990, pp. 22-45.

Chattopadhyay, Suhas, 'Operation Barga', *Social Scientist*, Vol. 8 (87), October 1979, pp. 41-48.

Chima, Jugdep S., 'The Punjab Crisis: Governmental Centralization and Akali-Center Relations', *Asian Survey*, Vol. 34 (10), October 1994, pp. 847-862.

Cline, Lawrence E., 'The Insurgency Environment in Northeast India', *Small Wars & Insurgencies*, Vol. 17 (2), 2006, pp. 126-147.

Das, Susnata, 'Marginal Communities in Peasant Movement: The Sharecroppers' Struggle for "Tebhaga" In North Bengal (1946-47)', *Proceedings of the Indian History Congress*, Vol. 74, 2013, pp. 640-651.

Dasgupta, Biplab, 'Naxalite Armed Struggles and the Annihilation Campaign in

Rural Areas', *Economic and Political Weekly*, Vol. 8 (4/6), Feb., 1973, 173–188.

Dasgupta, Biplab, 'Naxalite Armed Struggles and the Annihilation Campaign in Rural Areas', *Economic and Political Weekly*, Vol. 8 (4/6), Feb., 1973, pp. 173-188.

De, Nilanjan, 'Bengali Immigration and Renovation of the Administrative Structure of Tripura: An Analytical Study', *IJRSS*, Vol. 2(3), August 2012, pp. 129-138.

Deol, Satnam Singh, 'Sikh Ethnonationalism and Militancy: Manifestation and Prognosis', *Asian Ethnicity*, Vol. 20 (2), 2019, pp. 183-209.

Dhanagare, D.N., 'Peasant protest and politics—The Tebhaga movement in Bengal (India), 1946–47', *The Journal of Peasant Studies*, Vol. 3 (3), 1976, pp. 360-378.

Dyke, Virginia Van, 'The Khalistan Movement in Punjab, India, and the Post-Militancy Era: Structural Change and New Political Compulsions', *Asian Survey*, Vol. 49 (6), November/December 2009, pp. 975-997.

Fazal, Tanweer, 'Peace Talks' as Strategic Deployment: the State, Maoists and Political Violence in India', *Irish Studies in International Affairs*, Vol. 26, Special focus: Conflict Resolution in South Asia, 2015, pp. 39-51.

Ghosh Ratan, and Nagaraj, K., 'Land Reforms in West Bengal', *Social Scientist*, Vol. 6 (6/7), Jan. - Feb., 1978, pp. 50-67.

Ghosh, Biswajit, 'Ethnicity and Insurgency in Tripura', *Sociological Bulletin*, Vol. 52 (2), September 2003, pp. 221-243.

Ghoshal, Anindita, 'Tripura: A Chronicle of Politicisation of the Refugees and Ethnic Tribals', *Social Change and Development*, Vol. 16, July 2017, pp. 46-56.

Girani, E., 'Hijam Irawat and his Movements in Manipur: A Humanistic Revolutionary', *Journal of Emerging Technologies and Innovative Research*, Vol. 7 (4), April 2020, pp. 1765- 1772.

Hassan, M. Sajjad, 'Explaining Manipur's Breakdown and Mizoram's Peace: The State and Identities in North East India', *Crisis States Programme Working Paper no. 79*, February 2006, pp. 1-32.

Hausing, Kham Khan Suan, 'From Opposition to Acquiescence: The 2015 District Council Elections in Manipur', *Economic and Political Weekly*, Vol. 50 (46/47), 21 November 2015, pp. 79-83.

Horowitz Shale, and Sharma, Deepti, 'Democracies Fighting Ethnic Insurgencies: Evidence from India', *Studies in Conflict & Terrorism*, Vol. 31, (8), 2008, pp. 749-773.

Hultquist, Philip, 'Countering Khalistan: Understanding India's Counter-Rebellion Strategies during the Punjab Crisis', *Journal of Punjab Studies*, Vol. 22 (1), Spring 2015, pp. 93-121.

Iyenger, S. Kesava, 'Land Reforms in the Hyderabad State', *The Indian Journal of Agricultural Economics*, Vol. 8 (1), March 1953, pp. 114-119.

Jason Miklian, 'The purification hunt: the Salwa Judum counterinsurgency in Chhattisgarh, India', *Dialectical Anthropology*, Vol. 33 (3/4), December 2009, pp. 441-459.

Jetly, Rajshree, 'The Khalistan Movement in India: The Interplay of Politics and State Power', *International Review of Modern Sociology*, Vol. 34 (1), Spring 2008, pp. 61-75.

Kamei, Richard, 'Tribal Land, Customary Law, and the Manipur Land Revenue and Land Reforms Act', *Economic and Political Weekly*, Vol. 53 (19), 12 May 2018, pp. 52-56.

Kennedy, Jonathan and Purushotham, Sunil, 'Beyond Naxalbari: A Comparative Analysis of Maoist Insurgency and Counterinsurgency in Independent India', *Comparative Studies in Society and History*, Vol. 54 (4), October 2012, pp. 832-862.

Kom, Ch. Sekholal, 'Militancy and Negotiations: A Study of Suspension of Operation in Manipur', *Journal of Peace Studies*, Vol. 18 (1&2), January-June, 2011, pp. 70-87.

Kumar, Ashutosh, 'Electoral Politics in Punjab: Study of Akali Dal', *Economic and Political Weekly*, Vol. 39, (14/15) 3-16 April 2004, pp. 1515-1520.

Lacina, Bethany, 'The Problem of Political Stability in Northeast India, Local Ethnic Autocracy and the Rule of Law', *Asian Survey*, Vol. 49, Issue 6, 2009, pp. 998-1020.

Mazumdar, Arijit, 'Left-Wing Extremism and Counterinsurgency in India: The "Andhra Model",' *Strategic Analysis*, Vol. 37 (4), 2013, pp. 446–462.

Mazumdar. Charu, 'A Few Words about Guerilla Warfare', *Liberation*, Vol. III, (4), February 1970.

Mukhopadhyay, Ashoke Kumar, 'Through the Eyes of the Police: Naxalites in Calcutta in 1970s', *Economic & Political Weekly*, Vol. 41, (29), July 22-28, 2006, pp. 3227-3233.

Mukhopadhyay, Ashoke Kumar, 'Through the Eyes of the Police: Naxalites in Calcutta in the 1970s', *Economic and Political Weekly*, Vol. 41 (29), 22-28 July, 2006, pp. 3227-3233.

Nripen Bandopadhayay, '"Operation Barga" and Land Reforms Perspective in

West Bengal: A Discursive Review', *Economic and Political Weekly*, Vol. 16 (25/26), 20-27 June 1981

Oinam, Bhagat, 'Patterns of Ethnic Conflict in the North-East: A Study on Manipur', *Economic and Political Weekly*, Vol. 38 (21), 24-30 May 2003, pp. 2031-2037.

Om Shankar Jha, 'Combating Left Wing Extremism: Is Police Training Lacking? Case Study of Chhattisgarh', *IDSA Occasional Paper No. 3*, 2009, pp. 1-38.

Parratt, John and Parratt, Saroj Arambam, 'Hijam Irabot and the Radical Socialist Democratic Movement in Manipur', *Internationales Asienforum*, Vol. 31 (3-4), 2000, pp. 275-288.

Prasad, Archana, 'The Political Economy of 'Maoist Violence' in Chhattisgarh', *Social Scientist*, Vol. 38 (3/4), March-April 2010, pp. 3-24.

Raju, D. Ramachandra, 'Protective Laws in Scheduled Areas of Andhra Pradesh', *Cochin University Law Review*, Vol. IX, 1985, pp. 149-156.

Ramana, P.V., 'A Critical Evaluation of the Union Government's Response to the Maoist Challenge', *Strategic Analysis*, Vol. 33 (5), September 2009, pp. 745-759.

Ramana, P.V., 'Taming India's Maoists: Surrender and Rehabilitation', *Strategic Analysis*, Vol. 37 (6), 2013, pp. 716-728.

Rammohan, E.N., 'Armed Forces Special Powers Act', *Dialogue*, Vol. 14 (4), April-June 2013, pp. 114-120.

Rangaswami, Amrita, 'Making a Village: An Andhra Experiment', *Economic and Political Weekly*, Vol. 9 (36), 7 September, 1974, pp. 1524-27.

Rao, S. Laxman, Deshingkar, Priya and Farrington, John, 'Tribal Land Alienation in Andhra Pradesh Processes, Impacts and Policy Concerns', *The Economic and Political Weekly*, Vol. 41 (52), 30 December 2006, pp. 5401-5407.

Ray, Subhasish and Dutta, Mohan J., 'Insecure peace: understanding citizen and local government relations in a Maoist-affected region in India', *Critical Asian Studies*, Vol. 50 (1), 2018, pp. 37-57.

Reddy, N. Subba, 'Crisis of Confidence among the Tribal People and the Naxalite Movement in Srikakulam District', *Human Organization*, Vol. 36 (2), Summer 1977, pp. 142-149.

Rego, Stephen, 'Destructive Development and People's Struggles in Bastar', *Economic and Political Weekly*, Vol. 29 (7), 12 February 1994, pp. 351-353.

Routray, Bibhu Prasad, 'India: Fleeting Attachment to the Counterinsurgency Grand Strategy', *Small Wars & Insurgencies*, Vol. 28 (1), 2017, pp. 57-80.

Sangpui, Lily and Kapngaihlian, Jenny, 'The Quest to End Illicit Poppy Cultivation in Manipur: Examining the War on Drugs Campaign', *Economic and Political Weekly*, Vol. 56, (32), 7 August 2021.

Sanyal, Kanu, 'Report on the Peasant Movement in the "Terai Region",' *Liberation*, November 1968, pp. 28-53.

Sarkar, Abhirup, 'Political Economy of West Bengal: A Puzzle and a Hypothesis', *Economic and Political Weekly*, Vol. 41 (4), 28 January-3 February 2006, pp. 341-348.

Shimray, U.A., 'Ethnicity and Socio-Political Assertion: The Manipur Experience', *Economic and Political Weekly*, Vol. 36 (39), 29 September–5 October 2001, pp. 3674-3677.

Singh, Gurharpal, 'Punjab since 1984: Disorder, Order, and Legitimacy', *Asian Survey*, Vol. 36 (4), April 1996, pp. 410-421.

Singh, Prakash, 'Impact of Terrorism on Investment Decisions of Farmers: Evidence from the Punjab Insurgency', *The Journal of Conflict Resolution*, Vol. 57, (1), Special Issue: Entrepreneurship and Conflict, February 2013, pp.143–168.

Srinivasulu, K., 'YS Rajasekhara Reddy: A Political Appraisal', *Economic and Political Weekly*, Vol. 44 (38), 19-25 September 2009, pp. 8-10

Sundar, Nandini, 'Bastar, Maoism and Salwa Judum', *Economic and Political Weekly*, Vol. 41 (29), 22-28 July 2006, pp. 3187-3192.

Telford, Hamish, 'The Political Economy of Punjab: Creating Space for Sikh Militancy', *Asian Survey*, Vol. 32 (11), November 1992, pp. 969-987.

Chapters in Edited Book

Bhaumik, Subir, 'Ethnicity, Ideology and Religion: Separatist Movements in India's Northeast', in Limaye, Satu, Malik Mohan, and Wirsing, Robert G., (eds.), *Religious Radicalism and Security in South Asia*, Honolulu, Hawaii: Asia Pacific Center for Security Studies, 2004, pp. 219-244.

Bhuyan, Jogesh Ch., 'Illegal Migration from Bangladesh and the Demographic Change in the North-East Region', in Kumar, B.B. (ed.), Illegal Migration from Bangladesh, Delhi: Asthabharati, 2006, pp. 79-89.

Fair, C. Christine, 'Lessons from India's experience in Punjab, 1978-1993', in Ganguly Sumit and Fidler, David P. (eds.), *India and Counterinsurgency, Lessons Learned*, London: Routledge, 2009, pp. 107-126.

Fair, C. Christine, 'The Golden Temple: A Tale of Two Sieges', in Fair, C. Christine and Ganguly, Sumit (eds.), *Treading on Hallowed Ground: Counterinsurgency*

Operations in Sacred Spaces, Oxford: Oxford University Press, 2008, pp. 37-65.

H. Kham Khan Suan, 'Hills-Valley Divide as a Site of Conflict', in Sanjib Baruah (ed.), *Beyond Counter-Insurgency, Breaking the Impasse in Northeast India*, Oxford University Press, New Delhi, 2009, pp. 263-292.

Jha, Sanjay K., 'Political Bases and dimensions of the Naxalite Movement', in Ramana, P. V. (ed.), *The Naxal Challenge: Causes, Linkages, and Policy Options*, Delhi: Pearson Longman, 2008, pp. 62-82.

Marwah, Ved, 'India's counterinsurgency campaign in Punjab', in Ganguly Sumit and Fidler, David P. (eds.), *India and Counterinsurgency, Lessons Learned*, London: Routledge, 2009, pp. 89-106.

Rao, C. Chandra Sekhara, 'What to do?', in Sen, Samar, Panda, Debabrata, and Lahiri, Ashish (Eds.), *Naxalbari and After, A Frontier Anthology, Vol.1*, Calcutta:, Kothashilpa, 1978, pp. 99-105.

Reddy, K. Srinivas, 'Revolutionary and Counter Revolutionary Strategies of the Naxalites and the State', in Ramana, P.V. (ed.), *The Naxal Challenge, Causes, Linkages, and Policy Options*, New Delhi, Pearson, 2008, pp. 90-100.

Reddy, M. Shashidhar, 'A Political Approach to Naxalite Problem: Viability and Prerequisites for Success', in Ramana, P. V. (Ed.), *The Naxal Challenge: Causes, Linkages, and Policy Options*, Delhi: Pearson Longman, 2008, pp. 39-61.

Ruchir Garg, 'Roots and Causes: The Case of Dandakaranya', in Ramana, P.V. (ed.), *The Naxal Challenge, Causes, Linkages, and Policy Options*, Delhi: Dorling Kindersley (India) Pvt. Ltd., 2008, pp. 25-38.

Sanajaoba, Naorem, 'The Genesis of Insurgency', in Sanajaoba, Naorem (ed.) *Manipur Past and Present,* Volume I, Delhi: Mittal Publications, 1988, pp. 245-290.

Smith, Chris, 'Light Weapons and Ethnic Conflict in South Asia,' in Boutwell, Jeferry, Klare Michael T. and Reed, Laura W. (eds.), *Lethal Commerce: The Global Trade in Small Arms and Light Weapons,* Cambridge: American Academy of Arts and Science, 1995, pp. 61–80.

Snahal, Rajkumar, 'Post-Merger Political History of Manipur', in Sanajaoba, Naorem (ed.) *Manipur Past and Present*, Vol. I, Delhi: Mittal Publications, 1988, pp. 175-189.

Website/Newspaper Articles

'The Role of Local Governance in Sustaining Peace', *International Peace Institute*, New York, February 2018.

Achuthan, Col. J.K. (Retd.), 'Tackling Maoists: the Andhra paradigm', *India Defence Review*, Vol. 25, Apr-June 2010.

Akoijam, Angomcha Bimol, 'Making Sense of Corruption in Manipur', *Kangla Online*, 4 September 2012.

Arun, Irengbam, 'A virus called AFSPA', *Kanglaonline*, 10 July 2016.

Bhadra, Sujato, 'Peace-talk Process in Junglemahal', *Mainstream*, Vol. 50 (1), 24 December 2011.

Bhaumik, Subir, 'Disaster in Tripura', *Seminar*, Vol. 510, 2005.

Bhaumik, Subir, 'Insurgencies in India's Northeast: Conflict, Co-option & Change', *East West Center*, No. 10, July 2007.

Bhaumik, Subir, 'Tripura: ethnic Conflict, Militancy & Counterinsurgency', *Politics and Practices*, Vol. 52, 2012, pp. 1-28.

Bibhu Prasad Routray 'Unremitting Terror', *Outlook*, 3 February 2022 (updated).

Chhonkar, Pradeep Singh, 'The Creation of New Districts in Manipur: Administrative Necessity versus Naga Territorial Aspirations', *IDSA Comment*, 23 December 2016.

Dominika Sokol, 'The Sikh Diaspora in Cyberspace: The Representation of Khalistan on the World Wide Web and Its Legal Context', *Masaryk University Journal of Law and Technology*, Vol. 1 (2), 2007, pp. 219-230.

Gill, K.P.S., 'Freedom from Fear-Sukma attack: Chhattisgarh police cannot hold back and fight Naxals in their stronghold through proxies', *SATP.*

Harad, Tejas, 'ST Status for Manipur's Meiteis: What is at Stake?', *The Quint*, 6 May 2023

Hausing, Kham Khan Suan, 'Manipur impasse: The hills are alive', *The Indian Express*, 22 September 2015.

Jha, Sanjay, K., 'Naxalite Movement in Bihar and Jharkhand', *Dialogue*, Vol. 6, (4), April-June, 2005.

Jitendra, 'SC dismisses petition challenging functioning of Tribal advisory council in Chhattisgarh', *Down to Earth*, 24 November 2014.

Justino, Patricia, 'Governance Interventions in Fragile and Conflict-Affected Countries', IDS Working Paper 496, *Institute of Development Studies and Swiss Agency for Development and Cooperation*, October 2017.

K.P.S. Gill, 'Endgame in Punjab 1988-93', *Faultlines*, Vol. 1, May 1999.

Kleinfeld, Rachel and Majeed, Rushda, 'Fighting Insurgency with Politics: The Case of Bihar', *Carnegie Endowment for International Peace*, May 2016.

Maoist Documents, *Strategy & Tactics of the Indian Revolution*, Central Committee (P) CPI (Maoist) 2004, South Asia Terrorism Portal.

Mathew, Rohan D., 'The Telengana Movement: Peasant Protests in India, 1946-51', *ritimo*, 1 July 2021.

Myrdal, Jan and Navlakha, Gautam, 'In conversation with Ganapathy, General Secretary of CPI (Maoist)', *Sanhati*, 12 February 2010.

Navlakha, Gautam, 'People's War as Strategy and Peace Talk as Tactics', *Frontier*, Vol. 44 (44), 13-19 May 2012.

Ngaihte, Thangkhanlal, 'Manipur's blighted bills', *The Statesman,* 18 October 2015.

Panag, H. S., 'How India's Maoist counter-insurgency is being undone by a flawed security strategy', *The Print*, 15 April 2021

Panang, H.S., 'Religious intolerance main driver of insurgency in Punjab of 1980s. State's watching it again', *The Print*, 10 February 2022.

Phanjoubam, Pradip, 'The Assam Rifles lesson for Manipur', *The Telegraph*, 21 September 2021.

Ramana, P.V., 'Maoist People's Liberation Guerrilla Army', *IDSA Comment*, 12 December 2011.

Ramana, P.V., 'Peace with PWG Naxals: A wishful exercise?', New Delhi: Observer Research Foundation, 2 July 2004.

Rammohan, E.N., 'Manipur: A Degenerated Insurgency', *USI Journal*, January-March 2002.

Rammohan, E.N., 'Manipur: Blue Print for Counterinsurgency', *Faultline*, Vol. 12, May 2022.

Reddy, K. Srinivas, 'The Maoist challenge', *Seminar*, Vol. 569, 2007.

Routray, Bibhu Prasad, 'The State of Militancy', *South Asia Intelligence Review*, Vol. 4(26), 9 January 2006.

Routray, Bibhu Prasad, 'Tripura: Creating an Unenviable Record', *South Asia Intelligence Review*, Vol. 2 (14), 20 October 2003.

Sahaya, D.N., 'How Tripura overcame insurgency', *The Hindu*, 9 November, 2016.

Sahni, Ajai, 'Delusion of peace', *Frontline*, 21 October 2005.

Sahni, Ajai, ''Naxalism' The Retreat of Civil Governance', *Faultline*, Volume 5, May 2000.

Sahni, Ajai, 'Survey of Conflicts & Resolution in India's Northeast', *Faultline*, Vol.12, May 2002.

Sahni, Ajai, 'The State Advances, the Maoists Retreat', *South Asia Intelligence Review*, Vol. 6 (10), 17 September 2007.

Sahni, Ajai, 'Tripura: The Politics of Ethnic Terror', *South Asia Intelligence Review,* Vol. 1 (6), 2002.

Sanatomba, Kangujam, 'Was Irabot in favour of complete independence', *E-Pao*, 2 October 2013.

Shahikumar, V.K., 'Operation Nandigram: The Inside Story', *Indian Defence Review*, Vol. 23, 1 Jan-Mar 2008.

Sharma, Sushil Kumar, 'Naga Peace Accord and the Kuki and Meitei Insurgencies in Manipur', *IDSA Policy Brief*, 5 January 2016

Shimray, U.A., 'Naga Integration Movement: A Historical Perspective', *Nagaland Journal*, 22 April 2013.

Shinder Purewal, 'Sikh Diaspora and the Movement for Khalistan', *The Indian Journal of Political Science*, Vol. 72 (4), Oct-Dec 2011, pp. 1131-1142.

Singh, Aheibam Koireng, 'Suspension of Operation with Chikimz Outfits In Manipur Part I', *E-PAO*, 17 November 2016.

Sood, Sanjiv Krishan, 'Is Assam Rifles stretched with its dual role? Manipur ambush raises key questions', *The Print*, 17 November 2021.

Srinivasulu, K., 'Caste, Class and Social Articulation in Andhra Pradesh: Mapping Differential Regional Trajectories', Working Paper No. 179, New Delhi: *Overseas Development Institute,* September 2002.

Sudhakar, 'A Saga of Twenty-Five Years of Glorious Struggle, an Epic of People's Radical Transformation', *People's March*, Vol. 7 (1), January 2006.

Suvarna Damle, *A study of contribution of the Tribal Parliamentarians in strengthening Panchayats (Extension to the Scheduled Areas) Act (PESA),* Parliament, 2012.

Swami, Praveen, 'Failed Threats and Flawed Fences: India's Military Responses to Pakistan's Proxy War', *India Review*, Vol. 3 (2), 2004.

Yenning, 'Corruption scam and issue of governance', *E-Pao*, Imphal, 23 February 2015.

Ph.D Thesis

Ravikant, Rajeshwari, *"People's War" and State Response: The Naxalite Movement in Telangana, India (1970-1993)*, Ph.D Thesis, Vancouver: University of British Columbia, September 1995.

INDEX